WRIGHT'S

COMPLETE
DISASTER
SURVIVAL
MANUAL

WRIGHT'S

COMPLETE DISASTER SURVIVAL MANUAL

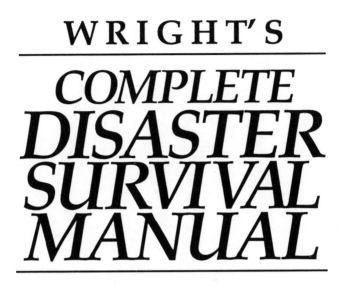

Ted Wright

HAMPTONROADS
PUBLISHING COMPANY, INC.

For information, write:

Hampton Roads Publishing Company, Inc.
891 Norfolk Square
Norfolk, VA 23502

Or call: 804-459-2453
FAX: 804-455-8907

If this book is unavailable from your local bookseller, it may be obtained
directly from the publisher. Call toll-free 1-800-766-8009 (orders only).

ISBN 1-878901-80-X

10 9 8 7 6 5 4 3 2 1

Cover design by Patrick Smith

Printed using acid-free paper in the United States of America

Dedication

To have faith in oneself, to believe in a cause so strongly as to place it above all other priorities in your life, is to be either a fool or a fanatic. . .but one man *can* make a difference. History is full of those who, even in the face of ridicule, believed in their cause and its positive outcome.

To my wife, Kacey, for her constant support; to my family who believed in me for they knew my truths; to the many kind friends and the strangers who encouraged me, this book is dedicated.

There can be no greater comfort in facing even the most trying of situations than to be as fully prepared as possible. Taking the *true* facts of the situation into account.

Fear of the unknown has plagued man since the beginning of time. To place *known* facts into this category is to encourage either ignorance or laziness!
This manual is dedicated to the elimination of ignorance.
"Long may *Gooberz* reign!"

CONTENTS

FOREWORD

In 1980 a chance news flash on my car radio was to change my life. Coming over the airwaves was a report of a minor earthquake somewhere. At that moment, my car and I were on a remote highway at a time when traffic was at a low volume. It was autumn and just about to get dark. For some unknown reason the car pulled onto the shoulder and we both sat, my car and I.

In a while I turned off the motor. My thoughts began to wander. . .disaster. . .pictures of London and streets with no houses. . .huge mounds of bricks and wood not yet cleared from the roadway. . . .

I knew from experience that deep under a lot of that rubble were people. . .unknown to me. . .long departed from this life. How long? Who knew. . .they were the victims who, for reasons unknown, were in the wrong place at the wrong time.

I thought of my Aunt Amy, how I had come home on furlough to spend a few days with her. . .the door was not locked and as I entered her small house, I could see the table set for supper. . .for two.

Aunt Amy never came home, and, though I spent all my leave time searching, the truth was that she had just disappeared. The mystery was never to be solved. Did she go on a last minute errand and get caught in a surprise air raid? No doubt under a pile of rubble, her remains would one day be moved by bulldozers. . .

My thoughts wandered for hours as I sat there on the shoulder of that quiet California highway. Suddenly the thought struck me that if *I* didn't get going, *I* would be declared a missing person!

On the way home, one thought kept running through my mind. "If the earthquake happened now, what would I do?" To my surprise, my thought pattern was very clear and concise:

You will decide whether to go, or to stay.
If you go, you will need certain supplies; if you stay, you will need different stuff.

9

Since that time I have spoken those words at seminars and lectures all over Southern California, for from that stop on the lonely road was to develop Earthquake Survival Services (my little company), books, tapes, cassettes and a video, all of which I am very proud. On that day so long ago I realized that I had a wealth of knowledge that most of you did not have.

For me, the simple basics that I learned in London, climbing in and out of the rubble, came as naturally as camping lore comes to a Scout.

My years of combat, in the Middle East and the Italian Campaign, etched pictures of broken cities and suffering people on my brain in such a manner that, even though these thoughts lay dormant all these years, they, with London, were once again crystal clear.

My first book, *Survive, I Dare You, The Earthquake Awaits!**, was written in 1980, when the best I could muster for an audience was a group of sleepy-eyed Lions at a 7:30 A.M. breakfast! My aim then was to challenge, attempting to stir my audience with word pictures they could not, at that time, comprehend.

Today, even all that has happened—the half dozen earthquakes now a reality, even the recent San Francisco event—has not served to create a sense of awareness in us Californians. I have learned to accept that, just like my Aunt Amy, many will be in the wrong place at the wrong time. I cannot change that. What I can change, however, is the condition of the survivors after the "Big One."

My writings have always tried to portray, in as plain a manner as possible, the facts as I see them: *Survival is for those who care.* I always try not to "throw daggers" at you, my audience. If you are not stirred to take action now, all the dark pictures of blood and gore will not help. Rather, those who may have decided to take a little tentative action could be deterred.

Since that news flash those many years ago, survival has become my business. "I will go anywhere, any time to talk about earthquake survival" has become my slogan. I am still appalled at the lack of preparation, but can only do what one human being can do, period!

This new version of the survival manual will be widened a little to be an aid book for disaster survival in *general*. This, I hope, will benefit those in other states who also must prepare for nature's onslaughts in forms other than earthquake.

All writings from my company are original. All products offered were either developed by me or well-tested before my endorsement.

One final word: it has been very difficult for me to accept that some people seem to lack knowledge of basics. So many times in the seminar and lecture scene I have not stressed these basics enough. If, for some of you, I "keep it too simple," please bear with me.

Survival for our families and especially our children is truly our own responsibility. The Bureaucracy has not yet figured how to get the aid we need down to our level. Until then, let US get US ready for the catastrophe that may come at any moment.

J.E. "Ted" Wright
Lancaster, California

*Note: *Survive, I Dare You, The Earthquake Awaits!* is no longer in print and therefore no longer available.

INTRODUCTION

The world is plagued by sudden major disasters that take many forms. Conversely, very rarely does Mother Nature strike without *any* warning. . .the disaster, either by location, environment or due process, was a known something-or-other just waiting to happen.

The tornado has many symptoms, the hurricane takes time to develop its "eye," the list goes on. This is especially true of floods and other localized disasters. If you choose to live and build your house in an earthquake fault area, or on a flood plain, or in tornado country, and do not prepare, who is to blame?

Preparation for catastrophe involves assessing *known facts* and taking countermeasures. Pictures of citizens in a war zone with gas masks at the ready is one example; storm cellars in tornado country is another.

It is true to say that once you have experienced a disaster you become a believer. Europeans have seen broken cities, displaced families, and hopeless situations. Tell them such and such is about to happen and they will respond in *some* way. . .they *will* take ACTION.

I still have a hard time accepting that my fellow citizens, for the most part, completely ignore the known fate that awaits the un-prepared. Or even worse, through lack of understanding, they *accept information given to them* and are therefore lulled into a false sense of complacency. What makes it worse is that the people who give out false information are well-meaning and honest for the most part.

Examples:

1. An earthquake drill held inside a building is not only foolish, but holds to the assumption that the building will survive as it is and remain in full operating condition. Like storing the fire engine *inside* the building in a major fault zone and expect to drive it out after the quake!

2. The hospital holds a drill with perhaps a dozen "casualties" lined up for attention while ambulances arrive with more injured, all

carefully laid out in the accepted manner: neatly placed on those nice stretchers that have a set of wheels that drop down so the victim is pushed smoothly into the waiting Emergency Room.

All of the people who see this misrepresentation of facts are led to believe that this is indeed how it will be. Filled with a sense of well-being, they go to their beds with the rosy thought that there really is a system to take care of them. Those who put on the show also go to *their* beds in the delusion that their disaster plan will swing into gear and do a great job. Every time I see this sad scene I want to scream!

3. Here's the well-meaning school. They have drills; food is set aside; all the students are aware that they may stay at school for a few days. . .but the drills are carried out in *silence.* No preparation has been made to sleep outside, and no one thought to talk about toilets and hygiene under field conditions.

4. Now consider a town with a hazardous waste problem. In the event of a misfortune, some rotten poison is going to come in the form of a lethal cloud. . .does anyone have any gas masks? Or a sealed room as a first priority?

This piece is called an introduction. For me it is an introduction to survival, which means before you can hope to take any precautions you must first know your enemy. Know his potential to cause you harm. Then, having assessed the potential, assume that the worst possible situation will happen. For it most likely will.

It would be ridiculous for anyone to suggest that you book into a hotel for a five-day stay if you only have two days' money, then assume that the manager will smile and say, "Hope you enjoyed your stay; send us the money sometime!" It might just happen that way, but the worst scenario is that you could end up in jail until someone bailed you out with the needed funds.

To prepare for this worst situation, surely you would have a back-up friend or relative waiting for the urgent call that is most likely to come?

That's my approach to survival and I use this kind of logic all the way through this work, as I did in my first manual. Although there is no "update," the disaster still awaits; I have, however, paid greater attention in this manual to minor detail, as it has been pointed out to me that not everyone has my basic knowledge of the "simple" facts. So I am going to be very basic.

You know, preparing for the worst will not prevent the worst from happening. . .going down into the storm cellar will still be required.

That tornado will not go away, it *will* pursue its chosen path, but the difference will be that going into a *prepared* cellar is a lot more comfortable than if the cellar were as cold and damp as some I went into in Minnesota!

Preparing for an earthquake will not stop it from happening, but I would sooner leave the place where I am with a backpack and supplies with water for my unknown journey than start off with just myself and no supplies. Having to stay in a dangerous place just because I know I cannot make it ten feet the way I am makes no sense to me.

Disaster is an immediate introduction to stress of the worst kind. Although you may have seen pictures, this is the real thing. In my time, I am sure I have seen every movie made concerning natural disaster, from the old Jon Hall *Hurricane* to forest fires and earthquakes. The one thought that always remains is that, in the end, it all comes out "good." After the great San Francisco quake and fire movie, a battered Clark Gable holds Alice Faye and says something like. . ."Out of this ruin will rise a better city."

The statistics of today belie these romantic notions. As an idealist, I hope that the fallen towns will be rebuilt elsewhere. After all, who would be foolish enough to re-build where Mother Nature has already said "unstable."

Facts also show that, after major disasters of most kinds, 60 percent of all businesses do not re-open, and aid from agencies is slow in coming. In many cases, homes affected by disasters of the last ten years are still not back to normal, mainly for lack of funds.

Reality always has to be faced. For those of us who are of a survival nature, we do well to fully assess our situation. Not from a safety point of view, but from the hazard standpoint. . .do not ask "How safe is my home?" but rather "How hazardous is it?"

If we determine the hazards in a particular room, what remains must be safe. Looking for what is safe tends to overlook the hazards that exist, such as something that can fall and break a limb.

When we look at the hazards of our surroundings, we should always view them from the same perspective, no matter what type of hazard exists. That perspective entails focusing on the *potential* danger of the hazard, rather than the actual danger that we have witnessed in the past; in other words, we must not become complacent because a hazard has, in the past, never actually endangered us.

Living in flood country is one example. Rather than making the statement "Oh well, we always have floods here," we should be voicing the precise consideration "But when it does flood, look out. The water rises awful fast." This outlook considers the actual danger itself, the water.

Obviously, if the flood condition has a history of a very sudden rise in water level, and if certain areas have repeatedly been "cut-off" over the years, it would seem to be good survival practice to have a boat or raft stored somewhere in the upper floors of a house located in such an area.

This kind of original assessment is the first step in any survival considerations. Following this first examination of the known history of your area should come the assessment of the "performance" of the particular disaster.

How long did the flood last?

In the past, how many days did it take for relief to arrive?

After the tornado, how long did it take for emergency shelters to be established?

The facts which follow such questions will lead to the obvious. . .food for x number of days in the attic of the flood areas, and some tents, etc. stored in the basement in tornado areas.

I use this simple approach to all aspects of survival preparations. *The quality of survival after a disaster is dependent upon the quality of the preparations taken before the disaster happened.*

In most of California today, disaster preparations for first aid, search and rescue, and transportation for injured citizens, are, except for some private efforts, *non-existent* at the state, county, or township levels.

After disaster, the familiar pattern of "Such and such has been declared a disaster area" seems by now to have become an attention-getting media requirement. This gets the rest of us to pay attention as the six o'clock news shows the usual aerial shots of the human and sometimes animal misery down below.

In these days of tight economies and shrinking budgets, one wonders why the almighty computer has not been drafted to delve into the dollar values of both action and non-action in known disaster areas.

Certainly, one feels that, in the light of the known facts, survival of a severely injured victim, the result of *any* disaster, is dependent on prompt action of a medical nature if life is to be sustained. Surely the question must follow: "How many lives have been needlessly lost due to lack of survival preparations of even a most *basic* nature so far?"

Couldn't the computer tell us which system is best dollars-

and-cents wise—preparation or non-preparation?

After over ten years in the survival business, it has become very clear to me that, in today's fast-paced society with budgets so severely trimmed, survival of the masses is going to have to be on an individual level.

As a follow-up to this statement, I present this:

> Given a good, broad assessment of all known facts, successful survival on the individual level using common sense and common every day items for survival preparation is not only possible, but *essential* if misery and loss of life are to be avoided.

This purpose of this, my second book, *Wright's Complete Disaster Survival Manual,* is to provide a more comprehensive, practical guide to individual and family survival than in the original version, *Survive, I Dare You, The Earthquake Awaits.*

In the following pages, I will deal with earthquake first and follow with other catastrophes when applicable. And, as I always stress to either the reader or the listeners at a seminar, merely being attentive is not enough. Take the *action* necessary to have made my time worthwhile. . .please!

Somehow, the message has to be made clear. In the event of a major quake, survival *during* the initial shock waves is a matter of where you are at that precise point in time. Obviously, there are places of high and low risk. The facts are unalterable. Call it fate, or whatever you will.

However, survival in the post-disaster period is *very much controllable,* by both authorities and public alike.

If the authorities are too involved with red tape to be involved with the man in the street, the people, Mr. and Mrs. John Q. Public, must be involved with and for. . .themselves.

Please read this manual from the first page forward. Hopping from section to section will cause you to miss the continuity and the many cross references made from one section to another.

Thank you.

CHAPTER 1
Facing Facts

The devil you know can't hurt you

I am a survivor. At age 16, I lived in my family's backyard shelter for almost a year. It was called an "Anderson" shelter, named after the British minister whose fancy title indicated that he was responsible for civilian preparation for war. Like thousands of others, as soon as the air raid siren sounded, if we were at home we dashed into the backyard and into that shelter.

During the time I waited to be old enough to go into the military, this shelter was almost a home. After our house was hit, it was all I had to call home. My mother went to stay with relatives in a safe area, and I stayed to "keep an eye on things," "things" being a small back yard and a pile of bricks!

As soon as the all-clear sounded, I, with all the other able-bodied men, went at once to the Civil Defense Post (there was one on every block) and reported for duty as a "Civilian Volunteer, Search and Rescue Brigade." We were given a hard hat (military helmet), a first aid shoulder bag, a portable stretcher, and an assigned "buddy." Very often you got a new buddy because the old one "bought it" the night before. Oh yes, we also were given an arm band, a big wide thing with the letters C.D. on it. Boy, was I a proud sixteen-year-old with that arm band on!

After being assigned an area, we went off as fast as possible to the newest devastation and proceeded to "search" and, when we found a live victim, "rescue." We were not paramedics by any stretch of the imagination, but under these tough conditions we became adept at the very necessary and basic first aid. Then, with a great sense of urgency (having found a live victim, our pride demanded we keep it that way), we climbed, stumbled, and, in many cases, clawed our way over the rubble with our victim holding on for dear life. Sometimes it was possible to make only one or maybe two rescues. The work was slow and painstaking, extracting the victim then having to get to the first aid station. Often it would take many hours to effect just one rescue.

Once the rescue was accomplished, we returned to the site to repeat the process. At a very heavily populated site, often many teams would get together and share the work, younger men doing the heavy clambering and carrying, older ones doing the digging.

How did it all work? The organization itself was fairly simple. Through the regional unemployment offices, all eligible people were recruited. On the federal level, all retired people were contacted. At the county level, through police and fire agencies, sites were designated similar to the Neighborhood Watch programs here.

Pay was very small. At first, the men who manned these Civil Defense posts and directed the volunteers were all either retirees or physically handicapped and not able to be in the armed forces. Each warden, as they were called, was responsible for a post. Each post was equipped with stretchers and first aid supplies and had radio communication linking it to a network of other posts, as well as the local hospitals, police, and fire units.

Each warden was responsible for the inventory, keeping up to date with the situations regarding hospital status, acute disaster areas, etc. For each warden on payroll, there were many of his friends helping as volunteers. Many of them slept at the post for weeks at a time; woe betide anyone caught trying to steal these vital supplies!

The outcome of all this was that, at the citizen level, thousands of lives were saved every day. Obviously, the system functioned without the aid of the bureaucracy, which could organize only to a certain level; the man on the scene did the rest.

Here in California, all those memories seem so far away. Yet, as soon as I hear the word "earthquake" or face an audience to give a seminar, the thought of that very effective program becomes as clear as that day long ago when it functioned so well.

Today, I am trying to teach survival preparations knowing that the system, as I have outlined it in the preceding paragraphs, does not exist. There are no teams of volunteers trained in search and rescue. . .the fate of victims will be left to chance and the hope that the injured can hang on until. . .

Having come this far in my life, chance is not an option. After all, I do have the experience, I do have survival knowledge; I can do the best I can for *me*. What about *you*, my fellow citizen?

Just as I was motivated those many years ago to prepare for my own survival and motivated to undertake my mission of spreading the word, so now I take you along on the journey of self-survival. But I warn you now: there will be no glossing over the truth. Facts are facts and must be faced. We cannot control loss of life; we *can* control conditions of survival, so let's start.

Myth:

During World War II and since, due to the devastation of cities and populations resulting from various disasters such as floods, earthquakes, and events like Mount St. Helens, the "experts" have accumulated vast amounts of information in their computers to be able to cope with just about anything; therefore people believe "It can't happen here!"

Fact:

Facts are history; to be useful they have to be extracted and tabulated. Today, after millions of dollars spent in the scientific area, it still takes a long time to determine just where a major quake occurs.

Why these millions of dollars are spent to occupy a few scientists in the pursuit of this knowledge is beyond me. The victims in the area already know, *at the moment of the first tremor,* where the event was. The rest of us being told avails them nothing that aids in their continued survival.

Today there is still much we do not know, for example:

—How much water is required to support 1 million people's survival for one week?

—How much vaccine is required to protect the same number from plague, rabies and other such epidemics that accompany disaster?

—How much antibiotics, blood, plasma, etc. will be needed for the estimated 50,000-70,000 casualties, and, more importantly, *where is it*?

—Then the vital question—how are these life-saving supplies to be distributed to those in need, one of whom could be you or me?

Myth:

T.V. newscasters who brag "You won't see ducking under the table at this station" and shows that depict a smooth delivery of injured to the well-organized hospitals encourage a sense of well-being that insulates the general public and supports the belief that "they" have it all in hand.

Fact:

During the height of the L.A. riots, this statement was made by the news media: "Centinella Hospital has so far received twenty-five casualties and are completely jammed up!"

The sad fact to be faced by us all is that we must prepare to survive with a loss of:

—Electricity. . .
—Natural Gas. . .
—Running water. . .
—Telephone. . .
—Radio/TV. . .
—Food and other essential stores. . .
—Public services, police, fire, and paramedics. . .
—Ability to drive.

Myth:

As soon as the shaking stops, the authorities will spring into action manning command posts and setting up communications networks to organize and dispatch paramedics and fire fighters, etc. The Red Cross will set up food kitchens and distribute needed supplies.

Fact:

Only those on duty at a command post will be there to run the controls. The rest of the required personnel will be in the same boat as the rest of us. . .stuck on the streets and freeways. . .trapped and unable to move. The earthquake is no respecter of persons.

Remember watching the firemen working the L.A. riots try to battle all those major fires and then add the fact that there will be a loss of water pressure.

Let's talk about paramedics. Even if they are able to travel, let's consider a few facts time-wise. How long does it take to render aid to a victim—just render the first required aid? Five minutes? Ten? That equates to six, at most twelve, victims an hour. That's leaving them on the ground where they lie. Now how can we expect paramedics to provide service for an estimated several thousand victims? County Sheriff Sherman Block in June of 1983 estimated that 12,000 to 55,000 injured would require hospitalization.

Trivia question for computer buffs: How many paramedics would it take to attend to 30,000 injured people so that the last to be treated was cared for within a time of, say. . .five hours?

Some further facts? In the report following the 1971 San Fernando earthquake, in the section dealing with "things to attend to as a result of this study" one of them was: "Steps must be taken to reduce the number of injuries due to flying glass." To date, not one county or government office has taken any steps to help the legion of clerical workers sitting under windows for the full eight hours of every day. Neither have schools, hospitals, law enforcement agencies, or most businesses of any kind!

The truth is that there is no possibility of a sudden surge of rescue workers coming to our aid. Law enforcement, the fire department, and the paramedics will be just as impotent in a major earthquake as they were in the L.A. riots. As for the Red Cross, they neither now have nor ever have had massive stockpiles of supplies, so there is no hope there.

I will not pursue this aspect further. Surely by now I have convinced you that you are "on your own" *totally.*

Myth:
Children at school are as safe as possible. They are drilled in what to do and, in the event of a major quake, will be well taken care of. They have plenty of food and water.

Fact:
In the event of a quake, children are taught to dive under the desk (tuck, duck, and hold) and, as soon as the shaking stops, leave for a designated area outside. Sounds great and very simple. The truth is that, in the average school, class size is now at about thirty (and getting worse), with no classroom aides.

Taking an average-size school of twenty classrooms, this equates to a student enrollment of approximately 600. Each classroom having one teacher equals twenty adults. Assuming this was a well-budgeted school, there might be about ten aides, which would equate to thirty adults. Add three clerks, one administrator, three cooks, and a custodian, and we have thirty-eight adults to care for *all* the needs of the 600 students under disaster conditions (provided all the adults survive; this is further discussed in Chapter 5)! If you are as concerned as I am, call your school and ask what the survival plans are (especially first aid, transportation, etc.). When you do call, please bear in mind that the primary concern of all school personnel is *education.* Funding and energy for survival needs is, after all, an extra burden for which they are not paid. Improvement of this situation will come only as a result of strong parental and public support.

Myth:

In the event of an earthquake, run to the nearest doorway, under a table, etc. Once the quake stops, go outside. If you are in your car, pull over and stay in it. Turn on the radio and wait for instructions.

—How long are you prepared to wait?
—What instructions do you think will come?

Most people really believe that, in the event of a major quake, the scenario will be something like this. Here are some more typical myth scenes:

Driving on the freeway.
The ground shakes, the steering feels funny, you stop and sit there while the shaking goes on. If you are religious you pray. . .others do whatever it is that they do. Others curse, "Damn, I'm going to be late for work!" Finally, the shaking stops. You wait, look around, notice that the driver next to you is doing the same thing, so you get out and join the throng of drivers now "visiting" on the freeway. Everyone seems a little nervous, but all are "hanging in there."

The general consensus of opinion is that there must be some damage up ahead, and soon the police helicopters will circle over-head and tell you what ramps to use to exit. "They have it all planned you know." All is calm; there is no panic. Some people have some beer or a bottle of liquor, and little parties break out—kind of fun, really. It breaks the routine. How pleasant an adventure it all is!

At the shopping center.
It is quiet in the store. The fluorescent lights create a bright, shadowless world. A sale is on and the place is packed. That smell that is always in the air of a large store—a mixture of perfume and air deodorant—creeps up one's nostrils.

Suddenly, the lights flicker once or twice, the ground starts to move beneath your feet, your body sways in a way that you cannot control. You notice things around you. The overhead lights are all swaying. . .one of those mannequins with the fixed silly grin falls over. . .the shaking goes on. . ."Must be a big one," you think. Then, just as quickly as it started, it stops. "Whew!" you breath a sigh of relief. Right away everyone starts talking at once, sharing thoughts with each other. Perfect strangers seem to be close friends.

A voice comes over the P.A. system: "Good day, shoppers. We understand there has been a major earthquake, but there is no need to panic, and to celebrate we have reduced everything in Ladies Wear by 30 percent—hurry for the bargains." (Ever notice that it is always Ladies Wear?)

The at-home scene.
The kids have left for school and "he" left an hour ago. You have a cup of coffee in your hand and are about to call your closest girlfriend down the street. Your thoughts are on everyday things: the children, the mortgage. Why was he in such a bad mood this morning? After all, it was his idea to move to the suburbs. So he has to drive a lot. But it's nice having neighbors so close, kind of like our own little town.

Just as you reach for the phone, a strange feeling comes over you. You pause, phone in hand. Then it starts. You feel it in your feet first; the ground kind of flutters. Then, the real shaking starts. You dive under the table. . .now it is really rough, bumping and rolling. . .the sound of things falling and smashing on the floor. "My God, how long will it last? Will the house stay up? Will I be hurt?"

Suddenly, you notice that the shaking has stopped but you are still crouched under the table shaking. Then you jump out of your skin. A small scream leaves your mouth by itself, as though you are not in control. It's the shrill ringing of the telephone and it seems twice as loud. Scrambling out from under the table, you hear the voice of your girl friend: "What did you think of that. . .my house is a *mess*. Now I'll have to stay and clean up and I was looking forward to going out. Oh well, it's the broom for me. How about you?"

Now let's explode these myths. But first remember that we are considering a *major* earthquake, not the trembler that affects only a small area. We must all be aware of and prepare for the major quake that will affect the whole of Southern California, from Bakersfield to San Diego, all happening at once.

First example, the school scene.
In the event of a major quake, all the kids *will* go under their desks. The dedicated teachers *will* calm the children down, somehow. Stories of great heroism be forthcoming. . .afterwards. But what of the now?

Those who can will evacuate the buildings. As for the injured, again, stories of great heroism will be forthcoming; but the sad fact is that our schools are sadly lacking in medical skills and supplies, while the transportation of the injured is totally in the hands of

25

chance. No preparation has been taken to secure transportation for, in some cases, many miles to the nearest hospital for those schools in outlying districts.

Of as much concern to me is the state of school buses, traveling not only country roads but busy freeways. One driver to, in most cases, fifty school children, with not one ounce of preparation other than instructions to "Pull over and get on the horn."

Even after the initial shockwave is over, what most schools are lacking is a supply of food and water on anything like a realistic level. Nor have they prepared for real survival—*outside* of those buildings that are, in many cases, doomed to fall down.

Recently, I heard a woman say to her second-grade son, "Don't worry; as soon as the quake stops and they call me, I'll jump in the car and come and get you." Little junior went off to school secure in the knowledge that "Mommy will take care of it." Mommy, on the other hand, really believes that there will be a phone call, and she will jump in the car as planned!

The fact is, there will be no phone and no roads to travel on. The radio will tell you to stay off the streets, and little Junior is going to have to stay at school and "tough it out," limited supplies or not.

After ten years in the field, it continues to amaze me that there are still school administrators who really believe that calling 911 will bring assistance for injured students after a major earthquake and still have not accepted the reality and potential of a disaster never seen in this country.

Second example, the freeway.

Morning and evening, the freeways of the greater Los Angeles area are jammed with over a million speeding cars. Coupled with this is another group, of close to the same number, using the surface streets in buses, cars and on cycles (motor and pedal).

This mass of travelers is so confined that any disturbance of the flow of one affects the other. Change on the freeway affects surface streets and visa versa. Ramp speed is affected, creating bottle necks in both areas.

In the event of a major earthquake, several reactions will occur simultaneously:

1. Large fissures and buckling of the road surface will occur. Due to the high rate of speed, vast chain-reaction pile-ups will take place, involving hundreds of cars in all directions.

2. Major cloverleafs and overpasses will collapse, dumping cars and debris on the road below.
3. Surface streets will be affected not only by these events, but also by falling buildings, high-tension wires, and debris of all kinds.

Driving the freeway will be like this: you are driving along and, as fast as a rifle shot, your car becomes a bucking horse. If you react quickly enough, if you are not day dreaming, your mind on other things (the job, being late, etc.), you may be able to pull over in time to avoid a collision. Once you do come to a stop, you still have to be concerned about the "other guy" hitting you.

The surroundings will look like a scene from a fright movie. Thousands of cars will litter the freeways, some rammed into by others, some piled on top of each other. Under what once were overpasses will be heaps of concrete, twisted metal, and mangled autos.

If you can step out of your car, around you will look like battlefield. The dead and dying; cries for help that cannot be answered. The same scene will be repeated on the surface streets.

—Now what do we *really* have?
—What is the devil we *must* know if we are to survive?
—What grim facts *have* to be faced?

A major quake at peak-load period will produce a death toll on our highways in the thousands. The high average speed guarantees it.

The injury rate will be incalculable. Added to this grim situation is an even sadder one. At the present time, given the state of preparedness, victims will perish for lack of medical aid. The dead, dying, and injured will remain where they lie for days. Even if Army medics are dropped in, consider the enormity of the situation:

—What do we do with several thousand people suddenly injured?
—Where do you put the several thousand wrecked vehicles they were in?
—How many months will it take to clear the miles of littered freeways?

Picture yourself just as you are today. You are right in the middle of that mess and you step out of your car, with the majority of others, without a scratch. What do you do now? Or suppose you have a laceration that is bleeding, or some other treatable injury, and you don't even have a Band-Aid!

Third example, the shopping center.
The store is crowded for the big sales event. People jostle elbow-to-elbow looking for bargains. Then, it happens. The first slight tremor stops everyone in his tracks.

Then, as the shaking becomes more violent, it suddenly goes dark and chunks of ceiling and overhead lights begin to fall on the shoppers below, who, in screaming panic, claw and hack to get away. . .to get out. . .to get anywhere but where they are!

The air is full of dust. The noise level is ear-splitting. The floor space is taken up with falling objects, stumbling bodies, and darkness. It seems like an eternity, but finally the shaking stops. For a long time the noise goes on. . .

If you are lucky, you will somehow, not even knowing how, find yourself outside the store. The parking lot is a junkyard of squashed cars from downed lights and once-high wires. You listen to the noise from inside the store; cries for help that cannot be answered. . .but you are safe. . .now what?

Grim statistics? Yes. Bear in mind that, of the 20,000-odd inspected and found-to-be-faulty buildings, less than 10 percent have had any structural repairs carried out.

Malls are a fairly new item in the construction field, but the design of massive concrete structures is so far unproven. Now add the fact that in the downtown section of most of greater Los Angeles and the surrounding area, major buildings (libraries, city halls, municipal buildings, and such) are very old and unlikely to stand up to much intensity of shock waves.

Fourth and final example, the home.
Although not newsworthy enough to be widely reported, the quake activity of just the last few years has produced a high number of ordinary homes so badly damaged that they were unlivable. San Francisco and the Bay Bridge played a front-page role on both T.V. and in newspaper coverage. What was not covered as prominently were the hundreds of homes damaged by the same quake.

In many cases, homes damaged in Coalinga in 1988 are still not repaired. As recently as October 13, 1992, the *Daily News* reported that Oakland Mayor Elihu Harris defended his city's response to the

1989 earthquake. It was also reported that only 600 building permits have been issued to the 2,777 dwelling units destroyed. Of the 1,300 apartments and hotel rooms lost, only 464 have been replaced. It must be pointed out that these damages were the result of only 6.7 to 7.1 quakes! Your chances of coming through an 8.+ quake with a house intact are indeed slim. That is not to say that all houses will be flat, but one collapsed wall or a bulged-up slab can make the house unlivable.

Let's go back to the woman sitting in the kitchen in the early morning. The house is quiet; all the family have finally left for their day. She reaches for the phone and. . .WHAMMO, it strikes!

This newly developed sub-division with its freshly constructed pads becomes fair game for earthquake tremors which rip through the footings and split the fresh concrete slabs asunder (an existing undisturbed grade fares much better). As the pad and slab split, the walls are placed under great strain. Movement of the walls affects the roof (especially with two-story homes), which can slide, if not collapse outright.

Inside, the woman has ducked under the table as furniture, bookcases, and kitchen cabinet contents dance all over the place.

Dust fills the air as chunks of ceiling fall down. Soon, the shaking stops and the woman's first instinct (a good one) is to get out, *anyway she can!* The whole house is a mess.

Climbing over broken glass, finally reaching the outside, she stands in the backyard trembling and sobbing. It is some time before she notices that she now stands in a pool of blood from her cut foot. . .

Still in her robe, she looks at what was once her home and wonders, "What on earth do I do now?" Within a few minutes the first aftershocks strike. . . .

Let's review what we have just covered. *The devil you know can't hurt you*—remember? So far, has this chapter been fact or fancy? What do *you* think? More fact than fancy, as far as I am concerned, but I can hear the skeptics saying something like:

"Over dramatization. A doom-and-gloomer looking for publicity." Are they right? Could be.

Now let me ask you *these* questions:

Do you drive the freeways? Ever had to make a sudden stop as a reaction to the driver up front? As you came to a stop, have you ever sweated it out as you looked up and saw the vehicle behind you was still coming toward you? Have you ever sat for fifteen or twenty minutes hemmed in with nowhere to go as some minor fender-bender was cleared somewhere up ahead?

Think about a thousand fender benders. . .all at the same time! Still think it sounds far-fetched?

How about coming north through the Mullholland cut dropping down into the San Fernando Valley? Encino is off to the left, Studio City off to the right, ahead is Sherman Oaks and the whole valley stretching on north into Sylmar and Newhall. Now, imagine a major quake that devastates that whole area right before your eyes, even right back behind you—back to Irvine, Huntington Beach, Costa Mesa, all shaking to pieces. . .think of the results of such a continuous great upheaval!

This is the major quake we must all prepare for.

Focus on the remembrances of the L.A. riots witnessed by the world. As the fires burned and the looters ran amok, do you remember the feeling of hopelessness that permeated the whole scene? All those fires that were out of control—how haunting was the absence of sirens. No rescue vehicles; in fact, no traffic on the freeways at all. . .

Now activate that whole picture substituting a major earthquake at 7:30 in the morning while the freeways are alive with those thousands of commuters. Do you think I am still overly dramatic?

It is true that a quake at the wrong time can be more disastrous than one that hits in the night hours. But whether the survivors are standing in their backyards, on the freeways, or wherever, the challenge is still the same: *"What now?"*

Of all natural disasters, the one that hits without warning, the *only* one, is the earthquake. All the others—floods, storms, tornadoes, etc.—all can be seen developing before they are felt.

Even if we put all logical facts aside and follow a movie script showing the fleets of helicopters, the National Guard vehicles, the stirring music as rescue is effected, to even the most stubborn skeptic, reality is still inescapable.

—How much time before that type of scenario comes to pass?
—How much time does the injured person have?
—How long can *you* wait for water in 100-degree heat?
—How long can *you* survive in an unprepared backyard in unknown weather conditions?

None of this factualization is new!

Major earthquakes and disasters have occurred in cities around the entire area of the "Ring of Fire" in places with much higher population densities than ours. [Ring of Fire is the name given to the area in the Pacific Ocean that swings in a northerly arc from Japan on the one side to the North American continent on the other. It contains much volcanic and earthquake activity and is the home of the Pacific Plates.]

Please don't try that "But we build our cities better than they do" bunk! *It is not reality!!!* As reported by the Department of the Interior in their report published after the 1971 San Fernando earthquake (quoted further in another section of this manual):

> "Surprisingly large ground motions were recorded. They *exceeded* at some places the El Centro and Taft records, which have guided earthquake resistive design for *30 years.* The high *vertical* accelerations recorded on instruments and reported by witnesses *probably* contributed to increased damage to structures." (All italics are mine.)

What does this report tell us?

Obviously, all designs approved for buildings prior to 1971 (that's from the 1940s, folks) and for the years during which the codes were being updated (what is a fair estimate of time for code changes—three years?), all such buildings are not strong enough for present-day quakes! Remember, the San Fernando quake was given a 6.8! Now think of all the schools and public buildings built in this time frame. The statistics are staggering!

Even so, for those of us who study information as we are able to get hold of it, it is not that difficult to assemble the pieces of the jigsaw puzzle that is the greater Los Angeles area. Never lose sight of the fact that one of the great problems facing the L.A. subway builders was the lack of information of just where essential services of sewer, gas, telephone, etc. really were. They just kept drilling into the stuff!

Still want to stick to the better-building-code theory?

No, the real devil we have to face is that of our own apathy. Are we either too busy or too indifferent to want to take steps to ensure the safety of the very young, or the very old, or *ourselves?* No, I won't give up. To do so would be to admit to negativism!

At this time of going to press, less that 1 percent of drivers carry any survival supplies in their vehicle.

Not one police black-and-white officially carries any extra water or earthquake-survival gear!

Our challenge, then, is to survive without any public services or utilities, no stores or pharmacies, and, worst of all, no organized survival planning at the citizen level.

Each day, it seems, we are faced with graphic illustrations, through newspaper and T.V., of the realities of misery that is, by now, the accepted norm for life on our planet. Should that misery be the result of natural disaster (floods, hurricanes, tornados, and such), the media really has a field day. We always see the victims look so helpless; one feels this great empathy with the sufferers. They seem at a total loss as they present a brave face to the callous reporter asking those heartless questions: "How did you feel when you looked at the pile of rubble that once was your home?"

The brave answer always seems to be, "I don't know what we are going to do now."

Yet, if we were to investigate a little further, we would find in most cases of natural disaster:

1. There was plenty of warning given, or

2. The action was a repeat performance of previous years.

People living in flood-prone areas have known of the problem for years. The oft-heard remarks along the lines of "Hurricane Blaa, which tore its way through here was almost as bad as Hurricane Bloo of a few years ago."

Similarly, we see pictures of store owners and others nailing up freshly purchased sheets of plywood for protection from the impending storm. One wonders what happened in the period of time between then and now? Why haven't store owners and others developed a system of steel shutters that could be pulled down each time a storm was due? Why waste all that material?

In tornado country, why do people not have storm cellars to go to? Why do the codes not include them as a part of the home?

Knowing the hazards of the area and the likelihood of "losing it all," why haven't people figured it out?

As a proud and independent people, we shun advice and look down with scorn on people of other nations who, from time to time, are forced to flee their homes. Yet, for lack of effort, we allow ourselves to be put in the same situation when, despite our own particular traumatic disaster, we stand with just the clothes on our back and say "what do we do now?" and wait for the Red Cross or Salvation Army to rustle up some food, clothes and shelter for our continued survival.

Coming as I do from a very resourceful British heritage, it is only now, after hundreds of face-to-face presentations with audiences large and small, that an answer is coming to me.

We in America are handicapped in our approach to reality. We are:

1. Conditioned by the media to seeing all forms of adversity.

We have "seen it all." No gruesome scene has been omitted from our educational package. Not only are we shown the picture of the corpse wrapped in a sheet, but, when possible, a zoom-in close-up of a glistening pool of the victim's blood on the ground where it ebbed from his body is provided. Similarly,

2. We are transported as quickly as possible to the scene of the latest disaster (hang on, folks, our camera crew is standing by), no matter where on the planet the disaster occurred.

We follow close at hand as the interviewer asks the same questions, hearing the same mumbling answers. We become as callous as the question itself: "How do you feel now that your husband and your only two children were killed before your eyes?" Horror loses its impact; pain is not transmitted through the media, written or visual. The media justify this attitude as a means to crisp reporting. After all, horror must be presented in a *newsworthy* form. . .why mess it up with pathos and drama? Why express pain? Likewise,

3. We are carefully educated by the media in that we are fed the scenes of the dramatic on both ends of the scale: the negative situation of the victims and the positive of the recovery (the rescue, etc.). What we are not shown is the picture of reality, the too-boring sight of the majority of the victims affected in a manner that is not newsworthy. Their scene lacks impact.

A house destroyed along with a hundred others is not newsworthy, whereas the one house with relatives frantically digging to find a lost family member is. It is the opportunity for more heartless questions to further insulate us.

We have all been brainwashed into the belief that the government will be there to save us from this pariah disrupting our lives: "The National Guard will be called." We have come to expect this as a right and that it will be so. What we are not made to realize is that these forces are not standing by waiting for the disaster to occur. It takes great time and effort to assemble and disburse troops (look at the aftermath of Hurricane Andrew). In the meantime, the loss of life that will result is incalculable.

In Europe and other previously devastated (by war or natural disaster, or both) countries, we have a first-hand knowledge of the *real* reality. When the news media's narrow tunnel vision is presented to us, we have our own down and dirty experience to guide us. To me, the story of the little boy who rescued a snake after it had been run over sums it up. After the snake got well it turned and bit the surprised child, who remonstrated in a very indignant voice, "Why did you do that to me, who befriended you and saved your life?" The snake replied, "But you knew I was a snake!"

The word "survival," to those of us who have experienced such devastation, means a whole inventory of *actions* to be *taken*, not just to be *considered* in passing and then *dismissed*. Actions that, once taken, will result in a very positive and comforting situation. People trying to cope in their own backyard, neighbors helping neighbors, and teachers saving students are just a small part of those actions. It is in this unheralded and unpublicized realm of reality that most of us live. And it is in this same realm of reality that many of us will die, unfortunately and unnecessarily.

That is the reality that hit me those many years ago as a result of that one news flash. It is that difference in our attitudes that I am attempting to rectify today.

Remember, this book is called a survival manual. By taking a few well-planned and relatively inexpensive steps, successful survival becomes a possible reality.

Which would you choose? An earthquake and no preparation, or a whole lot of preparation and no earthquake?

What happens in the first five hours is a matter of life and death for some. What happens in the first ten days is the difference between my own well-prepared backyard with my own loved ones or a tent city and someone else's loved ones for some time down the road!

If you feel that way, too, let's take up the challenge together with our families! Let's have some fun as we put into action the positive steps outlined in the following chapters.

CHAPTER 2

The Positive Side

Knowing not only how, but when and why

The great majority of people faced with a sudden disaster (natural or otherwise) *survive the actual event*. The *majority*.

An earthquake that kills 1000 people has 100,000 who survive the first shock-wave. The atomic disaster at Chernobyl killed fewer than 100 people as a result of the original explosion. (Hiroshima and Nagasaki were exceptions to this rule.) So what is the point?

Few of us will die in the disastrous event itself. The hazard is in those few critical hours *immediately following the disaster*.

How sad to survive the event only to perish afterwards for want of medical or other services. Or to be so emotionally traumatized as to be affected for the rest of one's life!

The answer? The quality of life *after* a major catastrophe depends on the quality of preparations taken *before*.

How can we achieve this "quality of life" after a major disaster? Primarily, the question arises, "How badly do you *want* a decent quality of life after a disaster?" In the light of recent disasters, both natural and man-made, the sight of refugees (made so through no fault of their own) waiting for relief with gaunt faces and hopeless expressions should at least be an incentive to do something!

Using my formula, basically all that is required is a simple evaluation of your own particular circumstances and the details of your daily life, then taking the actions necessary for your own and your family's welfare after the event.

I consider my formula to be the "three legged stool of survival planning." These three legs are:

Where will you be?
What will you do?
What will you need?

I use these three simple questions as the foundation for my survival plan. These are the legs of a three-legged stool that will enable me to sit in comfort at my time of need!

This survival plan will allow you to logically formulate your own survival requirements. It is designed to allow for individual needs and adaptations, but should be followed as closely as possible.

The fundamental question really is whether you are one of the do-bees or one of the do-nothing-until-it-happens crowd.

I'd like to share with you one of my nightmare scenarios, the one where I wake up in a cold sweat because a terrible 8.8 earthquake has happened. After the shaking has stopped, I am standing up on a hill somewhere looking down at all the devastation, the smoking ruins, the muffled moans of injured people, and nothing is happening. . .*nothing.*

I sit there on my hill and watch for a long time; still nothing is happening. Then I realize that the whole population has gone into shock. Being so insulated by the media and soft platitudes, the terrible reality was hidden from them. Now that it is here, they are spellbound with the enormity of it all. . .

Usually, I continue this muse as the waking state becomes my measure of dream to reality. Then I go into my "if only" phase. "If only I could have done more." "If only X could have happened." "If only. . ."

DIAGRAM 1—THE THREE-LEGGED SURVIVAL STOOL

Like to hear some of them. . .those positive things we *could* do something about?

Out there somewhere are people who are on life-support systems in nursing homes and even in their own homes. What of them when the power goes off? Hospitals have a built-in safety system for this eventuality; what about these others? There is a whole population of "legal drug-dependent people" out there somewhere: diabetics, cardiac patients of all kinds, cancer patients on a treatment program, epileptics, this kind of thing. Some of their medications must be stored at constant temperatures.

What a great undertaking for an organization of service, like the Boy Scouts or Girl Scouts.

I see all these close-knit congregations in churches everywhere. Safety in numbers? What a glorious opportunity for a simple home-based, two-way radio network housed in the rectory with a "walkie talkie" in each home. Now all the shut-ins and the sick can really be taken care of.

I worked out the dollar expense once. . .tried to interest our pastor. It was a realistic figure.

In every city and town in "Quakesville," Southern California, there is a great predominance of warehouse-style building material stores for us "Do-it-yourselfers." Next time you are in one, look up. (You are going to be taught to do often this as you read on!) There, above your head, you will see pallets of all kinds stacked to the rafters (How do they do that?) with all kinds of materials from roof shingles to wood of all sizes.

As the first tremor starts, these stacks of pallets are already on the way down, and the shoppers below do not even have time to look up. I wonder whose job it is to see that this is not allowed. Do we need an ordinance?

In my nightmares, I break out into a cold sweat as I see so many stores and supermarkets explode before my eyes. . .at peak shopping time, too. Yet the shaking stopped half an hour ago? If only they had been told to hold an earthquake drill, somebody would have been designated to turn off that six-inch gas main. . .I wonder whose job it is to see that this is not allowed to happen. Fire Marshall? City Inspector? Perhaps we need another ordinance?

In these days of strange things happening due to "budgets" and stuff, I've watched the emergence of the "portable school syndrome" all over the place. Most of the seven or eight new schools or additions in my own city are like this. Why are those double-wides sitting on scrap wood pieces when I know the code calls for "one approved stand every six feet in any direction"? These installations would not be allowed in any mobile home park in the Los Angeles County. Those structures hold only families; these schoolrooms hold thirty to forty kids!

Then there's that huge "portable assembly hall" (portable my eye) I watched them build on the site! "Why are the few windows so high off the ground?" I asked. "Because that's the way it was designed," I was told. I looked up at forty tons of steel girders sitting on the flimsy two-by-four walls and in my nightmare saw seven hundred children in that building at quake time. Then I remembered that there were three such buildings on other school sites.

"But these buildings are not in the jurisdiction of the City Building and Safety Department, you know." Then I wake up and wonder, "Why not?"

What if the parents only knew? How many "what ifs" can you think of? Wonder if we could do something about it? My address is in the back of the book!

Let's go on then. . .

Take a moment to consider *your* natural disaster.

Here in California, it is mostly earthquakes. The emphasis of this manual is primarily in that direction. Since earthquakes give no warning, we can use this negative in a very positive manner. If we were to prepare for all natural disasters as we should for earthquakes (at least ten days' survival needs), we would be far ahead of the game!

To pursue this reasoning further requires that we be prepared for survival for each twenty-four hours of any given day!

Since "where will you be?" is the first question, we should start right there, at the first leg of our stool (see Diagram 1).

Where Will I Be?

The usual first reaction to this question is "How the heck do I know?" Such an answer, of course, is a cop-out. At first glance, this would seem to be a very difficult question. Not only where will *you* as an individual be, but where will each of your other *family members* be? When starting my journey as a survival specialist, this was the first obstacle I had to overcome. Once it was overcome, the rest of the actions became routine.

How do we find the answer then? During the research period of my work, a very prominent fact became clear:

Most of us lead very dull and humdrum lives.We get up at the same time, we leave the house at the same time, go to the store, do our errands all at about the same time. There seems to be a security in routine. I fit very much in this category. Most of us who are self-employed do, at least if success is expected!

It follows, then, that most of us could work out our own "Where will you be?" question very well. Given a time of day or night we know exactly where we will be. We will be at home, on the job, driving, or some other place (the store, the dentist, running some other errand). Simplified then, this set of facts leads us to a new rule:

There are only four places we can be at the time of any major disaster:

1. At home
2. Traveling
3. On the job or at school
4. Those other places

Now the question "Where will I be?" should make a little more sense. I will be in one of four places! Let's study Diagram 2.

We see that in the period of twenty-four hours, the twelve o'clock position has us in bed. For all but night-shift workers, this will apply. Each of the four circled positions is linked to its next circle by a thick line that represents time. The circle is complete, as the day will be, when we are back at "square one," in this case, back in bed. It follows that, if we take an eraser and rub a space in one of the thick joining lines, we will have our progress around the circle interrupted. BAMM!!! This represents the earthquake event, the point of time at which our normal progress throughout our day was stopped. Now all we have to know is: what part of the circle were we in? That is the answer to "Where will I be?"

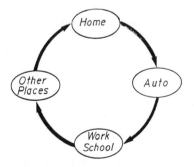

DIAGRAM 2—WHERE WILL I BE?

We have determined how to answer the question "Where will we be?" Now we must find the answers to the questions "What will I do?" and "What will I need?" We have established the four places we are likely to be at the moment the problem arises; considering those four likely places, what is our *action*? Let me give you a little "lecture," some points for consideration.

When we consider these four locations, one very important fact must be accepted and understood. Of the four places we occupy on a regular basis during our day, only two of them are under our own control:

1. Home, because we live in it (and in many cases own it); and

2. The automobile, because we own our vehicle.

The rest of the places are *not* under our own control. As soon as we enter the workplace, we surrender our freedom to our employers, very few of whom have any intentions of taking care of their own needs, let alone the employees, us. Likewise the other places in item four. I have yet to see a sign in a store that states "In the event of disaster do this. . ." What's the lesson then?

From the time we get out of bed in the morning, we are in control of our survival needs in only two places: right where we are (at home) and in our automobile! Does that mean that we have no control over the rest of the time? No. But it does mean that we have to adjust our thinking to accommodate these facts. There are only two places that I can prepare for my own survival: my home and my vehicle.

Now, since I drive my vehicle to get to work and to the other places, it must follow that if my home and my vehicle are *disaster ready,* then I must be ready!

I have spent ten years of my life trying to get that message across! Preparing for disaster is as simple as that.

Prepare the home. Prepare the car. And the rest takes *care of itself.*

Today, as we sit here, me writing and you reading, thousands of people have discovered the futility of running to the backyard unprepared after an earthquake:

"It just can't be done."

"It is hopeless."

Yet, just a little effort and preparation will take the "less" out of the situation, and leave the "hope" intact! This is the journey we are now going to take together. We will look at where we will *be,* what we will *do,* and what we will *need* in each of the situations of our day. Then, we will consider the other persons who are living in apartments and who use public transportation.

Before we go on, I would like you to turn back to the first paragraphs of Chapter 1. There, I outlined what was a very successful system for that time in London. Realize that there is no system at the citizen level yet here in California or in the rest of the United States. If a "Ross Perot" type of energy could be directed to the problem, there would very soon be, of that I have no doubt! As a logical human being reading this manual, keep the facts *as they are,* in clear perspective.

There is a whole new industry that has come into being whose sole business is "survival." Its representatives are found at swap meets, county fairs, and "earthquake preparedness shows." Their products usually fall into two main categories:

1. First aid kits, and
2. Survival packs and/or supplies.

The sales persons often have fancy titles such as "Support Counselor," and I have seen one whose card read "Crisis Management Consultant." I would love to tell you to go buy a kit and forget about everything else (including reading this manual), but it doesn't go that way. If it did, it would be like buying a car and not taking driving lessons!

Learning to survive in the backyard is not a difficult task. Preparing to do so is merely putting together items you already have (in most cases), and knowing where they are when you need them.

Common sense must tell you that having a good first aid book is of no use if you haven't opened it! The thought of standing with a huge gash on your thigh (a result of flying glass), trying to stop the bleeding with one hand and attempting to turn the pages with the other, looking for "How to stop bleeding," sounds ludicrous. . .or does it? If you are one of the 95 percent who are not prepared, don't laugh. You may one day be in a similar situation!

Following the directions given in this manual and putting together your own survival needs is a personal thing (like buying your own clothes). Having these items on hand for when they are needed is a wonderful added bonus.

Going out into the backyard and, with the family, making decisions like, "We'll put the fire pit over there, the toilets over there," etc. is a strong step to confidence-building that puts you far ahead in the survival game!

Confidence.

This is a most neglected word, often forgotten in survival manuals. It is the antidote for mental and emotional trauma, the type of trauma that is the by-product of disaster. All the experts agree that the finest weapon in the survival arsenal to fight this kind of trauma is *confidence.*

The sooner my self-*confidence* returns, the sooner I know I am going to make it. To me, there is nothing more *confidence*-building than going into my *own* backyard, putting on my *own* change of clothes, and pouring a nice glass of water out of my *own* supplies put away several years ago!

"Survival after the earthquake will take place one way or another," say the cynics. Of course this is true. How many lives and how many minds can we save with the types of preparations recommended in this manual we will never know.

For me, who has survived for almost a year in a backyard, I know it can be done. I am living proof. Whether it can also be fun is debatable and depends on a person's life style! What a surprise it would be if families were able to survive with restricted radio time and no T.V.! What a joy to rediscover the realm of books (that time-honored escape of yesteryear), and real family communication.

Now let's move on before we get too bogged down in detail.

I have tried to keep the text lively while, at the same time, paying as much attention to detail as possible. I have also had to be aware that there are very few people with any prior knowledge of this kind of activity.

For many of my readers I realize that the thought of being in the backyard for a long period of time is almost unthinkable, and sleeping out for the first time a nightmare! Trust me; you are going to have to sleep somewhere, and your own backyard sure beats a public shelter with strangers. It is well worth a little effort now in this, the quiet time!

The following chapters will try to be as broad as possible to cover actions that can be taken for all disasters. Let's go on now—and good luck.

Chapter 3
Travel

The automobile

Throughout the rest of the world, it is believed that we in America have a love affair with our automobile. It is claimed that we, above all others, lavish loving care and many hours of hard work polishing, vacuuming, and washing our cars. Others support an industry unique to us Americans, the "car wash," where our pride and joy is soaped, scrubbed, and polished. Traveling any distance in many states (California especially) poses a distinct problem, making the automobile a cared-for necessity.

Daily, for a variety of reasons, millions of us perform what I term the ritual of "slamming the door." Leaving the house we slam the front door. . .open and slam the garage door. . .and (usually minutes late) we scream off down the road after having slammed the car door!

Meanwhile, the second car also gets into the act as taking the kids to school or running off to those "other places" becomes the next order of business. In those "other places," we become especially vulnerable.

For whatever the reason, the journey for the late commuter is mostly a hazard. Racing each other in the futile pursuit of lost time, the journey in many cases (accidents happen) is not completed as planned. For the rest of the travelers, arrival at the destination is a time of "coming down" from the journey just completed. Often, the start of the day is ruined by the leftover anger caused by the actions of some other driver.

So, for the millions of us who are traveling, the question "Where will I be?" is easily answered: in the automobile.

Remembering our previous conclusion, that there are only two places under our own control, and accepting the fact that, with few exceptions, we do not go anywhere except where we drive, the automobile (from a survival point of view) is first on our priority list.

We spend more time *in* it and *with* it during our time away from home. In these hard economic times, many commuters spend very little time at home during the week, being home only for short periods on weekends. Many in the work force cannot wait for the weekend to dash off and become "recreation junkies," thereby spending even less time at home.

I have always recommended the auto as the number one "survival pod," for even in extreme disaster situations, the good old auto is always there somewhere close by! In the recent Florida/Louisiana hurricanes, it was significant to me that many buildings and homes were down, but, with few exceptions, the auto was sitting there totally accessible. Oh, it may, in some cases, have had a tree across it or was up to its hubcaps in water, but if there had been an adequate survival kit on board, what a difference it would have made for the well-being of the owner!

Perhaps we do give too much T.L.C. to our auto. Adding a little more T.L.C. for *us* is really what this chapter is all about. My aim is to slow you down a little and ask you to view your travel patterns from a different angle, as it were. We must first, however, define the finer points of our travel and more clearly define the first leg of our survival stool, "Where will I be?"

For those millions who journey each day, a classification of the journey must first be undertaken. I ask you now to consider your journey using the format which follows. Rate yourself as to both hazard and risk.

TRAVEL SURVEY

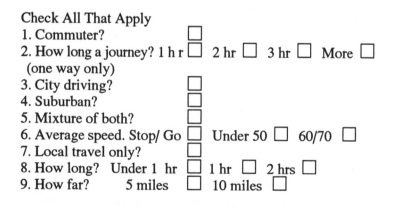

Check All That Apply
1. Commuter? ☐
2. How long a journey? 1 h r ☐ 2 hr ☐ 3 hr ☐ More ☐
   (one way only)
3. City driving? ☐
4. Suburban? ☐
5. Mixture of both? ☐
6. Average speed. Stop/ Go ☐ Under 50 ☐ 60/70 ☐
7. Local travel only? ☐
8. How long? Under 1 hr ☐ 1 hr ☐ 2 hrs ☐
9. How far? 5 miles ☐ 10 miles ☐

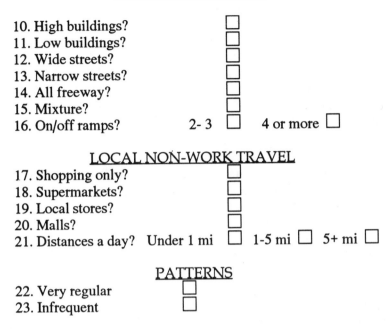

TERRAIN TRAVELED

10. High buildings? ☐
11. Low buildings? ☐
12. Wide streets? ☐
13. Narrow streets? ☐
14. All freeway? ☐
15. Mixture? ☐
16. On/off ramps?   2- 3 ☐   4 or more ☐

LOCAL NON-WORK TRAVEL

17. Shopping only? ☐
18. Supermarkets? ☐
19. Local stores? ☐
20. Malls? ☐
21. Distances a day? Under 1 mi ☐ 1-5 mi ☐ 5+ mi ☐

PATTERNS

22. Very regular ☐
23. Infrequent ☐

As you rate your time in the automobile, several points should jump out at you. Let's do some simple "fact finding." Obviously, I have no idea of your journey, nor you of mine. One thing we all have in common, however, is the hazard and risk factor of our daily journey. Remembering the sentiments of Chapter 1, *The devil you know can't hurt you*, I believe that the main reason most of us ignore survival preparation for the automobile is because we really are unaware of either our *hazard* or our *risk* factor.

Let's see if we can't put this into focus. Examine the two ends of the scale of the first section, items 1 through 9. First, let's take a high-volume traveler, the long-term commuter. The stats would be something like:

—Long time commuter, with a two-hour journey.
—Mixture of both city and suburban driving (travels in from the suburbs each day) at 60/70 m.p.h., has a stop-and-go journey.
—With a two-hour journey at 60/70 miles an hour, this person travels more than ten miles a day—that's for sure!
—This commuter is an old hand at his/her journey, drives a

total of four hours a day, and knows every turn in the road!

Now let's look at the other end of the scale, the commuter who drives:

—Local travel only.
—Less than one hour each way.
—All city driving.
—Under 50 m.p.h.
—Low buildings
—Wide streets.

This is a suburban or town dweller who daily travels a shorter, non-freeway journey. This person may use a freeway, but only for a short time, and travels probably less than two hours a day. Knowing the journey, this driver uses the same route each day.

What is the comparison of these two drivers?

The first driver is obviously in a high-risk category—long journey, high speed, and in with a mass of others doing the same thing. The hazard factor is high due to the mixture of the city and suburban driving and the high speeds maintained.

Directly opposite is the second driver, who is a "local yokel" type. This person travels around town to a local job and stays pretty close to home driving at a slow, fairly safe speed each day, with a total travel time of two hours or less.

Now let's talk about these two examples from a survival point of view. Obviously, the risk and hazard factor is high for the one but does not seem that bad for the other. Yet both face the *same challenges* immediately after the disaster.

Where will they be? On their journey.

Both are familiar with the route, both could drive it blindfolded, as they say. Both, then, have a clear similarity or common denominator: they both suffer from inattentive driving. Even though their average speeds differ, both are likely to have a rear-end collision, the curse of this type of driver. The high-speed commuter is more prone to a serious injury situation, but the slow driver is not immune to this type of hazard.

We could go on with the study of these scenarios, but I would rather leave you, my reader, to investigate the facts of your own journey first. Then perhaps you can study the journey of your friends? How about making copies of the travel survey and carry out a little survey at the workplace. (Listen to all the "speed drivers" protest their innocence!)

My aim with the survey is to bring your attention to several important "survival" tools you should develop:

1. Stop daydreaming in the morning and renew acquaintance with your journey! Think about it from its best and its worst points. If a disaster happened, where would you most *like* to be on the ride, and where is the place you would most *not* want to be? Get the idea?
2. For the long-distance driver: Where on your journey is your point of no return, the distance from which you could not walk home?
3. In the most hazardous, built-up area, if you had to stop for disaster, are you able to walk your way to safety from any point you may happen to be? Do you know in which direction safety lies? Personally, I am a "tumbleweed"—I can get lost in a large store! Being downtown anywhere requires a map to get me out of the area. How about you? You may have to hightail it out on foot, you know. So be familiar with your location.
4. Do you feel that your city hazardous driving might warrant such a "getaway"? You might consider carrying your supplies in the vehicle with you.
5. If you have to, could you stay at the workplace?
6. Finally, have you discussed your possible intentions with your family?

There are, of course, many other factors to consider, but these main points should be taken care of first. The rest will become obvious as we progress.

From a safety point of view, look at your own scenario. If you fall into the "high speed/long journey" category, consider the law of averages; it might be a good idea to quietly re-evaluate your journey patterns. Perhaps leaving five minutes earlier could add a little safety factor on your side. Combined with the six points talked about earlier, it most certainly will make a big difference at the time of disaster.

Where will you be? In the automobile, going to the job, coming home, or at some of the other places we go (to the store and such).

Before going on, let's also consider the weekends, vacation times, or going for a night out with friends. All times spent in the auto may have different characteristics regarding the type of journey, speed, etc.; yet the *basic needs* will always be the same.

Perhaps we do have a love affair with our automobiles. Since we are so dependent on them, our attention may indeed be warranted. Looking at the other side of the coin, isn't it time we gained a return for our investment?

The tragedy to me is that so few of us realize the advantage of the fact that the auto is always there. Except when we go into our residence, it can, indeed, be made into a true "home away from home" on wheels. With really very little effort, the car can be made into a "survival pod" that can sustain and shelter us for a very long time. (Out there, in every big city, there are hundreds of people doing just that, living in their cars.)

Now let us move on to the second leg of our survival stool:

What Will I Do?

Progressing from "Where will I be?" (in this case, the automobile), we must now move into action—the phase of *doing*.

Once again, let's take a step back before we dive into the pool! Remember the travel survey? You will fit somewhere in those scenarios! Remember the pointers that followed? I hope you will take a moment to reflect and consider your reactions to them as we move on through the next paragraphs.

In Chapter 1, the myths and facts of freeway driving at disaster time are documented. Please turn back and read them again to refresh your memory. Thank you.

Now we are back together again, but hopefully with an acceptance of a more realistic picture. Imagine you are traveling on your day's journey (you recreate your own scene) when suddenly, *It* happens (remember, earthquakes give no warning). Let's not spend time indulging our imagination on long descriptive passages on *It*. You will, by a series of actions, come to a *Stop*. Slowly and controlled or suddenly and violently—however it happens, you and the vehicle will eventually become motionless. Now comes the "Do" part.

1. First assess your physical state.

If it was a nice, controlled stop, you are not injured. If, however, it was one of those rending, tearing, metal-on-metal jobs, your first task is to check for injuries.

Now you can see why just *having* a first aid book is not of great comfort at this time. It is also important to have understood before you arrived at this point (as arrive you will) that there are not going to be teams of paramedics flying down the freeway to attend to you. *You are all you have!* Part of your survival plans *must* be a rudimentary knowledge of first aid. Knowledge of pressure points to stop bleeding is essential, as is a practical idea of fracture first aid.

2. Are you able to get out?

Again, according to the type of stop, you will have a clear idea whether getting out of the vehicle is a problem or not. If you are in a collision situation, getting out may present a problem, but, for obvious reasons, getting out is top priority, both for your own morale and for your safety.

Facing the devil you know is always worthwhile to me. And, considering the risk of fire or inhaling chemical fumes from radiator coolants, etc., it is knowledge that should enable you to deal with your situation in a positive manner.

How to get out, then? Under your seat you will have your wrecking bar (it's included in the "needs" section further on). Your best way out is through the windshield. Move to the passenger seat, if you are able (if you are injured you will of course have attended to your own first aid). Then, being careful to protect yourself, smash the windshield totally. Be sure to clear the *bottom* of the windshield, over which you are going to crawl out.

Now reach forward, wrecking bar in hand, and pull yourself forward as far as possible to attempt to get you head and shoulders out of the open windshield. You will arrive at a position where you are bent over the dash to about the waist. Place your feet on the seat and then, pull yourself forward as you lie flat on the hood of the vehicle (you will be face down). Pull, wriggle, and squirm until your feet are clear of the windshield opening. Now you should be able, one way or another, to place your feet on the ground. Using a combination of the wrecking bar and your hands should effect the exit from the vehicle. Continued survival may depend on getting clear. Now that you are free, you must determine:

3. Where are you?

Earlier we talked about the best and worst places on your journey. Remember? It is important that you now assess where you are. Perhaps we should enlarge that statement to include what state are you in, surroundings-wise? Obviously, if you had a quiet stop you are not in immediate danger from an injury perspective. Now the environment becomes the issue. A wreck situation may pose different issues. . .both injury and environment have to be considered.

Consideration of these facts is required so that you can determine your next step, which is your decision:

4. Do I Go or Stay?

I expressed the opinion that all of us travelers have one thing in common. I refer, of course, to the point in time when, after the major disaster that has interrupted the smooth flow of our lives, we have to decide "Do I go or stay?"

A variety of circumstances will have to be reviewed in this short moment of time. Obviously, *hazard* will be number one. *Physical condition* will follow closely behind. Finally, your *emotional state* as an individual must be considered. Staying calm and logical, what are our options?

First is hazard. What is the immediate situation location-wise? A city street with high-rise buildings all around? A country suburb? Or a chain-reaction scene with piled-up vehicles everywhere? Without considering aftershocks, are you in physical danger?

Second in consideration, physical condition. How are you? If injured, are you mobile? If you have to go, can you? Even if only a short distance? Apart from injuries, what is your general health situation? Being realistic is essential now. This is not the time to be "macho," male or female (what is the feminine for that word, I wonder?). Leaving on a long hike is not smart if you are not in good shape! If you have a serious injury, the question may well be answered for you.

Finally, your emotional state. We will talk later about communication. For now, let us assume you are part of the 96 percent who have not even thought about survival or disaster in any way, and suddenly you are standing or sitting outside your vehicle wondering what on earth happens next. It is tempting for me, who has labored for so many years to try to prevent you being in this position, to now say "Sorry Charlie" or "I told you so!" This is a negative attitude and would not help you. It is far better for me to say "Remain as positive as possible. You cannot change events. Your concerns for family and loved ones must go on the back burner for now. The priority at this moment is *you.* "

Now you must stay calm and reevaluate the hazard/health factor, making the decision we will all one day have to make: to go or to stay?

This is a nice lead-in to the third leg of our stool of survival: "What will I need?" Before we move on, let us re-cap and establish what we have accomplished so far:

1. We firmly established our whereabouts. In the automobile.

2. We evaluated the type of traveler we are using the traveler survey chart.

3. Hopefully, we learned some lessons to help us in our daily journey. Like paying more attention, perhaps even slowing down a little!

4. We evaluated the journey itself. The best and the worst as it were.

5. We ran through a possible scenario of the disaster itself (the "What will I do" phase).

6. We talked about a possible evacuation of the auto using items not yet discussed. They were items from our "needs" list. To supply the answers to those missing details, we need the third leg of our survival stool, especially since:

7. We discussed possible injury and the evaluation of our capabilities resulting not only from the present physical state, but our health in general. This leads us to the decision,

8. Do I go, (even for a short distance dictated by the present environment) or do I stay for a longer time?

What Will I Need?

Now is time to consider that other leg of the stool: What will I need?

Our needs will fall into two categories: Go gear and Stay gear. Obviously, if we decide to Go (and hopefully most of us will), the gear to support our journey will be needed. If we are part of the Stay group, remaining will also require support. Now the value of being prepared becomes obvious. Unprepared, we will endure needless suffering, not to mention the humiliation of becoming a refugee.

Needs then? First, Go gear.

The very phrase "Go gear" conveys what this gear is.

It is those items that we will need to support us in our evacuation from the place we are to the place we need to be, either for an immediate safety factor or as part of our prearranged plan of action.

Remember, we talked about the one thing all travelers will have in common as they arrive at this point in time? This common denominator is the making of the decision to Go or Stay. That's how the term "Go or Stay gear" originated.

What is this mystery gear to which we keep referring?

Once again let's back up a little and take a look at where we are. All of us are at a standstill. The disaster has happened. We have, one way or another, gotten out of the car, or we are stuck in it injured (unless we are very badly injured, we *will* get out). We must now stand and ask ourselves the millions of questions that flash through our minds:

—How bad was it?
—How are the family members?
—What shall I do now?

If we are not careful, we could go haywire at this point, but we will not. We have considered this situation ahead of time and have made preparations for it.

Now we *DO*. Go or Stay?

First let's consider Go. Go means we are going to leave where we are, either singly or with others, but we are going to leave. We had planned to go either home or to a pre-designated place. We may have a relative or friend nearby. Perhaps we are a public servant who must report for duty. For whatever the reason, we have a need to leave.

It surely makes sense to have supplies and support items for the journey. Since there is more than one item, we need something to carry the stuff in, and for that purpose we need a carry bag of some kind. I have always recommended a backpack. This item has the advantage of allowing the hands to be free; at the same time we can carry a good amount of weight without fatigue.

Backpacks come in all shapes and sizes, from the very light, plastic, simple types to the very complicated ones carried by back-packers who hike off for days into the wilderness. Stay with the simple kind. One with a good strong zipper with easy access and a small pocket on the outside. These packs are not expensive and usually run from under $10 to no more than $18.

According to the length of your journey, you will need the amount of supplies to support you in the task of survival. No matter the length of the journey, however, the *basics* will be the same. The personal support items (food, water, medications, etc.) as well as the creature-comfort items (clothes, toiletries, etc.) are required.

Let's make up a list, then talk about the whys and wherefores later. Packing from the bottom on up, you will need:

BACKPACK LIST OF ITEMS

1. Several pairs of good thick "sport socks."
2. T-shirts and undergarments.

3. A towel laid flat, with a dry washcloth in a zip-lock bag.
4. A box of large lawn and trash bags.
5. Transistor radio and batteries. Leave in packing.
6. A roll of toilet paper, sealed in zip-lock bag.
7. A 16- or 20-oz bottle of mouthwash in a plastic bottle.
8. At least two plastic containers with good tight lids.
9. A plastic drinking vessel, cup or glass.
10. Eatin' irons, metal (knife, fork, and spoon).
11. Flat box of baby wipes.
12. Flashlight, metal "Magnalight" 3-battery type.
13. Address book and diary in zip-lock bag.
14. High-protein wafers in zip-lock bag.
15. Individual packets (single-serving size) of soups, coffee, etc.
16. On-the-go food items. Must be dry.
17. First aid packet.
18. Map and compass (optional).
19. Water filter.
20. Portable cook stove and fuel.
21. Packet of paper face masks, type used by painters.
22. Pair of work gloves.
23. A pair of jeans (or shorts if summer).
24. Medium-size wrecking bar.

This completes the inside of the pack. Now in that outside pocket:

25. Toothbrush (travel type in case), toothpaste.
26. Comb and brush.
27. Deodorant.
28. Foot powder.
29. A good dry-skin creme.
30. Pair of scissors (medium-size) or Swiss-type knife set.
31. Any special medicines, vitamins, etc.
32. Personal needs, feminine items, etc.
33. Pens and pencils.
34. One or two pocket lighters.

You will need in the vehicle at least two canteens of water (the one-gallon over-the-shoulder type is preferred), a good pair of walking shoes, and a sweat suit if it is winter. These last two items should be in a plastic bag. This completes the Go gear.

We will go over the list in detail in the text to follow.

Now let's compile the list of Stay items. These are the things that will make all the difference if you have to stay with the vehicle:

1. Sleeping bag or blankets.
2. Pillow(s).
3. Camp stove and utensils.
4. Kitchen items (can opener, slicer, etc.).
5. Food stuffs.
6. Water, at least a five-gallon container.
7. Books, games, hobbies. (The one book you never had time to read!)
8. An "Auto Torpedo."

All these stay items will be packed in the trunk.

This then, is the list of the Go gear and the Stay gear; not that big a deal, is it? Nearly all of these items you already have around you; it's just a matter of getting them organized and into the pack. Take a pad and pencil right now and go down the list and see which items you do have, and which things you will need to get.

Together we are going to go over the list item by item, discussing the merits of the kit in general and why we need all this stuff! Before we do, however, let's go back in our mind to the scene as it will be if we had no survival kit at all. What it would be like if we were part of the other 96 percent!

Here you are, at point zero—the disaster has just happened and somehow, miraculously, you are still alive. Shaken, you get out of the vehicle, take a look around, and guess what? Either by choice or necessity you have to make a decision!

Know what it is?

All together now! "Do I go or do I stay?"

With no survival gear, make that. . ."Can I go, or can I stay?"

Imagine it is winter and you are dressed for a white-collar job (suit or dress, etc.). As you stand there, the cold quickly comes through the soles of those flimsy dress shoes and the wind nips at your bones. Or it is summer. . .you step out of the air-conditioned car and "Wow, I thought it had cooled down." Now the heat of the scorching road burns through the thin soles of those dress shoes.

Let's get on with some positive stuff! I would hate to think that any reader of this manual would end up in that position! Let's go over these items and talk about them.

First the Go stuff. Let's start with the empty backpack. Here we go with item #1.

1. Several pairs of sport socks. What do I mean, sport socks? Remember that I have no idea of where you will be, how old you are, or how long your journey may be. We must all look to our own situation. Preparing for any type of long walk, we always consider both comfort and health. In the case of feet on a long walk, they need all the help they can get! By sport socks, I mean those thick wool-type socks that act as a cushion and soak up sweat. Always get good-fitting socks, and when you put them on make sure to smooth them on the foot with a smoothing-out motion from the toes to the heel. This avoids possible creases in the material that could cause blisters. . .the last thing we need!

2. T-shirts and undergarments. This is a loose term, isn't it? We are talking here about a situation where, after you are on your journey away from the car, you stop and think about getting out of these grimy duds! Whether you packed T-shirts or sport shirts is really up to you. Your underwear is, of course, your own affair. One thing for sure—there is no bigger morale builder than being able to change your clothes!

3. A towel with wash cloth in a zip lock bag. This should need no explanation. The towel should not be a large, thick, space-taking one, but the smaller, hand-towel type. After all, you are not going to wash very much. You will take a small amount (that's a *small* amount) of your precious water to wet the dry face cloth and, after freshening up, put the cloth back in the zip-lock and seal it up for next time.

4. Large lawn and trash bags. These products come in such a variety of shapes and sizes. Which type to use? Well, what are we going to use them for? Cut off the corners and cut a small hole in the middle and you have a poncho either for the rain or to rest in and keep warm. With bags placed over sticks or tree limbs or branches, a small privacy screen can be made. This facilitates toilet needs when in a fairly open or non-private area. For rest times, these plastic bags make good groundsheets and covers to preserve warmth. In extreme heat conditions, they make excellent shades and covers.

5.Radio and batteries. This is another item that comes in all shapes and sizes. What are our criteria? Light in weight, not too bulky, and good range potential are really all that we are concerned with. Batteries, of course, are required! Now, this is very important: *leave these items in the manufacturer's packing.*I cannot stress this too strongly. Why? I have yet to find any radio, anywhere in the home or car, that, if it were not still in the packing, did not get used. Leaving the radio and batteries in the packing, for some strange reason, deters people from using them. We need these items when we are out there alone, not only to find out what's going on, but for our own comfort and morale. To try to use a radio that has no power is a very demoralizing experience.

6.Toilet paper in zip lock. No comment needed!

7.Mouthwash in plastic bottle. At seminars, this is an item that is always a "show stopper" as soon as I mention it. Those tall plastic bottles of green or blue mouthwash are so handy for us survivors because they have so many uses. Here are just a few:

—Of course as a mouthwash,
—Great as an antiseptic,
—A real pick-me-up for those poor tired feet,
—Saves water when cleaning the teeth,
—Great underarm freshener when changing the top gar-
  ments,
—To wash out minor cuts and abrasions, etc.

The list is long; perhaps we should have a competition for most uses!

8. Two containers with tight lids. This is a "your choice" item. For myself, I like the 10-oz. flat type (for easy storage). In one of mine I put one of the many fruit juice powders on the market. I choose one with a high mineral content. In the other, I like to keep a good malt-type protein powder. Again there are several. I pack my containers out of the jars that the product comes in. The object is to have a good supplement to enrich the water that will be consumed, thus increasing protein and mineral intake.

9. Plastic drinking vessel. Again, this is a "your choice" item. I use the tall, colored tumblers in which I wrap my eating irons (item 10) in a couple of paper napkins to stop them rattling around, thus supplying a further need.

10. Eatin' irons. I stress metal because they can be easily cleaned in sand or soil and are used over and over. This saves space over a package of plastic disposable utensils.

11. <u>Box of baby wipes</u>. On a long hot day there is nothing better than to wipe off the dust and grime with a nice, sweet baby wipe. Good enough for baby's tender skin? Must be even better for my old, razor-scraped jowls. Sometimes when dining out and they give you those little plastic pouches with the wet wipe inside? Save them and throw them into the old backpack. (When a baby is onboard, use only baby wipes—not alcohol-based wipes—on his tender skin.)

12. <u>Flashlight, metal</u>. I always recommend the three-battery "Magnalight" metal flashlight for the twofold reason that it is sturdy and easily fits into the side of the backpack. Also, a metal flashlight of this type, used by security personnel, makes for an excellent defense item.

13. <u>Address book/diary</u>. At first this may not seem to qualify as a genuine survival item. However, chances are that all your important phone numbers are in the memory of either your answering machine or the cordless phone. Out on the road, are you lost? The reason I include this item in with the survival gear is for the very good reason that you should have your personal statistics with you. Not only phone numbers, but insurance policies and Social Security information, as well as all credit card and bank info. Tough to consider, but in the time it takes you to get home, your house may be lost. If not in the initial shock wave, by fire or aftershocks. Also, as much as I don't like to have to say it—but it must be faced—there is the possibility of being robbed of your valuables while you are on the way back or while staying where you are. Having your vital information down on paper, tucked away, is a must.

14. <u>High-protein foods</u>. 15. <u>Individual food packets</u>. 16. <u>On-the-go food</u>. I have lumped these items together so that we may have a more meaningful discussion on survival (to-go) foods. As members of our free American society, we are really spoiled when it comes to food! Our stores are so full of such a variety of choices that we have, indeed, become shoppers of choice, sticking to our own favorite foods, good for us or not! No, this is not going to turn into a health lecture! But from the survivalist aspect, we are governed by certain criteria. The food must be able to stand variations of high and low temperatures in a car trunk. It must have a long shelf life. And it has to be as light as possible. To-go food needs to be of a very high-energy-producing material. For the most part, we need to have foods which do not require further preparation during travel. The

food items need to be in single-serving size as often as possible.

With these guidelines, then, we are directed to the grains, cereals, and high-protein/high-carbohydrate foods. You must, however, make your own choices as to what you pack from these sources. I cannot make specific recommendations. When I do, it always seems to lead to controversy from other authorities. The last thing we need as we prepare for survival is controversy! Speaking for myself, I pack the malt powder and fruit juice powder in item 8, then my "on-the-go" items I divide into three sections:

a. Meal items,
b. Snackin' food, and
c. Try-not-to-get-bored munchies.

Each section is contained in a large zip-lock plastic bag.

a. Meal items. By this I mean the type of food that you sit down and prepare as a meal. Those packet foods are ideal for this purpose—individually packaged soups, bouillon, etc.; just add water and instant rice and in a few moments you are eating! For desert? How about some trail mix with extra raisins or nuts? These menus are limited only by your own imagination!

b. Snackin' food. Into this group fall all of the items that are consumed as a "quick fix" at your regular rest stops. Many of these items also fit into the next category. These are nuts, raisins, beef jerky, dried fruits, well-packaged protein bars (preferably foil-wrapped), this kind of thing.

c. Try-not-to-get-bored munchies. We will talk later on about hiking regimen, but for now let us say that a long hike of ten or more miles for the inexperienced can become not only very boring, but also very demoralizing! To help offset this syndrome, food items that can be reached for without stopping are a boon. In this group we would include wrapped hard candies, beef jerky (careful with this—it tends to make you very thirsty), chewing gum, nuts, raisins, dried fruits, etc.

What have we emphasized? I hope the lack of canned food is obvious! Also that the items I have mentioned fit into the qualification criteria (light, long-lasting, and so on). The stress on nutrition and food value can also, hopefully, be seen.

Make your survival fun! Spend time in the market looking for new items that appear in single-serving packages. The list is enormous as manufacturers use this packaging for so many items these days (from tea and coffee to soups, nuts, and fruits).

Your survival supplies can be re-vamped many times and kept up-to-date. Try to avoid the Well-that's-done! attitude. In time you will have forgotten what it is you have—or do not have—in the old backpack!

This should give you enough to work on. I always try to stimulate rather than direct when it is possible. Many of you are experienced backpackers and campers and are very familiar with all this stuff. Help a friend, share your knowledge. Perhaps groups of knowledge-sharers could be organized amongst church and social clubs? Now let's move on.

17. First aid packet. Notice I said first aid packet, not "kit"! Now we have to break away again and have some dialogue. In seminars, I spend a lot of time on this subject, for it is a most important aspect of our individual survival. Remember that we will have no outside help in the area of our own and others' first aid needs. We are indeed on our own. For that reason alone, the more things are familiar to us at the moment of crisis, the easier it is to function. It must become very obvious then that nothing is more familiar than that which we do ourselves. . .surely the first aid items put together by us are more familiar to us than the purchased kit which has, in most cases, never been opened?

Further, what are the types of injuries we can expect?

Band-Aid type scrapes? Hardly! We can expect and must prepare for the *dramatic. . .broken bones. . .heavy contusions from falling objects. . .severe cuts from glass*. In summation then, we will need supplies to answer this need.

—Large, 4"x4" pads with compression bandages to stop bleeding. We also must have a basic knowledge of pressure points to further this endeavor.
—Ace-type bandages of 2", "4" and even 6" should be in the bag; used with the wrecking bar, an emergency splint can be quickly applied, even if sufficient only to assist our exit from the vehicle.
—For the cleansing of wounds we already have our bottle of mouthwash, but a small bottle of iodine or similar skin cleanser should also be included. I have an eye-cleansing

kit in my own back. Dust in the first few hours will be a problem.

—Include a package of butterfly-type strips, as well as a roll of zinc oxide tape, the kind used by athletic trainers, to serve as stitches for deep lacerations.

—We have already have a pair of scissors in the backpack.

—Finally, a bottle of non-aspirin type pills may be in order. You may also choose to carry things like antacid tablets.

You notice that the first aid supplies are both simple and basic. I know what I have, and where it is. In my time of need I may have to go to work with only one hand. Or I may be in a difficult contorted position. Whatever the situation, my first aid bag is handy and familiar to me. I prefer the zip-lock type bag tucked right near the top of my pack.

As a re-cap, the first aid bag I have outlined is a simple collection of necessary items for, just as the name implies, *first aid: the items required for on-the-spot treatment as a first step to recovery.* Knowing the types of trauma we are likely to encounter, we prepare accordingly. I am always dismayed when audiences ask questions about first aid "kits" or I find people selling expensive and bulky first aid kits that are so complicated they cannot be used. One imagines the owner in some of the scenes we have already talked about, and the complexities are obvious!

In case of blisters, all right, throw in a few Band-Aids! But please. . .keep your first aid packet *simple.*

18. Map and compass. In the formation of the list you remember I said "optional." I believe you should not try to go cross-country by compass and map unless you are very experienced using these items. Having a map to study freeway routes is one thing, but trying to cut corners can be very risky and perhaps life-threatening. A person can wander for days lost on a simple hike that takes the wrong turn. Even under normal circumstances, the search and rescue brigade out on the job would have great difficulty finding you. To take such a gamble in time of disaster is far too risky.

19. Water filter. Modern technology has produced for us a whole series of bacteriostatic water filters. These products come in many shapes and sizes. These filters have silver components in the filters which enable them to filter very brackish water, making it safe to drink. Simple in operation, this type of filter is recommended to carry in the pack.

20.Portable cook stove and fuel. There are many very simple portable cook stoves on the market, usually in the better hardware stores. These are compact units that use chemical fuel, like those used under food warmers in restaurants. Although not really essential, for the space/weight involved these inexpensive items make a world of difference when a tired traveler needs a hot cup of soup or coffee in a hurry!

21. Paper face masks. One of the by-products of a falling building or collapsed ceiling is dust. Thick clouds of swirling, choking dust. These inexpensive little pre-shaped paper masks are indispensable as a breathing aid under these types of conditions. When a hasty retreat from a built-up area is in order, the mask is a must.

22. Pair of work gloves. At first, this item may appear somewhat of a "nit-picky" item. Ever a stickler for detail, I assure you that this is a very necessary item, one that is easily overlooked. Clambering over debris. . .moving items from one's path. . .getting out of the vehicle. . .even keeping warm on a cold day. . .are only some of the uses for these gloves. The choice should be very simple; the inexpensive cloth-backed, leather-palmed type is ideal.

23. Pair of jeans or shorts. Many of us in the workplace are not dressed "tough." Women, especially those who face the public each day, are expected to dress fairly formally. Moving from the job site to evacuation is not an easy transition. A dress is not exactly "to-go" gear! By all means, the pair of jeans or shorts is a mandatory item. In the trunk or with you inside the vehicle is that pair of good walking shoes if you are already a on-the-go person. This is the time to combine the two. Now, it will be noticed that the shoes were not packed in the pack. Under normal circumstances we would change before leaving the scene. However, if a rush evacuation is required, all we have to do is pick up pack, shoes, and water, and "we're out of here" as they say. Besides, shoes are a bulky item.

24. Medium-size wrecking bar. Of all the survival items, the wrecking bar is the one that never leaves my side. It is my trademark. I take it with me to meetings and seminars. In the vehicle, it is always under my seat, and I recommend all travelers to have one. Its uses are many, and throughout this text you will have noticed my constant referral to this handy implement! *Don't leave home without it!*

This completes the itemized list; now to the front pocket. Most of the items should be self-explanatory (toiletries, etc.). Some mention may need to be made about other items: foot powder is most necessary for those of us whose feet are not used to the sudden abuse of long periods of walking! As for the dry-skin cream, in summer or winter the atmosphere alone is enough to dry out the skin. Add a little wind and the result can be very painful. A small bottle or jar of good moisture creme is worth its weight in gold.

On the more personal side, please be aware of the special medications that you may need to take, especially if, like me, you are a vitamin/food supplement person. In this time of stress the last thing we want to do is break routine. Speaking of routine, ladies, don't forget that menstrual cycles are not aware of disaster and will need to be provided for.

Pens and/or pencils are a necessity for that diary you are going to keep. And, speaking of necessity (I wish they were around when I was a Boy Scout), the butane or other such pocket lighter is essential. Carry at least two, thus removing the menace of wet matches forever!

This completes our Go gear. All that is left of this topic is some discussion of just what we have to contend with as we Go. Now I have to put the ball in your court, for we are entering an area of consideration in which only you know the details: your journey. Just how long a journey are you planning? Obviously your supplies must support such a journey. How does one compute a journey?

Backpackers and hikers may do it differently today, but in the Army we did it like this:

—Travel for fifty minutes in each hour, stopping at ten-minutes-to-the-hour; rest with the feet above the head for this ten-minute period.
—Take a meal break every four stops, and wash out the mouth every single stop.
—Calculate distance as follows. On level, flat, hard surface, a good comfortable pace of forty steps to the minute will produce about four miles an hour in distance. Climate and time of day will make a difference, as will the state of your own energy.
—Learn to pace your efforts so that you stiffen up your pace after a rest period and during the early morning.
—For a short hike (of say twenty miles), you may decide to travel almost continuously.
—For the longer journey of five or six days, you should limit

your travel time to a given routine. Avoid deviation from a steady pace, which produces miles.

—Always remember: no matter how desperately you need to get home, pace your efforts to your experience. If, as a result of the travel survey you took earlier, you find that the reality of your situation may require a journey of several days, perhaps you could introduce a little walking into your present leisure-time activities. At least to get the feel of things!

We come now to the Stay gear. You may say, "I travel only a few miles each day. I do not even consider staying with the car; I'm going home no matter what!" Fine, but consider this before you go on:

—The roads may be in very bad shape not far from you, making crossing that wide crevasse beyond your physical capabilities, or
—You may be injured and unable to travel at all.

Another possible problem is time. The disaster may have hit late on a blustery winter's night. Prudence may dictate that a morning trip would be more practical. The moral of the story is: even if you think you are the type that will never stay with your vehicle, a little reflection of the current situation is not that much to ask!

Suppose that you never travel more than a short distance from home. You may ask, "What do I need all that gear for anyway?" Please consider taking just a blanket and a pillow. It would make even one night in the car more pleasant and put you in a much better condition for a morning hike!

For the rest of us, the Stay gear, as outlined, needs discussion only as to the length of stay anticipated. Let's look at it this way:

—"For me, getting home is out of the question." Fair enough.
—"Unless circumstances beyond my control dictate, I am staying put!" Fine.

Now the question arises:
—"For how long?"

First, from the study of the disasters that have already taken place, we know that an event of the magnitude we are preparing for will be greater than anything that has happened so far. All vehicular travel will, most certainly, be impossible. The situation on the major freeways will be unbelievable. Clearing the dead and injured, not to mention the debris and wrecked and abandoned vehicles, will take weeks.

If you are one who has to stay because the distance or your physical health demands it, doesn't it follow that the only way you'll return home will be via an assisted means. . .

In other words, *you must be able to survive unassisted for as long as it takes for the authorities to set up reasonable shelters.* Public travel will have to come later. What would be your assessment of that time period, in your own opinion, before all this happens?

In all practical situations, preparations for survival for at least ten days is a minimum requirement. Considering that the Stay gear does not have to qualify for the Go-gear requirements (weight, dry condition, etc.) this is not such a tall order!

Let us approach this problem of ten days' survival as though it were a camping trip.

For one person, a minimum of five gallons of water, plus the two one-gallon canteens in the Go gear supplies, equals seven gallons total. At one-half gallon a day, this would last for fourteen days, even if, during that time, no new water were available.

Food-wise, a good supply of canned food can easily be put together. Choose items like a medium-sized can of ham, for example, that can last for several meals. Rice, beans, and other dried grains and cereals make easily prepared meals. Remember that we have provided a camp stove and utensils in the list of supplies.

Also on the list (as was in the to-go list) was an item referred to as a food torpedo. The food torpedo is fully explained in Chapter 4, in the section on backyard survival. An even better alternative for Stay food storage would be an auto torpedo, a smaller version of the food torpedo and also described in Chapter 4.

Now let us recap our situation:

—We prepared for the *event* by determining where we were.
—We prepared for the *situation* of being in the automobile.
—We have prepared for *either* the to go or stay situation.

Now all that is left is to wait it out in a prepared manner.

This chapter will be referred to many times in the coming text as we fit the pieces together for our overall family survival planning. Before we leave this section, there are a few things we should talk about.

To Go, and Subsequent Travel Considerations

Be aware that you are in the minority. Face the reality of having your own supplies while most others do not.

If you travel in a group, set some ground rules. Your supplies shared with a others will last a very short period of time. Then all of you will be in the same supply-less boat!

If you are a woman, think carefully before you team up with an individual male or an group in which men outnumber women.

He travels fastest who travels alone is still a good policy.

At dusk, consider your location. Is it safe to go on, or should shelter be sought?

In towns or cities, avoid deserted neighborhoods, day or night.

Expect the worst. It will be a jungle out there; plan accordingly. Stay in the open where possible; rest and hide at night.

Be flexible in your plans. If a safe area is encountered (a police checkpoint, an Army camp etc.), consider your options. Inquire as to conditions in the area you are headed for. Perhaps your to-Go plans might change to Stay plans if prudence dictates.

To Stay, and What's Involved

You are all prepared and, unless you are injured, you are in a good position. If you are injured, be aware of your symptoms.

If your type of injury is likely to result in infection, look for signs of such (a temperature rise, etc.). If such a thing does occur, you will have to consider leaving to seek help or being watchful for air patrols for this purpose.

If not injured, set up camp for a comfortable stay; you have all you need!

Be wary of visitors. Hide all obvious valuables. Act low in spirit if the visitors are predators!

At dusk, put out all lights. Sleep when the sun goes down. If you wake during the night, consider the situation. Are prowlers on the loose?

Hide all supplies except those you are using. Use the engine compartment, under the car, or under the seats for this purpose. Prowlers will look to see what is available. Not sure if you are armed, they will usually keep a low profile unless you present an obvious picture of being well supplied.

If you are still on the freeway and there is open country around you, it is a good idea to move your camp to an out-of-the-way place where you can see without being seen.

Of course, the ideal would be several prepared survivors grouping together. If enough of us do prepare, this could become a positive situation!

I realize that these sentences may appear to be over-dramatic, but I continue to stress that *the devil you know can't hurt you!* I would be remiss if I did not face, in print, the facts that I know you will face in reality!

We have talked so far from an earthquake point of view. What about other types of disasters?

Floods

If you live in a flood zone, you should always have a semi-prepared To-Go kit ready. As the water rises, finish your kit and pack it in the car prior to leaving.

If this is a fairly regular annual occurrence, you will have a good idea as to how long it will be before you can return. Extra supplies for that period of time can easily be provided. Time is on your side. You have ample warning; use it!

If you are in a flood zone that you normally live through without evacuation, you are one of those the rest of us see on T.V. in a house surrounded by water. You will have your Stay gear in the upstairs part of the house, for this is your camping area. A rubber boat up there with you would be my own choice, just in case unforseen circumstances arise and "they" don't get to you in time!

Hurricanes

As I write this, Hurricane Andrew has just completed his work. As I watched those thousands of cars evacuating the area on T.V., I thought, "Boy, how great if they all had survival kits in the car with them." Later, as the days wore on and little relief was forthcoming, I thought of my recommended minimum of five days' supplies. . .what misery and anger those people could have been spared!

Hurricanes *always* give fair warning. Use that time to prepare your emergency supplies to take with you or bury in the ground for when you come back!

By now, all of you who are not in California, and have read this far, will have a very good idea of what this manual is all about. Surely, working out a disaster plan from the ideas given thus far is not that difficult a task?

For the want of a nail the shoe was lost. . .

As I repeat so often, "survival" has a totally different connotation for me than for my fellow citizens. I hope by now that the survival situation for you is a little clearer!

Before we go on, let me remind you of all the general rules of conduct mentioned over and over again by the media and others:

—Try not to park or come to a stop at freeway overpasses.
—Look out for fallen wires; they could be live and lethal.
—Try not to speed, and if you do, leave enough distance from the car in front to allow for emergency stops.
—If disaster strikes, slow down, come to a controlled stop, preferably on the shoulder.

That's about it for this chapter. Let us now go on to Chapter 4, the other area under our own control survival-wise.

Chapter 4
The Home

Backyard survival

We have agreed that of the four places we are most likely to be at disaster time, only two of them are under our own control. One is the auto, which we have just discussed. The other is the home.

Home is indeed the most important element of our family life, affecting all members of the family unit. In the past, treatments of this same subject (both written and spoken) have shown that the problems of clear presentation are as difficult as the variety of shapes and sizes of homes themselves! Split-levels, tri-levels, ranches, cottages—the list is long. Take into account condominiums, apartments, and mobile homes, and the complexities grow!

Obviously then, the best approach would be to establish a general plan of attack, then work from there toward the specialization needed for each area. This is the approach I shall use for this manual. Here we go.

First, let's have some food for thought. Despite all you may hear to the contrary, your chances of having an undamaged home after a major earthquake are slim. After the tenth to fifteenth aftershock, it is even slimmer.

If you are in a new home, should you have asked, your builder/realtor will have assured you, "This home incorporates all of the latest earthquake codes." Feeling secure, you went on with the "walk through" and then bought the house. Sorry to burst your bubble, but even if your home does comply with all the latest codes, it is not (repeat *not*) earthquake-proof!

Let me clarify that statement. The building codes in force at the time your house was built incorporate what the ruling authority felt was the most *practical* and most *inexpensive* measures to make the building as safe as possible *in that price and quality range*. This is a lot different than having a custom home built by an architect with instructions to "make it earthquake-safe!" See what I mean?

In all the earthquakes so far, the first things to go on a house is the chimney, then the patio cover. Overhangs and porches are next.

I spent two years in school learning about drafting and design, and when I built additions to our house I incorporated many features that were "above code," much to the amusement of the City Engineer!

Earthquake-proof? There is no such thing. Doing the best we can with all known facts. . .yes. As safe as possible. . .yes. But not being aware of what Mother Nature has in store. . .expect the worst!

Another point to consider is the quality of your builder. Putting on extra "sheer" panels (required by most codes) is not effective if the panels are put on with staples instead of nails and glue! These are the types of details I mean.

What's the point I am making?

What is a safe home?

From a survivalist point of view, for me in particular, there is no such animal. In my diagrams for a safe shed, and in the other plans that I offer, you will notice some incorporation of ideas that will make as safe a structure as possible. To build a house this way would be great, but I would hate to have to pay a professional for all that custom work!

Prepare for survival with your home *flat,* and start from there. Everything else is a bonus!

Fact: Earthquakes are measured in "magnitude" here in America. We hear very little about "intensity," which is the International Scale established by the Earthquake Folks in the rest of the world as a communication tool. It is a means of expressing to each other the quality of the quake.

An earthquake with low magnitude, say 6.7, with a high intensity can be very devastating. The 1971 San Fernando quake would be a good example. It was only 6.3 in magnitude, yet it did tremendous structural damage for its duration, with a measured vertical movement of up to nine feet, and a .5-.75 G force. In some places a 1.00 G force was registered, an intensity of a very high order in the sixty seconds of its life.

On the other hand, the San Francisco quake in 1989, which was given a 7.3 rating, did very little damage apart from the Bay Bridge, the Nimitz Freeway, and the Marina. It had a low intensity. The only known recorded quake in excess of 8.0 was the 1964 Alaskan earthquake which was given 8.5 and created damage over 50,000 square miles!

Just for the record, the latest shakers in 1992, Big Bear and Landers for example, have all been low-magnitude, high-intensity affairs.

The moral would seem to be, "Prepare for the worst, but expect the best!" Accept that we are due, and let's get on with it!

The first step in home preparedness is to become familiar with your home. "Wow," I can hear you say, "I have lived in this house for a long time; no one is more familiar than I with my own home!" That's not what I mean! "Familiar" means knowing, for example:

—Where on the lot does the house sit, front or back?
—Which side do the services come in? Over or underground?
—Housing tract or large lot?
—Single- or multi-story?
—Wall or fence?
—Where are the services located? All on same wall?
—Which are the bearing walls?
—What is around you in the neighborhood?
—Where is the nearest open ground?

This is what I mean by being familiar with your home. So familiar that, in time of stress, you can run instinctively to the service panel, or away from that power pole on the south corner of the lot. (That's what I have. Soon we hope to have our electrical service underground.)

Next, we have to become familiar with the inside of the home. Which way are the exits? If you have an upstairs, which is the way out from there?

I want you to take a fresh approach to your home, to look at it from its hazard point of view rather than from its safety aspects. A good, strong, safe house is one thing, but *each room* can present many hazards in the form of items that can fall and injure you (e.g., large unprotected picture windows can shatter and cause severe injury). We must go room by room and look for and, as far as possible, correct the hazards we find.

Next we must go back outside to the yard (the European term "garden" sounds so much nicer) and design our backyard survival plan.

It is true that the quality of your survival after a disaster will depend on the quality of the preparations before the disaster happens. What are our priorities? What about our three-legged survival stool?

—Where will I be? Somewhere in the house obviously.
—What will I do? Do what I can to be safe.
—What will I need? The means to continue to survive, of course.

Can we define that even further? I believe so:

1. Protection of self and family,
2. Protection of property,
3. Establishment of survival needs and supplies,
4. Protection of survival needs,
5. Assistance to neighbors,
6. Maintenance of self and family post-disaster, and, perish the thought,
7. Evacuation plans.

These seven steps comprise the very comprehensive list upon which we shall develop our survival program.

From the outset, let me stress (as I always do) that 90 percent of what we need to meet all our needs we already have around us. It's just a matter of "getting it together." Adapt all that you are about to study now to suit your own situation. In some cases, I will make notations myself. When I do not, you can think it out for yourself.

For example: When I talk about supplies in the backyard, if you are in hurricane or tornado country, you will instinctively know that, to be safe, your supplies will need to be below ground. If you live in flood country, your survival supplies will need to be in the upper floors of the house. A Californian would not think this way. Understand? Let's get on then.

1. Protection of Self and Family

First we must go room by room and look for the hazards. Remember? Each room must be evaluated.

Bedrooms

Is there a way out other than through the door? Prepare a rope or ladder for evacuation. Secure one end around the leg of the bed or other object. If there is a closet near the window, secure the rope around the closet pole right near the end where it is strong. The rope can be coiled up out of the way, ready for use if needed.

What shelter is in the room? How about the beds? Are they strong enough to be protective if you were to roll out and lie on the floor next to them? (I saw a person on T.V. who advocated, "If in bed, stay where you are until the shaking stops!" I wondered at the time if I would have the courage to stay on top of my bed as the roof or ceiling fell in on me.) Look at the legs of the bed. Are they strong

71

enough to stand up to a lot of weight? If not, figure out how to improve the situation. Often, a simple addition of a nut and bolt can work wonders. Even consider adding extra legs under the spring frame to turn a weak frame into a strong one (see Diagram 3).

Always remember that there is a roof up there (your house's hat, if you will), and it is waiting to come down! Always look for likely "caves" to shelter in.

Look at your windows. Glass is our number-one enemy, from an injury standpoint. If you do not have blinds or drapes of any kind, especially in upstairs rooms, cover the glass with criss-cross strips of clear tape.

Bathrooms

Usually the window is high up and difficult to reach. If you are in the bathroom when the shaking starts, open the door. This will ensure that you have a way out and will be able to avoid getting trapped if the door should jam up. Bathrooms are safe to be in. They are small, which means that the weight is carried on walls that are close together, and they also have extra bracing to hold pipes and other things in place. This all helps to make the bathroom a fairly safe box-like structure.

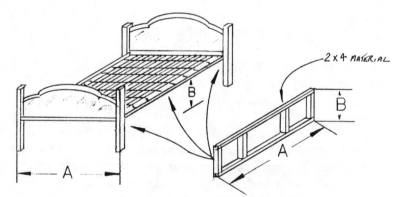

USING DIMENSIONS A AND B AS GUIDES, CONSTRUCT 2x4' FRAMES TO STRENGTHEN A BED FRAME AS INDICATED BY ARROWS.

DIAGRAM 3

Kitchens

I recommend that, even if you do not have children, you put those child-proof locks on each of the cupboards. These very inexpensive gadgets prevent the kitchen cabinet doors from opening unless the lock piece is released by hand. These are great for protection if you find yourself in the kitchen at quake time. Just think, you crouch down in front of those nice safe cabinets, then whammo. . .the doors shake open and dishes and/or canned goods rain down on your poor head and body! An injury situation to be avoided, to say the least!

The kitchen has another hazard that I must mention, and that is your stove (or range as some call it). Usually, we are in the kitchen to either make a mess or clear one up. I call making a mess preparing a meal, which entails using the stove (either the top, the oven, or both). If the shaking starts, *stay away from the stove!* That hot pot full of soup or that casserole in the oven is another serious potential injury to be avoided!

Take a look at the design of your kitchen. In the older homes the kitchen is often long and narrow with the stove and counter on one side, sink and fridge on the other wall. Often, there is a window over the sink. Watch out for that window! Glass could fly in on you as you stand there doing the dishes and looking out at the garden view. That's the kind of hazard I want you to get used to looking at! Become survival conscious; look at the rooms in your home from the hazard point of view, not the safety it affords! Now let's go on.

Living and Family Rooms

I could spend many pages in the details of each of these rooms. All of us like to establish a character to our rooms, especially the living room. (Some used to call it the parlour in the old days!) This makes for so many varieties of decor and furniture fashions: furniture that varies from the large and heavy to the ultra-modern spindly types that some prefer. It seems, then, that some ground rules would be helpful.

Whenever I go into a home to give advice, there are basic rules that I work by:

—How much window area is there?
—Where are the seats in relation to the windows?
—How many ways out?
—Where are the possible "caves"?

We already talked about windows and glass. In the government report about the February 9, 1971, San Fernando earthquake, there was a list of thirteen items to be considered for future preparedness. Item #11 focused on attention to measures to prevent injuries from glass. On the face of it, this seems such an innocent statement. The precise wording in this government paper is:

11. Greater attention to the hazard of broken glass is needed.

To date, I can honestly say that I have emphasized this very real danger every time that I have had an opportunity, both on and off the lecture platform. It is to my intense dismay that, so far, few if any have heeded this warning. I think I probably am more intensely conscious of this danger since I had a very dear friend who was blinded by flying glass while rehearsing with a dance class in his studio. The room had floor-to-ceiling glass.

I am especially concerned about school classrooms that, in the main, do not have any drapes or blinds.

After considering window area, I ask where the seats are in relation to the glass. Ever notice that couches are so often placed in close proximity to windows? How often we sit watching T.V. with our back to a window?

Next, I consider the number of ways out. I always have this built-in awareness that, after the shaking stops, my first impulse is to get out. This is, of course, the correct thing to do. In your home, always be aware of the ways out of each room. This does not confine itself to doors!

Finally, I look for the sign of "caves." I have already mentioned this phrase. So let me now give you the Law of Caves:

All objects not on the ground, *always* have the desire to return to Mother. In this case Mother Earth. *All Objects.*

That lovely, treasured vase would, if it were not for the shelf it sits on and its own broad base, topple and crash to the ground, unfortunately destroying itself in the process. When given the op-portunity, objects will "go to Mother" unless prevented by another object in the way.

Example?

In disaster (fire, earthquake, explosion, etc.), the walls of a structure may collapse, allowing roof and/or upper floor beams to fall to the ground. Very often, other objects (strong shelves, heavy furniture, etc.) get in the way, thus impeding the fall of the original beam or object. That portion of the object not so obstructed will continue to fall until it reaches its target, the ground. The other portion (usually the end piece) will be held up in its descent, and, after its falling end has come to rest, will itself be stationary, resting on its support object (whatever that was).

Now, if we visualize the picture in great detail, we will see that there is a space or "cave" formed by the action I have described (see Diagram 4).

In London, we learned to look for these caves, for from them hundreds of people were rescued.

Back to our evaluation. Be aware, then, of possible caves. In the event of that ominous rumble, dive for that pre-determined spot. In the calm of this moment, be aware that you must try to throw yourself down into a potential cave site with your head *toward* the exit (the door or window). The cave you may find yourself in will most likely be restricted as to your ability to turn around. Knowing which way the door or exit is enables you, as soon as it is safe, to begin to crawl out. It is very difficult to crawl out feet first!

A word to all standing outside a fallen structure about to attempt a rescue. *Stop.* Look for the caves. Walk around and look deep into the structure. When you locate caves, before attempting to walk or climb or start to pull at wreckage to get to victims, be sure that the cave is well supported and will not collapse as soon as you pull a key piece out.

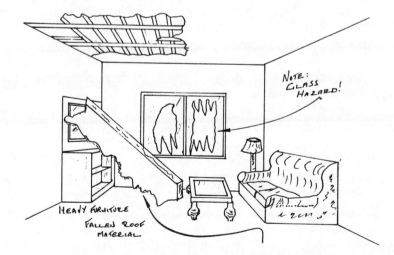

DIAGRAM 4—SIMPLE EXAMPLE OF A "CAVE"

How sad to survive the actual quake and then perish because some unsuspecting or untrained person wrecked your survival cave!

Secondly, *never* attempt a rescue without a "buddy." To rush to the aid of a victim without another person is very foolish. If you yourself become trapped in the attempt at rescue and your whereabouts are not known, your own family will spend fruitless time searching for you in the wrong place, and your own rescue may never take place.

I think I have given you enough to start you on a "hazard inspection" of your house. To find the bad spots and correct them and develop safe spots for your own protection is vital to your survival. Now let's go outside.

As I said, I have a large power pole on the south-east corner of my lot. Judging its height, and pacing out that distance (from its base), I can easily calculate its possible hazard factor. The worst scenario would be that the very tip (about four feet) could well end up in my living room. On the other hand, it could go the other way and end up on my neighbor's house. The point to consider is that the part of my garden in the possible danger zone is already established as a hazard right now. Until the shaking stops and that pole is down, it will continue to earn the respect it deserves. No person will ever, for instance, sleep in its path!

How about your yard? Do you have a block wall around you? Was it built with rebar (Steel rods down the hollow blocks)? If it was not, it will come down. Try not to put supplies under a block wall unless you are prepared to spend the time moving the bricks to get to them.

Where is the safest part of the garden? If you have to evacuate the house in the middle of the night, where is the safest place for the "family assembly" area? Alright then, where is a good place to put the clothes we will need at once?

Considering "protection of self," which is what this section is all about, accept the challenge of the worst scene you can think of:

It is 3 a.m. The shaking starts and is very violent. . .goes on forever it seems. Suddenly, almost before you are aware of the silence, you realize it has stopped.

Next to the bed you have placed a pair of solid-soled slippers, preferably leather (you are going to have to walk over unknown hazards, including glass). Grabbing the flashlight always near the bed, you evacuate, screaming to the other members of the family, "Get out, Get out!"

Now is where those drills come into play, for as you reach the opening (be it a doorway or a hole in the wall), you will stop for just enough time to be sure that debris is not still falling. When the first aftershock hits, what is hanging there waiting to come down does so without any further hesitation. Some things, such as patio covers and overhangs, may shake loose and hang there, but it takes successive shockwaves to bring them down. Getting out with care after the first wave stops is essential. There is nothing worse than to survive the first tremor and, due to a careless action on the way out, be caught and possibly injured in the second one!

You cough and choke all the way to the outside. Dimly, you are aware of others around you. You have headed for the assembly place (you had practiced it enough) and, hugging each other, you realize someone is not there. You look back at the wrecked house and see that the back wall is down. The roof is at a crazy angle. All of you rush to the rubble and scream the person's name. You hear a muffled cry and, rushing to the spot, you can see in the dark the figure of your missing family member trapped under a beam.

As you pull the victim to safety, you see that this loved one is little the worse for wear other than the gash on his head and some wooziness. Now let's do a review. There, at approximately 3:30 a.m., you and the whole family are there in the backyard. In the dark and in your night clothes, you give thanks for this bedraggled family member just rescued from the debris of what once was your home.

As a family, all of you stand outside and dejectedly but thankfully take stock of the situation. Most of the damage seems to be on the bedroom side of the house. The rest looks as though, in the morning, you might be able to get into the wreckage and pull out a few things. Just then, the ground starts shaking as the first of many aftershocks begins to hit. Suddenly, you realize that there is an injury to take care of.

At this point, our little narrative will take one of two roads:

The first, a negative one: What on earth do I do now? Why we are here in the clothes we stand in with an injured person and . . .*nothing.*

The second, and of course as a writer and a survivor, my favorite one, the positive: Mother says (firmly), "Well, let's not just stand around. Sally, go get the first aid box so I can fix your poor brother's head. You know where it is. John, (turning to her husband) better get the footlocker out so we can all get into some warmer clothes before the next shock hits. Arty, be a dear; let's put some of that Boy Scout training to good use. Why don't you get the fire pit going so we can all have a nice cup of. . ." (tea [British], coffee [American],

Cocoa [French]) or whatever *you* would say in this scenario!)

Far-fetched? Ask survivors in Coalinga, San Francisco, Big Bear, Landers, Miami, or Louisiana!

Protection of self and family include all of the above. We will detail specifics later on in this chapter.

2. Protection of Property

At first, saying protection of property may sound out of place when talking about a house!

A house is not a person. True, but look at the situation from a survival point of view. Shouldn't we do all in our power to protect our house from the dangers it may be exposed to?

Logically then, we should become familiar with our house. First from the structural point of view:

—In which direction do the bearing walls run? How can we tell the bearing walls?

—Where are the services? Gas? Water? Electricity?

—In which wall are most of the services?

—Are there any walls without any services in them?

—Is it a single- or double-story?

—What sort of roof? Tile? Shingle?

—Is there a lot of equipment up there? Air conditioner? Cooler?

These are the questions that you must be able to answer in order to do the best job possible for the protection of your property after the disaster. Why?

First, we must be familiar with the structure of the house. What are bearing walls? A bearing wall is a wall that has roof extensions running the whole length. These are the ends of the rafters and are known as "rafter tails." The weight of the roof is supported by all walls that have these rafter tails resting on them.

"What is so important about that?" you may ask. When the house starts to move and shake, it is these walls that are most likely to collapse, due to the fact that they are weight-bearing. They are certainly to be avoided at all costs from a shelter point of view. Hence, the need to identify them.

Some roof designs are "hip" roofs, and often have more than two bearing walls (see Diagram 5).

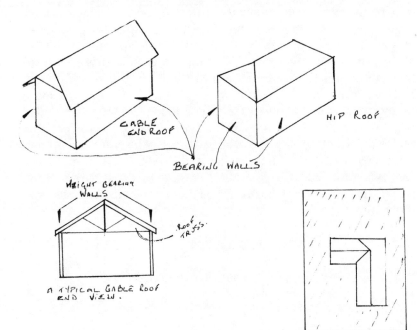

DIAGRAM 5

Next, the services. When the shaking stops, look for that wall that had most of the services in it. If it is damaged, then the chances of broken pipes of one kind or another are most likely. Do a quick survey:

—Can you smell gas?

—Is there water leaking in the house?

Remember, if you suspect a gas leak, turn off the *electricity* first, then the gas! Leaking gas will still be around after you turn off the gas valve. Turning off the electricity eliminates the chance of spark and explosion.

We need to talk about the services and practice shutting them off. Just in case, even at this late date, you have not already become aware of the procedure involved, the major electrical service box is called a panel and is that flat oblong box on the wall that has above it a round glass dome called a meter. At the bottom of the flat box is a clasp-type thing which, when you pull and lift, makes the lid of the box pull up toward you. Underneath this lid is a whole row of funny looking switches with the numbers 10, 15, and 20 on them. Don't even bother to try to figure out what they are (just for the record, they are called circuit breakers). If you lift the lid up until it is parallel to the ground, you will find that when you push it forward toward the wall, it will fit into something that will make it stay up! Now both hands are free. Now, look way up top to the very first of these funny switches and you will see two of them joined together with a metal connection. This is the main switch. Grasp the top coupled switches, which will be pointing left, and with your thumb and forefinger, swing or push the switch to the right. It will be quite stiff and, when moved, will give out a dull *thonk* sound. Now all the power to the house will be off. If you must, walk into the house and prove it to yourself!

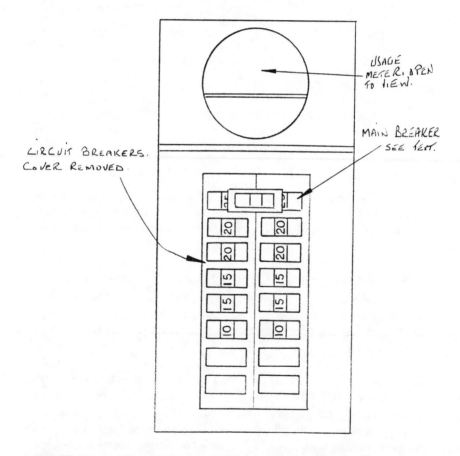

DIAGRAM 6—ELECTRIC POWER PANEL WITH COVER REMOVED

Now go back and reverse the procedure and turn all the power back on. Close the lid again, making sure that it is fastened down as it was before (see Diagram 6).

Sometimes in homes, you may find a security lock on the panel. If there is, it is a further problem to deal with. I never understood the thinking behind a locked power panel on a private home. After all, you cannot steal someone's juice without being incredibly obvious about it. If you decide to continue with the locked box idea, make sure you place a key in a safe place that is easily accessible when you need it. When you go back into the house, you will need to reset the video machine, clocks, and other things that have timers on them.

Now for the gas. The gas meter is always located close to the ground near a wall close to the front of the house. There will be one pipe coming out of the ground going into the meter. The meter is a large box-like thing with dials on it. On one side of the gas meter is a large saucer-like thing with pipes coming in and out of it. This is called a pressure regulator. Now, on a pipe close to the regulator, you will find a lump of metal sticking out, like a flat short bar.

Believe it or not, this is the gas shut-off valve, purposely made by the gas company, I believe, to be as near to impossible to turn off as they can make it! Now comes the exercise of turning off the gas. In your practice session don't, under any circumstances, actually do this unless you or a friend or relative knows how to go around and light all the pilots again! The gas company gets really irritated when asked to do this after you do a practice run. Since, in an emergency, even the gas company tells us to "turn off the gas," I think it is only fair that they should be involved!

This is the procedure used to turn off the gas. First, you need a large, strong tool called a crescent wrench. This tool has jaws on it, and when you turn the funny round thing with indentations on it, these jaws open and close. You can find out which way does what yourself. I have used them for years and still am not sure which way does what from memory! Anyway, open the jaws, and when they are wide enough, place them over the little bar sticking out of the pipe under the saucer-like thing. Now, tighten up the jaws of the wrench until they grip the bar and hold fast.

Now comes the fun part! Try to pull or push until the little bar *starts* to move. It will take all your strength to even get a movement out of the thing. Some shut-offs have not been used in years, so they are stuck (pros call it frozen). The reason I said "pull or push" is because of another puzzle understood only to the gas company; if the shut-off is facing right, it will pull toward you; if it is facing left

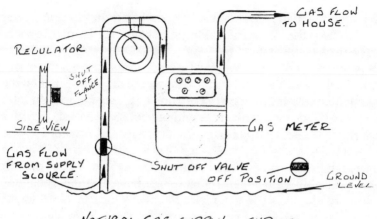

NATURAL GAS SUPPLY - TYPICAL.

NOTE:

SHUT OFF VALVE IS _ALWAYS_ BEFORE THE ROUND OBJECT CALLED THE "REGULATOR", OFTEN THE VALVE IS AT GROUND LEVEL.

DIAGRAM 7—NATURAL GAS SUPPLY

it will push away from you. So when you get to yours, it may be facing the front. . .or the back. . .oh well. Hence, the instruction I gave. Pull or push until something starts to move (see Diagram 7).

You can do a little practice movement and that will be O.K. A small amount of movement will not shut off the gas, only reduce it a little. Then, when you get the feel of it, you will not be concerned at shut-off time.

Now—and to me this is most important—if you cannot get any movement from your gas shut-off valve, call the gas company and say, "My gas shut-off valve is stuck and in an emergency it would not shut off. Please come and fix it!" In the real emergency, that darned valve might be the difference between safety and your house blowing up. Maybe with half the neighborhood!

A word for all of you who live in an area supplied with a propane or other stored liquid gas systems. Your storage tank is at least twenty feet from the house. The safety code requires it. In many cases, this is only a minimum distance. Many are much farther from the houses that they supply. In all cases, after a major earthquake, *shut off the supply at the tank*. That's a major earthquake. Shut it down!

The reason I am so emphatic about this procedure is this: your

82

main supply line is at least twenty feet from the appliance. Mostly, this pipe is buried in soft soil. The amount of earth movement, the twisting and turning that may have taken place, is an unknown factor. Liquid gas does not rise and dissipate as does regular natural gas. Consequently, starting the automobile or even lighting a cigarette many hours later could trigger an explosion. Especially in a sheltered, wind-free area, leaking liquid gas can hang around for days. Besides, why waste all that gas you are going to need for your survival!

Think you had fun with the gas? Wait till you get to our next chore, shutting off the water. This one they buried in the ground!

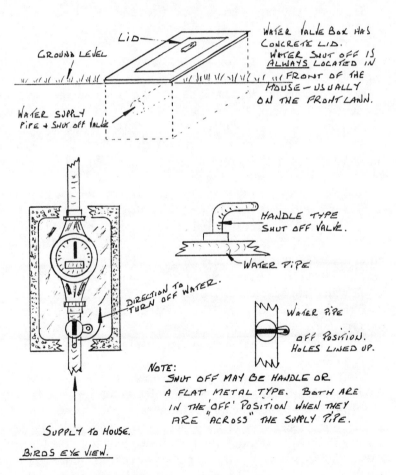

DIAGRAM 8—WATER SUPPLY, TYPICAL

Go to the front of your house by the street. Look for a concrete lid to a box that will be as large as 28" by 18" or as small as 18" by 10" according to the age of your house (things got smaller as the years went by). Now comes the fun! Under that lid is the water shut-off valve (see Diagram 8).

One of the first things that will become very obvious to you is that there is no handle to lift this concrete lid. "Ah," you say, "but if the shut-off is under the lid, what is the secret?" "Well," I say, "there is no secret. But if you look closely at this lid, you will see what appears to be a flaw in the design of this thing. It has an oblong slot up there by the top (or bottom if it was replaced the other way.) This is the way to open up this lid!"

Seriously, you now need a good strong screwdriver (or I have even used a tire iron). The gimmick is to create leverage that will lift the lid free. This is one of those chores that is so simple once you have done it. Trial and error will get you to the place where the lid is off. Hurrah! Now, stop.

Before we go any farther, look into the hole that you have just uncovered. According to the climate where you live, that hole can be the home of a large menagerie of a variety of beetles and creepy crawlers! The one we most have to watch out for is our friend, the black widow spider! So please, before we go on, take a stick or whatever and clean out the hole!

Now we can get on with the business of shutting off the water. Look down into the hole. The first thing that will catch your eye is that funny-shaped, almost-round thing sitting in the middle of that big pipe running from the bottom to the top of the box. That funny thing is the water meter. It may or may not have a lid on it. This is the meter that is read by somebody every month and determines how much water you have used.

Directly above this "clock" is either a large metal handle or a metal thing similar to the gas shut-off valve you used earlier. Actually, they are both cast from the same mold, as it were, and do the same job.

Your assignment, should you choose to accept it (as the T.V. series used to say), is to shut off the water by turning that valve off or pulling that handle down. I use the same type of crescent wrench as I use for the gas, only this time it is used "standing up" putting a bar or other object through the hole in the handle to obtain better leverage. For those of you not so handy, there is a solution! You can purchase, from your local hardware store or hardware supply house, a tool called (wouldn't you know it) a "shut-off key." There are two types (purchase according to the kind of valve you have). This key, which is no more than a "slot" welded onto a bar, with a handle that is about three feet long, enables you to turn off the water without even bending down! Not only that, the handle of this wonderfully simple tool can be used to lift that heavy concrete lid (Did you find out how heavy it was?).

No matter what tool you use, turning off the water is no mean feat. It will require a lot of strength, so don't be afraid. You won't break anything. Use a lot of force!

Study the diagrams. Go outside, look around, and practice. Hopefully this text will make sense and prepare you properly.

That takes care of the services. Always remember, don't be afraid to call the various service companies if you have any problems. They will gladly send someone out to check things over and even show you how.

Let's get back to the structure. The question about the type of roof finish involves weight. A tile roof is heavier than a shingled one. Think about the rooms that you sleep in. These rooms should be made as safe as possible, taking into account the amount of weight that is over your head. Add the weight of the Sheetrock that is used to construct the ceiling, and you have a fair idea of what is up there waiting to come down.

Remember caving? Think upwards. Remember that a roof-mounted cooler or air conditioner only compounds the problem. Is your bed directly under an appliance of this kind? Move it!

As soon as possible, learn these steps that increase the chances of your home's survival. Talk to your neighbors about these things. Think of the consequences if, due to neglect or ignorance, the house down the street catches fire from leaking gas, which in turn may put your own house in danger. The question will always arise, "Could the fire have been avoided if the gas had been turned off?"

Oh, one thing before we leave the subject of property.

So far, in all of the disaster situations, payment of compensation to the victims from government agencies and insurance companies can require up to four to six months processing time. One of the great problems causing this delay is documentation. Computers are out. The process of going back over records is a long one when one has to go "back to main office" (often out of state) or "back to the State Assessor's office for records of the deed, etc." The list of frustrations is long!

Copy all of your records now. If you are a renter, copy your rental agreement. These, together with utility bills (telephone, etc.) will verify your legal residency. There is the classic case that arose as a result of the San Francisco quake. An apartment building of twenty-six units had seventy-five claims for losses from people giving the building address to support their claims! Later, when we talk about food, I will suggest what to do with these documents.

Protection of self, protection of property. Oh, yes. Before we go on, let's not forget the old family auto, or those precious collectibles. They're part of property, too! Really, isn't it time to revise our thinking regarding the auto and other precious items?

After we had a fire at our house in 1990, I became aware of the importance of relatively inexpensive items and their value to me from a replacement point of view. For example, a couple of oil paintings of no great monetary value, but of great sentimental value, were priceless in my eyes (the friend of mine who painted them was long deceased). To the insurance company, replacement cost was $25 each since I had not had them appraised!

Often, when I visit homes, I admire those lovely collections of figurines and the like. Being survival-conscious, I immediately think of the vulnerability of pottery or porcelain items to the hazards of earthquake conditions. Isn't it time to review a collection from a value point of view? Saving and packing away some of the best pieces? How about a rotation system? Each month exchange the pieces that are in danger for those packed away. At least then you could enjoy some of the collection each month.

How about the auto? Perhaps it's time to start thinking about parking it in the driveway instead of the garage. It does have a second set of survival supplies in it! Digging it out of the rubble for those very supplies is a problem you don't need.

All of these details are part of the survival thinking process. If I keep repeating the principles involved, hopefully the process will become as much a second nature to you as it is to me!

Let's move on now to the next item:

3. Establishment of Survival Needs and Supplies

Now we come to the "meat" of this chapter (no pun intended), the actual hands-on of our survival supplies.

Going back over this text, and returning to the point where the family stood out in the yard after the quake (remember, I described the two examples), if you were of the first category (unprepared), you stood in the backyard asking, "What do I do now?" Most people, I believe, do not organize their own backyard for survival for the simple reason that, unless they have had some camping experience, they just do not know where to start!

For both the experienced and inexperienced, here is my presentation of a logical approach to backyard survival planning. This will enable anybody to get started turning the backyard into what it needs to become: the prepared disaster support system just waiting to be used!

Five categories need to be provided for. They are:

A. Personal Needs,
B. Tools and Utensils,
C. Food and Water,
D. First Aid and Home Medicine Chest, and
E. Well-being and Morale.

For those of you who purchased my video, this is the same format that I used then. Remember, as far as I am concerned, we are planning for an indefinite stay in the backyard!

The list is not in any special order (each item being as important as the others). As a start, I recommend that you set aside:

—A good footlocker or suitcase for item one,
—A good strong metal box for item two,
—Food and water we will come to,
—First aid, etc., again a good strong wooden or metal box,
—Another suitcase or small footlocker.

While you are in the process of compiling your survival gear, several innovative ideas will come to you. Look around at what you have tucked away in the garage or attic. The drive behind everything that I do is to keep costs down to a minimum. Most of our requirements are already around us.

Let's make a start, with our personal needs.

A. Personal Needs

Each member of the family unit should be made aware of the purpose and intent of our survival planning allowing, as a follow up, the assignment of each member to assemble his or her own survival preparations. This would eliminate a conversation likely to be heard after the quake, "But Mother, you know how much I need such and such; don't tell me that you didn't pack it!" I am attempting to show that "personal needs" is, indeed, an individual thing.

Let's define personal needs: Those items considered *by the individual* to be necessary for that individual's continued personal well-being under survival conditions.

Obviously, for all of us, the ideal circumstance would be to have a $100,000 motor home parked in a safe country environment (within walking distance of the house) where we could go and spend an idyllic time riding out the aftermath! Looking at the more practical aspects of things, it follows that I, as an experienced survivalist, can make do with a lot less than the average individual. I believe I have struck a common ground, though. Let's begin our individual preparations for backyard survival.

As a starting point, I recommend the use of a good footlocker as the container for personal needs. I am fond of these because they are durable and utilitarian (and probably because my footlocker did such a good job for me during my military career). Into it, then, go each person's private items.

First, clothes and personal-care needs (remember the scene standing in the backyard after the quake a few pages back?). Ideally, the clothes should be updated for summer/winter wear, but this is asking too much. Try to pack a good variety of gear.

Personal Items:
1. Sweat suits, pants, coveralls (outer wear in general),
2. Lots of socks (thick and thin),
3. Plenty of underwear,
4. Upper wear (T-shirts, etc.),
5. Sleep wear (practical),
6. Toiletries basic to the survival condition (tooth brush, brush and comb, deodorant, the stuff from the car kit, period),
7. Any special medications, vitamins, or health supplements (if you are used to taking them),
8. Toilet paper,
9. Shoes and/or boots,
10. Towels and a wash cloth (Don't forget the stuff you have in the car),
11. Your own sleeping bag or
12. Pillow(s) and blankets (if that is your preference),
13. Feminine needs (if appropriate),
14. A poncho or heavy coat, or box of large lawn and trash bags, and
15. Personal I.D. and papers (Repeat, personal papers).

Before we close the lid, it is a good idea to place several layers of newspaper over the top of the items. This acts as an insulating material. Then throw in a good handful of moth balls or other moth repellant.

Now for the next item on the agenda.

B. Tools and Utensils

It's important to remember that there will be no power, so all tools will have to be hand tools. As a basic kit, I recommend the following:

Tools:
1. A good, short, strong, rough-cut hand saw,
2. A good, medium-weight hammer,
3. A good, serviceable hand axe with a short handle,
4. A hacksaw,
5. If possible, an Army trenching tool (This is an asset because it is a digger and a mini-pick axe in one),
6. Both types of screwdrivers, phillips and common,
7. A good knife (pocket or sliding blade kind),
8. A ball of strong twine,
9. A roll of bailing wire,
10. A good assortment of nails,
11. Both types of pliers, common and wire cutter,
12. The wrecking bar from the auto kit,
13. As many of those blue plastic tarps as you can afford,
14. Fuels for your various lanterns, cookstoves, etc.,
15. Several pairs of work gloves,
16. An auger-type post hole digger,
17. An ample supply of plastic trash bags and a roll of plastic sheeting (I prefer 30 mil.), and
18. A good staple gun and lots of staples.

This is only a basic kit. I am sure that you handypersons can think of a much more complete kit. I base mine on possible needs: the ability to pull lumber out of the wreckage and make shelters; making improvements to the early primitive-type fire pit; toilets; etc. We will always be learning as we go, maybe moving the sites of some of the support services to a more practical location as the conditions dictate. Planning is good, but experience has the final say!

This takes care of the tools part; now to:

Utensils:

One of my favorite pastimes is digging around thrift stores and military surplus stores. I get not only items, but ideas for survival needs! Things like wonderful, old-style suitcases that are not in vogue anymore. For a few dollars, one can purchase good hand tools, footlockers, and utensils of every shape and size (for both kitchen and toolshed use), as well as pots and pans of all kinds. I always look out for the old, heavy, cast-iron types. Great for backyard survival, they maintain a high degree of heat and cook stuff without burning.

Unless you happen to have a extra supply of kitchen items standing by, I suggest that you give the second-hand stores a chance. In the past, I have found camp stoves, lanterns, and even tents in this kind of market. It sure saves buying new.

Back to the topic. What are our needs in this area?

Well, of course, we need to take care of our minimal requirements (such as making tea and coffee). But we also need to plan for the more complicated food preparations (making bread, cooking healthy soups and stews). Oh, yes! Backyard survival is not necessarily all that different from cooking in the house. The only difference is that the backyard kitchen doesn't have a roof, at least not at first.

Be sure you have provided for the basics of boiling, frying, and, as well as possible, baking. Always keep in mind that risking life and limb to go back into the house for a forgotten item is not too smart.

In with tools and utensils I include those special kitchen items like butcher knives, can openers, and such. These expensive-when-new items are a real find when discovered in your friendly, local thrift store.

Other basic needs (cutlery, plates, dishes, bowls and basins) come to mind. Your choice is whether you "go plastic" (no washing-up worries) or take the one-metal-set-of-each-per-family-member route and an all-clean-your-own approach for clean-up afterwards. For myself, keeping in mind the scarcity of water, I like to go plastic, knowing I always have a good supply of plastic trash bags around.

This is as good a place as any to say a few words about garden hygiene. Living in the backyard, for those not used to the camping scene, will present problems known and solved by even the youngest Scout, who was taught "Routine." Always:

—Keep the campsite picked up;
—Have a designated area for food scraps and keep a layer of soil over the old food and waste;
—Air out all blankets and sleeping bags each day;

—Establish toilet hygiene procedures from day one;
—Provide a shelter for firewood and kindling;
—Keep all food in good sealed containers. Ants can scent sugar a mile away;
—Keep sleeping areas swept out, clean, and dry.

Before we go on, let us include in the Utensils column the items that can be used for cooking and food storage. It is not all that long ago that many rural areas did not have the luxury of electricity at the end of a switch. Even today, a large part of Mexico, along with many other countries, does not have electricity. Yet, these same areas enjoy as high a living standard as we do from the point of view of cooking food and the storage of their supplies. How do they do it? Here are just a few ideas for you to consider; I have prepared most of these techniques for my own survival.

Let's think about cooking. For a start, the fire pit is the most primitive approach, and for many, all that will be available. For the real handyman, what about an old-fashioned wood stove? Grandma baked wonderful bread in those old ovens (not to mention all those delicious pies and other baked goodies). Kitchen woodstoves are not that hard to find. Next come the propane conversions of old gas stoves. Not a difficult or very technical undertaking. Your local propane supplier has a stock of the various interchangeable jets required. A propane tank and regulator are also readily available.

Once we break into the propane field, any camper or travel trailer dealer has a good supply of all sorts of models of both propane refrigerators and stoves of all sizes. Carefully used, a five-gallon tank of bottled gas should last at least ten days for cooking and the fridge. Figure three five-gallon tanks for a month, or three of the ten-gallon size and you are set for a long time!

If you live in the country and are already on propane, all you need to do is secure alternate appliances ahead of time. You can use the existing gas pipe for your supply to the new location or set up a new living location ahead of time, say out near the barn (not *in* the barn please!).

You know, for those of you who hate the idea of backyard survival per se, as you read what I have just written about wood stoves and propane appliances, doesn't the idea of eating food cooked on a conventional stove appeal to you? Does it not also serve to demonstrate that living in the backyard, even without a camper or motor home, can still be made to be more than just bearable with a little effort and ingenuity?!

We have yet to consider some other alternatives that use only natural methods. How about the straw box cooler? Ever heard of it? The principle is very simple and very effective. The straw box cooler is just what the name implies, a wooden box of any given size, with a smaller wooden box inside it. The difference in size is taken up by a layer of straw, kept continually moist with cold water.

To understand the principle, imagine that you open the lid of a box, and all that you can see is a layer of wet straw. Then, feeling in the straw, you find the lid of a smaller box. If you lift the lid of this smaller box, you will find items needing cold storage to be in good condition! The secret is, to be sure:

a. That the small inside box is *completely* surrounded and covered with a good layer of damp straw, and

b. That the lid of the outer box is a good tight fit.

This straw box is good for keeping baby formula and food fresh, as well as medications such as insulin. Obviously, keeping the box in the shade is a plus factor (see Diagram 9).

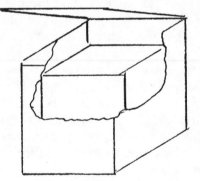

THE BOX WITHIN A BOX PACKED WITH WET STRAW.

DIAGRAM 9—THE STRAW BOX

How about the old root cellar idea? Again, this is not that difficult. I use six wooden pallets (see Diagram 10). These are readily available from feed stores, furniture movers, factories, and warehouses (usually free or at low cost). Measure the outside dimensions of the pallet. They are pretty standard in sizes. Let's assume you have the 48″ size. Dig a hole that is 4 feet 6 inches deep, and 4 feet square. Place one pallet flat on the bottom for the floor. Line the sides with one pallet per side (if they give you trouble, tie the corners with string). Staple plastic around the inside of this box, or slide the pallets into a large trash bag before use so that they are already "lined." Now you are ready to put on the lid, which will be six inches below ground. Cover with plastic (bag or sheet), and you have a mini root cellar that will stay at a constant 63 degrees!

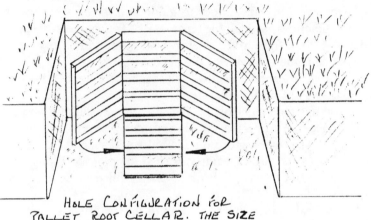

HOLE CONFIGURATION FOR PALLET ROOT CELLAR. THE SIZE WILL DEPEND ON PALLET SIZES

DIAGRAM 10—PALLET ROOT CELLAR

Having even a small root cellar opens up the possibilities for storage of properly prepared fresh vegetables. Wow! Root crops do well, as do all home canned goods. *Remember,* store as if the items were about to be moved across country in a covered wagon! Wouldn't it be awful to store a lot of supplies and have the earth movement smash all those jars! Lots of newspaper, sawdust, or plastic packing materials is the answer. Root-cellar living is a lost art, but there are many resource materials in the library. If you are motivated to this system, I suggest you study this fascinating concept that, after all, preceded the refrigerator.

Now we are coming to the essentials. Items that require outside storage: water and food (Yes, I changed them around for my own purpose!).

C. Water and Food

Always remember that the enemies of water are *heat* and light. Keeping these two things in mind, the next question is: How much water will I need?

The standard answer that we are all familiar with is "One gallon of water per person, per day."

We could enter into a tremendous debate on the merits of this statement. There is no doubt whatsoever that a person could exist on far less water a day than this. We have seen enough movies to know that! However, my aim is not to guide you to the very barest of survival practices, with all the tensions of "Touch one more drop of water and it's a fight to the death" syndrome. Rather, my aim has always been, and always will be, to convince you that, with a little conscious effort and a practical approach, survival can become a "normal" way of life! No question.

Let us not lose sight of the fact that we are talking about the continuance of life on a reasonable and *healthy* level. True, we have to skip personal bathing or doing laundry and such chores. But we must still eat and drink at fairly normal intervals (cooking meals, allowing a child to have a drink of orange juice made with water, this kind of thing).

A practical approach means facing the realities of any given situation. A school with 700 students needs 700 gallons of water a *day*. Put aside the "looks like enough" approach—it will not do!

One gallon a day. Let's compute this figure. We are preparing for a survival period of at least ten days with no outside help (I plan for much longer, myself.) This means, using a basic family of four as our unit of measure:

1 gal a day times 4 persons = 4 gals per day,
Times the ten days = 4 x 10 = 40 gals total.

On the face of it, that seems like a lot of water, but really it isn't. Get two twenty-five-gallon containers and you have a surplus!

Thinking about a family of four, under most normal conditions, at least one gallon of milk is consumed every two days. When I was raising my four sons, we used two gallons a day! As a rough average though, we could say a minimum of three gallons a week for a family of four. Taking and preparing those three gallon jugs when empty, filling them with water, then storing them, means that, in three and a half months, all the water you need will be in storage! Going a step further, once the habit is established, in six months (twenty-four weeks) you will have stored seventy-two gallons water (or enough water for eighteen weeks' survival). All this using a container you normally throw away.

The quality of your survival after the disaster is always equal to the quality of the preparations taken beforehand. Never forget this truism!

So, where were we? Ah, yes! Water storage. And the enemies of water are. . .light and heat.

This means that we have to store our water where it is both dark and cool. Since we are not storing it in the house, it follows that we should look around outside for a suitable place. In my video, I show the method of storing those milk or similar-type containers in the ground. This is a fairly simple process and involves digging a trench (6″ wide by 10″ deep and I suggest 36″ long). This trench will store six gallons of water, which is a two-and-a-half-day supply for our family of four (see Diagram 11).

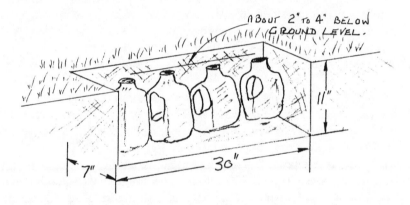

DIAGRAM 11—WATER STORAGE TRENCH

Once in the trench, the containers are covered with sand or soil to lightly cover the caps. Items stored this way are both dark and cool. If the trench is in an area that is watered by a sprinkler system or hose, so much the better.

Perhaps you have a sheltered corner in the garden with high bushes or a hedge that is cool and dark. Store the water there, on top of the ground. It is still sheltered from light and heat.

To prepare the plastic containers, first clean and rinse the inside.

Do not use detergent; you'll never get the soap out! After a good rinse (don't forget to do the cap as well), pour at least four ounces of undiluted chlorine bleach into the container. Replacing the cap, rinse the inside of the container and the cap by turning the container upside down, making sure that all of the inner surface is treated with the chlorine rinse. This results in a nice film of chlorine over the inside plastic surface.

Now empty the bleach from the container and fill with clean cold water. *Do not rinse!* If you have a water filter, so much the better. Once filled, store your container in a cool, dark place.

The next question that is usually asked at this point is "How long does water last this way?" My best answer is, "It depends how you are going to use it." This may sound evasive, but it isn't really. For example, if you are going to take the water, put it in a pot, bring it to the boil and make rice or stew, you will sterilize the water through the boiling process. Stored in a cool dark place, it should be safe to use for several months.

However, if the water has been stored for six months or more, and it is to be consumed straight from the container, I would suggest filtering the water first. Remember, we have a filter in the survival supplies, though it is putting the filter to work when it may not be necessary. Another method on a planned procedure could be:

We are in the backyard survival mode. We take out two containers of water for the day's use, and, opening each container, we place four drops of chlorine bleach per gallon into each container. After replacing the cap, shake well and allow to stand for a few minutes before using. A very simple procedure to adopt.

I think at this point it is important to have a little discussion about this whole water "thing." First, under the storage-and-use policy that most of us follow, we clean a container, fill it with clean water (the same water we use every day), and then, to the best of our ability, store the water in a cool dark place. It seems fairly logical that, when we come to use this same water, unless it was stored in the direct sun every day, and unless it was pretty lousy stuff to start with, there cannot be too much bacterial activity that has taken place.

On the other hand, if you are going to use (as I have heard recommended from time to time) the water from your toilet tank, hot water heater or water bed (remember those waterbed chemicals?) for any purpose other than washing, that's another matter. It isn't worth the risk. Most of the bru-ha-ha about water concerns the necessity to use brackish water found in the open or on the street from a burst water main. Only for desperate people in dire straits (like the unprepared survivor) is use of this type of water even considered. If any of my readers find themselves in this situation, I have failed. It is for this very reason (that of saving my readers from ever being in this situation) that I spend so much time on the nit-picky details!

I have found that, in the long run, taking time and labor into account, if you can afford the less-than-$20 involved, the twenty-five-gallon plastic container is the best bet. Place it in its storage "home" before you fill it, though. It is a bear to lug around when full!

There is a video in preparation covering this whole area of Food and Water.

Now, let's move on to one of my favorite subjects: food for the survivor. I always start my preamble as follows: *Our forefathers crossed this land in covered wagons without the aid of refrigerators or canned food. The answer to the question of what food is best for survival needs, is to study and adopt their methods.*

End of talk. Let's move on!

Seriously, how did they do it? They were, of course, bound by the same criteria we are. First, they needed food that had a long shelf life and was easy to transport. We have the same need, except we don't have to worry about transportation. What kinds of food then, are we looking for? Needs no refrigeration, has a long shelf life, and is easy to store. We should all arrive at the same conclusion: grains, rice, beans of all kinds, flour, sugar, and various kinds of coarse oats, usually already ground for use. Although I did not include it in the list of utensils, a hand grinder is a boon for those of you inclined to really get into this section of culinary art.

When it came to meat and fowl, all their stores were dried and/or smoked (cured). If you are of a mind to do this, all sorts of meat, fish, and fowl may be purchased already cured (along with a whole selection of sausages). Also, there are several good, fairly inexpensive smokers on the market that enable you to put up your own supplies. If they are electric, better get going before the disaster hits. Afterwards will be too late!

While talking about cured food, let us not forget the whole spectrum of dried foods (especially fruit, nuts, vegetables, and trail mix), together with those luscious and very nourishing granola selections. I have always found this section in the market to be very expensive. As a result, a good weekend exercise is to work as a family to prepare sun-dried fruits and veggies of all kinds. There are many excellent granola recipes available, too. A word of warning:

be very disciplined with all involved in this type of project or you will most likely end up eating more than is put in storage!

The process of sun drying is not that difficult, and there are many very fine pamphlets available for this instruction. Basically, the process is very simple. First you need a sunny, wind-free area; a table or good-sized piece of plywood on trestles; two medium-sized window screens; six clamps; and a supply of well-washed fruit and vegetables.

Place one screen on the work surface, and carefully fill the whole space with slices of fruit to be dried. Cover with the other screen over the top of the fruit. Clamp the screens at top, bottom, and middles, and let the sun do its work! Or you may hang or stand these screens upright. Tomatoes, eggplants, and potatoes do well with this method, but most salads do not (see Diagram 12).

Note that fresh produce to be sun-dried should be thoroughly washed, and any imperfect fruit should be discarded. Slice fairly thick and place between screens, whose primary purpose is to prevent excessive curling of the product. Once sufficient dehydration has taken place and the product retains a flat profile without any pressure, move it from between the screens to the top of the upper screen and start a new batch between screens. Continue this process with different fruits and vegetables as they come in season. This process will provide an abundance of both highly nutritious and versatile food supplies.

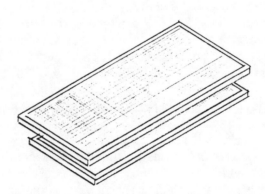

DIAGRAM 12—FOOD DRYING USING SOLAR ENERGY

Now we logically move into the area of canning. The Mormons are experts in this field of survival preparation, probably because they have been at it so long. If you are a canner, go to it. For backyard survival, why not. *But* (and it is a big *but*), there are some drawbacks to the canning system. The main one, of course, is storage.

Since we are not even considering storage in the house, outside storage for cans (glass jars) is the same as for water: in a place that is cool and dark. Ideally, an old time root cellar (which few of us have) would serve us well. You could follow my suggestion and make your own as we have already discussed. Failing that, please remember not to store all those lovely jars on a shelf. They make such a mess when the shaking starts!

Without a root cellar, what are we left with then? In the ground with a lot of space between the jars seems to be one answer. Dig a trench as you did for the water containers, as wide and as deep as your jars, making sure that the lids are about two inches below the surface. Leave a good distance between the jars so that the soil between the jars will act as a cushion against the shockwaves coming through the ground.

If you decide to store your canning jars in a footlocker-type deal, use plenty of newspaper and pack the container as though it were going to be shipped cross-country!

We have talked about food from the early pioneers' standpoint. Why? First, because all that they used (and all that I have recommended) is both cheap and very easy to obtain (very important to a struggling writer and exponent of an unpopular subject!). Also, it seems to me, why stack a load of *canned* beans for example, when a twenty-pound sack of any *dry* beans cost less than $5 and is so easy to store?

There are, however, many items that we can obtain that they could not. I refer to that great number of items that we talked about in both our Go and our Stay gear for the auto. All those individually packaged items that can be purchased usually in 20-, 40-, and up to 100-count boxes. Go to the wholesale suppliers for restaurants and institutions. There, to your probable amazement (it was mine), you will find small packaged items you never imagined existed.

How about all the soups served at your favorite restaurant? Yes, that delicious clam chowder, minestrone, and tomato, packed for individual servings, and all you add is water! Along the same aisle, you will see packets of gravies, broths, deserts of all kinds (Jell-O in two- and five-pound packets), all the fruit drinks, as well as tea, coffee, and cocoa. The list is long.

Why survivors are reduced to lining up with sad faces waiting for the Army or the Red Cross to supply them with the very basic handouts, when all this lovely food is waiting to be stored away in the backyard, is really beyond me. Then, of course, I have to remember, they did not have access to this survival manual. . .or did they?

There are a few tricks of the trade we have not talked about. How about the sourdough starter? Ever heard of it? No? Sourdough Willie would be shocked! If you are interested, your local librarian will show you where his book is, along with others on the same subject in the cookbook aisle.

Basically, it is a very simple procedure, and one I highly recommend. The principle is based on the natural reaction of certain ingredients to each other. In this case, yeast, flour and water. What could be more simple? The whole thing acts this way.

The ingredients are stored ready for use: a packet of dry yeast powder, flour, sugar, and water. To start off, mix together:

 1 package dry yeast
 ½ cup warm water

Add:

 2 cups flour
 2 cups of water
 4 oz. sugar

Stir ingredients in a glass jar or earthen pickle jar, cover, place in a warm place and wait about twenty-four hours. Boy, are you in for a shock! When all this stuff gets to activating, it produces a bubbling, rising demon in the pot!

The idea is that you can take out one cup of this stuff, mix it with water and flour to the consistency of pancake batter, and—presto—sourdough pancakes hot off the open griddle! Or you can make sourdough bread, rolls, or what-have-you.

"Each time you take, put back" is the law of the sourdough pot. In the example mentioned, put back a cup of water and a cup of flour. The beauty of the sourdough pot is that it keeps on going. . .forever! There are as many different "starters" as people who used them. In the old days of the chuck wagon, hot sourdough biscuits and bread were ready in minutes from when the wheels stopped turning. . .all from the starter pot.

In summary, then, there is no end to the variety of survival foods that can be stored. Remember that we are under a time of stress, and, in these days of working parents and fast-food mania, the diet of the average American leaves much to be desired, to say the least.

I gave a seminar for a group of Mormon ladies recently and, during the let's-all-talk-together phase, a story was told of this lady who put her family through a trial run of earthquake survival using the stored foodstuffs. The lady telling the story said, "The children just would not eat the food. They went hungry." I chuckled to myself and, when asked my opinion answered, "Come E plus about three, they'll eat whatever is available, especially when they go to their friend's house and they don't have any junk food either!" This woman was talking about prepackaged survival food and, frankly, I don't blame those children. Some of that stuff is tasteless.

It is somewhat ironic that the whole purpose of my efforts in writing this manual is to try to get you to provide emergency food for yourself and your family to avoid the bread line with all the other survivors. As an added benefit, all of the foods that I recommend you store will provide a highly nutritional and wholesome diet, far better than many of you normally consume.

Having time to have fun preparing the family meals in the backyard can also have many bonuses—the positive out of the negative situation, as it were. Think of the challenge of putting together meals from the stock of foods that you have! Need a typical menu for the day? How about:

Breakfast:
—Orange or other fruit juice, tea or coffee,
—Sourdough or other pancakes, or
—Biscuit and gravy southern-style,
—Nutmeat patty, hashbrowns.

That should hold us until Lunch:
—Sliced wholewheat pan loaf with honey or jam,
—Fruit juice cocktail,
—Trail mix and raisins.

A dried fruit snack in mid-afternoon should hold us until Dinner:
—Clam Chowder, or
—Chicken barley soup
—Nutmeat loaf, mashed potatoes and gravy,
—Choice mixed vegetables or corn,
—Jell-O pudding, or
—Mixed fruit cup with tapioca, and
—Fruit juice or other beverage.

Through these examples, I am trying to demonstrate that there is no limit to the variety of food that is available to a cook with a little time on his hands! Also, bear in mind that, for the first few days, there should be a good supply of freezer food that must be eaten before it goes bad.

At my house, we have an old, second-hand refrigerator that is kept outside. I realize that the contents will not keep unless a generator were to be run constantly once the power quits, but I have mentally prepared myself to the task of quick preservation of the food by barbecuing or boiling the meat and fish for use in the first week.

Backyard survival. It can be fun. But it has to be provided for, both mentally and physically.

I would be remiss if I did not give time and space to alternate types of foods that are available for the survivalist. These include the very fine line of freeze-dried items and, of course, the Army field rations sold at the military surplus stores. The main reason I have not spent a lot of time on this area is that I am from the "natural" survivalist school. As an individual, I am a label reader. Nothing goes in my shopping cart before the label is read. Apart from the expense of both the freeze-dried and the surplus military foods, I am far from satisfied with the amount of preservatives used in the preparation of these items.

Now before you all start protesting and writing letters, let me clearly state that I am not in any way condemning these products. Junk food is consumed by millions of people every day. I am merely pointing out that for me, a person on the low end of the economic scale, price is my main concern. And in my price range, quality is still a goal. So there are alternate foods out there, but, for the survivalist who shares my concerns, the items I talk about in this manual best fill the bill.

Now let's get back into our survival mode. There are certain rules to learn. The backyard should be set out to provide clearly defined functional areas. These will be for:

Kitchen and Food Preparation

You will need a fire pit area. If you have one, the barbecue should be moved to this area. Even with a barbecue, a fire pit is still a must. Fire pits come in a variety of sizes, according to need. Basically, they fall into two categories: above- or below-ground fire pits.

First, the above-ground model is just what it sounds like. Taking blocks from that wall that is down, make a long fire pit to put oven racks on. Scoop out a small amount of soil (not too deep), so that this unit will act as a pot-cooking place (see Diagram 13).

Then you will need a still-larger above-ground unit, probably round, to boil larger pots of water for beans and stews. As soon as water becomes available from the official sources, you will also need this larger area for boiling the family wash and bath water (see Diagram 14). What a happy day that will be!

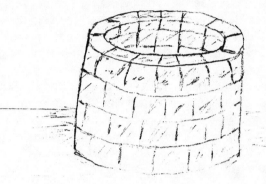

DIAGRAM 13—ABOVE-GROUND FIRE PIT

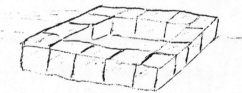

DIAGRAM 14—DEEP ABOVE-GROUND FIRE PIT

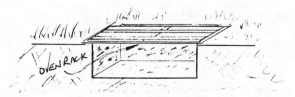

DIAGRAM 15—BELOW-GROUND FIRE PIT

Now, let's talk about the below-ground, or true fire pit. This will require the consideration of what the pit is for; but before we come to that point, let us think about what this type of pit does.

The below-ground pit is made by digging a hole, usually a trench configuration, in the ground, about twelve inches deep. This hole or trench is then filled with wood chips and pieces small enough to go in the trench. These are then set on fire. Now, the object is to wait until the main flames have died down, leaving nice hot embers remain in the pit. This resulting heat source can now become a stove, allowing you to cook casseroles and baked-type dishes under controlled conditions. Being below the ground, the embers remain hot for a long period of time, depending of course on the type of wood used. Hardwoods and roots last the longest. Some cooking hints are to be found in the food appendix at the end of this chapter.

These fire pits should be provided for ahead of time. If they are not actually made, at least the materials should be close by, ready to use at crunch time.

A rough table to provide a food preparation surface is our next topic. In Diagrams 16 and 17, I have sketched a few ideas for shelves and racks, just as a guide for you to work with.

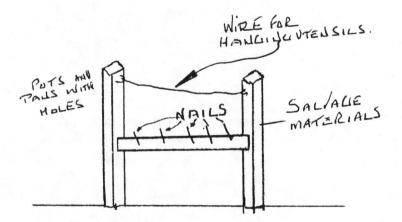

DIAGRAM 16—STORAGE SET-UP FOR COOKING AREA

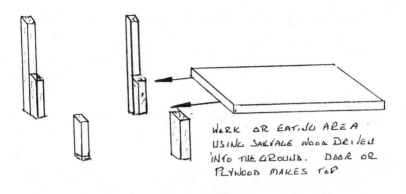

WoRK oR EATiNG AREA
USiNG SALVAGE WooD DRiVEN
iNTo THE GRounD. DooR oR
PLYWooD MAKES ToP

DIAGRAM 17—WORK OR EATING AREA

Once you get into the thought pattern of providing backyard survival ahead of time, inevitably you will find that, as you go about your daily life, little ideas will pop into your head from items that you see. A sale on lumber (say 2x4s for a dollar each), nails, tarps, etc., is a bonus. All such items purchased ahead of time really pay off later. Also, try to provide a large vessel, like a small metal garbage can, for boiling the water for washing of self and dishes (when water is available, of course).

I already mentioned the problem of food waste and flies. At the end of this chapter, you will find an appendix. It deals with food preparation in some detail.

Toilet Area

After the family planning sessions, you should, as a family, decide "one potty or two?"

For health reasons alone, I still have not found a better system than an earth outhouse as I discuss in my video. I recommend a hole dug with an auger-type post-hole digger to at least four feet deep. Pile the loose earth away from the hole, and then place flat bricks, cement blocks, or even thick wood pieces around the mouth of the hole to prevent cave-in of the top (see Diagram 18). From this point, your own ingenuity comes into play. You may construct a privacy screen with the plastic bags draped over sticks, or you may have a complete shelter made as in the old outhouse days.

Obviously, the preparation for this situation should be completed

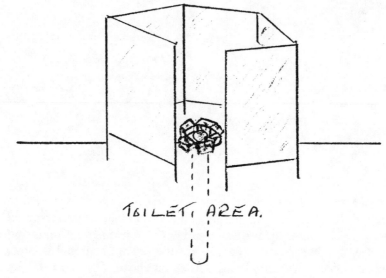

USING PLASTIC TRASH BAGS
ON STAKES DRIVEN INTO GROUND.
FOR ANY DESIRED PRIVACY AREA.

TOILET AREA.

DIAGRAM 18—TOILET AREA

in advance of the required day. Waiting for the time when the family is all collected in the backyard after the disaster is a little late to be asking "Where do we go?"

Look around your tool shed or wood pile and determine what you have available for the provision of your family's outside bathroom. Perhaps you will consider making a portable structure and then fold it all up in a safe corner of the garden, where it waits to be put into use. Don't forget to buy an extra toilet seat next time they are on sale!

The procedure for use is (having a sack of lime available) after each use, put two scoops of lime into the hole, followed by two scoops of soil. Natural action does the rest.

If you can afford them, chemical toilets are helpful, but they still have to be serviced. Nature provides that service for free with the earth toilet.

There are so many different ways to go. To me, a concerned bread winner will be the concerned survivalist who, in the calm light of *now*, will accept the challenge of the future *then*.

It was always a learning experience to witness, and sometimes take part in, projects of settling in that occurred when my Army unit was in a place that was going to be "home" for a while. Showers and all sorts of creature comforts were made overnight out of virtually nothing.

Before moving on, please consider this whole subject of the toilet in some detail. Young children not prepared beforehand will be placed into an unnecessary situation of stress, as will all family members. Our bathroom is a very personal place. . .we use it in our own time and in our own way. For many of us, the moments spent shaving, showering, and other tasks of toiletry are rare opportunities for a personal period and a meditation time for many. To be suddenly thrust unawares into a crude out-house situation, with no prior discussion, could create a stress that can be so easily avoided.

What did we say about the quality of survival depending on the preparation? Let's go on to;

Living and Eating Area

If you already have a picnic table in the backyard, you are home free. If not, you will need to provide some arrangement for eating and family association time. This area may well need some sort of cover from both the hot sun and the winter rains. Those nice sun rooms on poles that are so popular come to mind. Or you may consider making a shelter using a tree or some poles. Or follow the ideas in Diagrams 19 and 20.

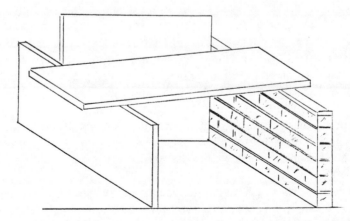

DIAGRAM 19—MAKING AN AGAINST-A-WALL SHELTER

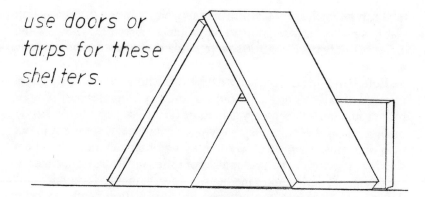

use doors or tarps for these shelters.

DIAGRAM 20—AN A-FRAME SHELTER

Certainly you are going to need a good eating area, one that will also serve as the recreation area to do hobbies and games. As those of us who are campers will remember, the tent or sleeping area is a popular place at free-time periods, but we still need to have a sit-down place for meals and fun times. Now on to:

Bedroom Area

Perhaps you have a tent or tents. Problem solved! If not, you will need to construct a shelter for your sleeping convenience. I have seen newsreel pictures of survivors in the backyard who had pulled mattresses from the house and, there in the open, they attempted to sleep. They did not, of course, last more than a couple of nights.

The sleeping area must be a *covered* shelter for many reasons. In the first place, the temperature and change in atmospheric pressure are both conditions we "inside" folks are not used to. We can get sick real fast. Sleeping with the head uncovered means that we are going to directly breathe in the cold night air. Lungs not used to breathing cold and damp air can become congested and quickly turn to pneumonia, a condition not welcome. If a covered shelter is not ready for the first nights, be sure to sleep with the mouth covered with a scarf or some other item that will warm the cold air prior to entering the lungs.

Secondly, flies and night fliers can quickly ruin a good night's sleep. Probably the most important reason to provide a shelter is a psychological one. It gives us a slight taste of normalcy. We are used to sleeping in a room. To offset the trauma of the disaster, we are advised to, as quickly as possible, return to "normalcy." Sleeping in a "room" is one of the quickest steps to achieve this goal.

The shelter can be very fancy or very simple. A pole and some tarps will do fine. I have drawn some types of shelters for you to consider. Your own location will be your guide (see Diagrams 19 and 20).

Always sleep with your head facing north. Always put the closed side of the shelter facing the windy direction; this helps to keep both wind and rain out. A good tip is to ask your son, the Boy Scout, for some advice. Or ask somebody else's son. They learn all this stuff. I did!

So we have our kitchen, toilet, bedroom and living/dining room all taken care of. What's missing? Purposely, I omitted the bathing area!

For the first ten days, or until a good supply of water is available, there will be no need for a washroom in its literal sense. We do not have water to spare for washing our bodies, taking showers, shaving, and all those other luxuries that are part of our way of life. We all have those bottles of mouthwash to clean our teeth with, and, until we are absolutely sure that our precious water supply can be replenished, personal hygiene is out!

So far, we have acted as if the backyard was to be our permanent home, and I am sure that, as cozy as I hope I have made it sound, you are feeling that, "It's not going to be so bad after all!" It is my sincere hope that this rosy picture I have painted will remain. However, as your advisor it is my duty to place all the facts before you. Now it is time to face and plan for the dreaded fact that all concerned survivalists fear. That fact is the circumstance of evacuation.

As a society, living as we do in both the city and the suburban areas, it follows that the one always affects the other. Suburbanites drive in droves to the city for their employment activities each day, while the inner-city dwellers, many unemployed, occupy each available living space which, in most cases, are run-down and neglected. All the available development monies are poured into the suburbs, leaving the inner city to fester and rot.

This unfortunate circumstance is a fact of life for all of us. But for the survivalist, it is like a death knell. It is the time bomb that threatens us all. Mother Nature is unforgiving:

—She cares not that you let structures deteriorate to the danger level.

—She is not dissuaded because thousands of people call
these slums home.

—She destroys the property of all, rich and poor, who are not
mindful of the enormity of her power.

—Put nuclear power plants on a fault? Fine. Expect an
American Chernobyl!

—Neglect the safety codes? Prepare to face the consequences!

The consequences are that the very heart of the city will, and does,
endanger the whole population. Where are the oldest sewer pipes,
whose routes are mainly unknown (ask the Metro Rail engineers!)?
The oldest gas lines (many deteriorated to less-than-allowable
limits)? The oldest water pipes and mains (those same lines we
depend on for fire fighting)? How much illegal toxic chemicals are
used and stored in this same inner city sprawl?

What is the probable outcome of all this?

—Fires.

—Explosions.

—Possible toxic clouds.

—Mass confusion and conditions so dangerous that, even if
they are able to penetrate the area, fire personnel will be
at risk of the gravest nature.

For us backyard survivors, it means that there is a very real threat
to our safety, thus leading to the need for mass evacuation. Now all
our careful plans are possibly in jeopardy.

I have struggled for years with this problem. Having provided so
diligently for our survival, what are we to do if fire, racing across
the city, causes us to run and leave everything behind?

Many years ago, I was invited to an "earthquake seminar" that
was put on by a very high-priced promotion company. I was new to
the business myself then, still developing my own technique for
telling it like it is. When the subject of possible evacuation came up,
they handled it this way.

Using slides drawn by a very talented artist, the scene was
portrayed like this:

The background was a brilliant red sunset against which the
figures were silhouetted. There were four in the family: a very
tall, slim, young mother, an Adonis-type male figure straight

out of the nearest gym, and two adoring children looking up at them (wouldn't you know it, a boy and a girl!). The family was straight out of the 1940s. With backpack in hand (one backpack for the four), they turned away from their undamaged suburban home and walked off into the sunset.

The polished studio announcer's voice droned out in a syrupy baritone as these slides were flipped in sequence. "Should evacuation be necessary, our family shows that they are well prepared for whatever comes!"

I am sure that somewhere that slide show is still being shown. Just as surely, somewhere audiences are just as gullibly being sold a bill of goods that is so far from the truth.

The problem I had to try to solve was "How can we avoid the very circumstances we have been planning to avoid? How can we not end up wandering around like the 'don't cares?' To be in a similar position to *them*, with what *they* have, *nothing?*"

To solve this problem I developed the food torpedo (see Diagram 21), a carefully packed portable food carrier that can provide enough survival food for the individual or the family. This food torpedo is both light and durable. It is made from a four-foot length of four-inch plastic pipe with rubber seals (J-caps). In its sealed state, it is both airtight and waterproof. After packing, the food torpedo is buried in the ground.

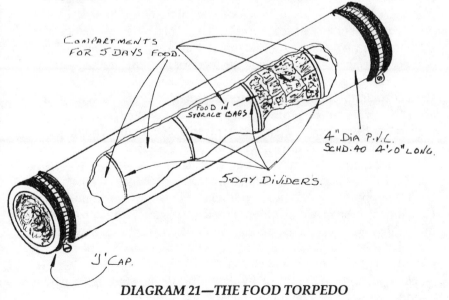

DIAGRAM 21—THE FOOD TORPEDO

111

If evacuation is called for, the food torpedoes will be dug up and taken with us, together with a couple of cooking pots; we are still able to provide for ourselves until we can return to our homes.

As you will see from the diagram, the torpedo is packed with four days' food for a family of four, in four twelve-inch layers. Each layer is complete in itself.

Three light meals (breakfast, lunch, and dinner) are thus readily at hand. Commercial food torpedoes are planned as funds become available. To develop supplies of these food torpedoes for distribution to distressed areas after disaster has struck would be an ideal. Since they are very durable, they can be dropped from the air to isolated or cut-off places as in flood conditions.

The contents of the food torpedo have been carefully calculated to provide a basic nutritional diet. Grains, nuts and cereals, protein powders, and dried fruits are placed together with baby formula, if it is designated as a need.

You remember that when we were packing the Stay gear for the automobile I said that I would talk about this subject in the section on backyard survival? Here we are!

The auto torpedo is slightly smaller. It's only three feet long, but still packed with the same highly nutritional products. However, with this smaller torpedo, you do not have to be concerned primarily with separating the days' supplies from each other. The types of foods and snacks packed in this container are of the on-the-go type (high-energy, high-protein kinds of foods). When we were at the Go-or-Stay decision time, you remember that great emphasis was placed on the details of making your own decision. Now some of the reasons for that advice will become clearer as we discuss the food for that time frame.

Are you a "goer?" If so, how long is your journey going to be? Reflect this time period in your travel torpedo! Conversely, if you are a "stayer," you will probably have packed stay-type foods in your tube, more like a food locker with items that will require cooking as opposed to the high-energy travel stuff. Get the idea?

Food torpedoes will never be an alternative to a full survival set up. But for evacuation, they maintain the aim of the survivalist. . .to be self-supporting under all conditions. Many survival families I have talked to have adapted food torpedoes as storage bins, packing one with flour and grains, another with dried fruit, etc. You may consider this as a viable approach to your own survival planning regardless of your disaster situation.

Now, sticking to our nit-picky-detail format, how do we prepare a food torpedo? Let's do it together.

First you need a length of plastic pipe, four inches in diameter. There are two grades available. Schedule 40, which is very thick-walled and the most expensive, and schedule 200, which is thinner and quite cheap. There is also a black variety called sewer pipe that is somewhere in the middle. All are adaptable, but I prefer Schedule 40. Buy your pipe in eight-foot lengths, which will make two torpedoes.

You will also need to purchase four J-caps. They are rubber and are sold with the steel locking bands as a set. You need two for each torpedo.

Cut the pipe into two four-foot lengths. Most supply houses will do this for you for free. Smile nicely and assure them you are not a plumber (they love do-it-yourselfers!). Now you are ready to go.

The best way I know to instruct you is to show you how I do it. (There is a video on the way!) You need a lot of space on a table top to lay out your supplies. As you look over the list of available items, you need to write down your menus for your family for the four days you are going to pack into each torpedo.

This list is by no means complete. You will find a tremendous variety of packaged dry goods out there. The restaurant supply house will surprise you! All of these items are sold in bulk packaging: the flours and grains probably in ten- and twenty-pound sizes, the small packaged items in from 100- to 200-count boxes (that's the tea, sugar, jams and stuff).

Have fun going around and listing all the items available, and then sit down and write your own menus. As you do, think of the challenge of having to cook with a minimum of utensils. One frypan and one saucepan will get you by. Here's a basic list to start you off:

Breakfast

Tea/coffee	Mush	Oat meal
Hash Browns	Jams, Honey	Dried Milk
Fruit juices	Sugar	Cornmeal
Pancake mix	Soy flour	Dried fruits
Biscuit mix	Smoked sausage	Nut Meats
Gravy mix	Southern	Dried egg

Lunch

Biscuit mix	Granola snacks (Foil wrapped)
Raisins	Nuts
Fruit roll-ups	Protein flakes
Honey	Hot cocoa mix
Dried fruits	Soups

Dinner

Beans (black, red, white, navy etc.)

Lentils	Peas (green, red, split)
Soups, all kinds	Soup starters
Rice	Beef jerky
Sugar	Raisins
Dried fruits	Milk powder

These lists are, of course, not complete. You would add those items that are used by your family: ketchup, salt and pepper, these kinds of things.

Now, I realize that many of you wise gourmets out there are saying, "but what about this or that group of good wholesome foods?" Noodles of all kinds come to my mind (especially those green spinach ones I love so much). Why are they and other items not on the list then?

Please remember that we are talking about survival at the minimum level. Some items do not pack well, some take up too much room and do not compress. On the other hand, there are many other excellent foods that are suitable for this purpose. I hate to get into the middle of opinions about which foods are better than others (vegetarianism for example), but there is a whole group in the dried yogurt, bulgar, and nut-meat families that are great nutritionally and do pack well. So go to it!

You have studied the lists, made up your menus, and now we have to turn our lists into reality before we can proceed.

From these lists then you will go out and buy your supplies. Perhaps on the trip you will see other adaptable items. Once back home, we can prepare to pack our torpedo.

First let me point out that we are going to pack in such a way as to waste no space at all. In order to make the torpedo work properly, all the items must be packed into smaller bags to comprise the day's supply for each meal.

Let's break that down even further. For example, that box of forty tea bags? You would put into each day's packet only those tea bags you are going to use that day. I put all my beverage needs into one bag (e.g., two tea bags, two coffee bags, four sugars, four creamers), seal it, and it's ready to pack. Get the idea?

We have to do the same with all the bulk items. One cup of rice? Bag it. One cup of split peas? Bag it. And so on, until all the food for each day is not only individually bagged, but is in separate piles for each day. Two torpedoes, eight little sections on the table!

Leave the caps off for now and, placing the end of the tube on a chair, or on a piece of cardboard on the floor, pack in the little bags of foods like the backpack in the to-go gear; the last-needed items go on the bottom. In this case, it would be the eighth day's supplies. Now proceed to pack the next three days' into the torpedo. Use napkins as separators for each day. You may find that it is difficult to push the items down the tube. Air is trapped in between them or on the bottom. Lean the tube forward to let this air out and continue to pack all four days' supplies.

Now, carefully lift the tube and lay it down on the table. Place a "J" cap on one end and tighten it. Bang this sealed end on the floor, and you will notice all the packets of food go down even more. Perhaps, there is even room for a roll of toilet paper! Put on the second cap, and that tube is complete.

Now, pack the second tube in the same manner. Your eight days' food supply is ready to be buried in the backyard, hopefully never to be required. Oh yes—tape a penny or a dime to the outside of the tube to be sure that you will be able to open the torpedo when you need to.

I keep a couple of leather straps in a plastic bag next to my torpedoes in the ground. These are used to make over-the- shoulder carrying straps for the evacuation journey.

Before we leave the subject of food torpedoes, I would like to go back to our dialogue about documentation: the need for proof of ownership or rental verification. One of the biggest problems after a disaster is the inability of government agencies to deal with compensation of various kinds (property and structural loss, etc.) promptly. Time and again, delays of six months or more are being experienced by claimants because of the loss of records in the disaster (proof of who you are, what you lost, and so on). It is vital that you have a copy of your documents (deed, rental agreement, insurance paperwork, etc.) readily available to begin the restoration process. The small document torpedo is the answer.

Using the same procedure as the food torpedo, only with two-inch pipe and J-caps, an excellent storage for vital documents and even jewelry is quickly made. *Bury it safely in the ground where only you know its location!* We should also mention at this point that "plastic" (credit cards) will not be of any value after the quake, or indeed in any disaster where power is out. Consider using the small plastic tube as a money safe also.

An interesting little aside is the story of many Londoners after the war. Picture the scene. Rows of rubble piled high by bulldozers on each side of a street. Some piles as high as twenty feet! Life and traffic went on, in some cases, for years after the war before a particular street was cleared for rebuilding. What would be required of course before this could happen was that all those piles of rubble, once homes, had to be cleared. . .so, bring on the bulldozers!

How the word ever spread or how people ever remembered, I do not know. . .but as soon as the first clearing procedure began, groups of people would congregate alongside the roads. As soon as a section was cleared, the people would swarm like a flock of birds and begin digging and scratching on the freshly cleared ground! These were the former residents who had once lived on the very spot they were now on. Now they were digging in their own back yard! For what? Storage containers of precious belongings! A complex assortment of cans and old ammo boxes, metal thermos bottles, you name it, and someone had thought of it! Family heirlooms, precious (though perhaps of little value) jewelry, medals from previous wars, old photographs. All buried in their own "time capsules," fashioned for protection against the ravages of war.

When I started my research on survival needs and methods I determined to pass that scene on to my audiences. Having done this, now I pass it on to you, my readers!

Let's go back now, to the garden areas all laid out for us. Our supplies are prepared and ready as far as we have gone.

Now back to that night not so long ago when we stood in the backyard at E plus about five minutes! Before clothes, what was the first thing we had a need for? Right. First aid kit! So let's do it.

D. First Aid and Home Medicine Chest

As you are now well aware, I do not advocate first aid kits, per se. When I say "kit," I refer to the type of small metal box usually found in the trunk of one's car. I think these are a waste of time and money. Until the manufacturers of these products take the time to research what a *survival* first aid kit should look like, they will go on selling the public (who buy in good faith) a generalized first aid kit that does not have adequate supplies for use under these conditions. These kits do not come cheap. I saw an advertisement for one said to contain his-and-her Band-Aids!

What would be far more appropriate for the home is the type of first aid box or "station" found in industrial workshops and factories. These are equipped for far more comprehensive injuries than the kit

I spoke of a minute ago. As these tend to be expensive purchased outright, you can easily put one together on your own. If you can afford to purchase one, it would be easier.

As we did with the car kit, let's start at the beginning; we are going to make our own first aid "box" for want of a better term. Into it goes:

First Aid Supplies
1. Ace bandages and 4x4 pads. We are concerned with bleeding, cuts from glass on any part of the body, especially on the feet in the rapid home evacuation process. We need then, a good supply of 4x4 sterile pads and compression-type bandages. Ace-type bandages in 2-, 4-, and 6-inch widths are the most effective.

2. Gauze bandages, butterfly strips, and Band-Aids of various sizes.

3. Cleansing solutions and swabs.
Small bottle Merthiolate   Cotton Balls or Swabs
Bactine   Peroxide
Iodine   Eye flush kit

4. Antidotes.
Bee sting kit.
Snake bite kit.
Diuretic.

5. Burn kit.
Burn creme or gel.
Saline solution.

(If we escaped from the house with or without injuries, the next injuries we are most likely to encounter are in the backyard. These are likely to be burns in the first instance. We are using open fires. Cooking over an open fire which we are not familiar with can be dangerous, so burns and scalds are likely.)

6. Thermometer.

7. Sterile wooden stick applicators.

8. Several pairs of rubber gloves.

This kit will enable us to provide aid to all of the injuries associated with backyard survival. We can also render aid for even serious wounds and possible fractures, but of course we also need to have a *basic supply of knowledge* as to what to do with the supplies.

This is my kit. Now I am sure that many of you can improve the inventory in your bag. As a nurse, you may have a suture kit. The potential is wide open. Remember, though, that we are talking about *first aid* needs that will apply to backyard survival and, of course, those first vital moments after the initial shock has happened.

We must always be aware of the possibility of the shock factor, as well as the observation for the onset of early infections. These usually require the assistance of a professional.

We also have our car kit to supplement this home kit. But, at best, we must exercise caution at all times to avoid unnecessary injuries. We need to stress to younger family members that there will not be doctors and paramedics available for a while.

Just about every survival manual I have read stresses the need for a first aid book. The thought of a family after a disaster rummaging through the kit to locate the manual to find out what to do is too sad for words. Prepare yourself now.

Now I would like to move into an area not touched on in my first book or any other manual I have read so far.

Home Medicine Chest

One of the finest home medicine chests I ever saw was put together by a mother who incorporated all of the medicines and over-the-counter medications that she had used for herself and her three sons in the preceding year.

As you can imagine, it was a pretty inclusive little box, but as she said, "I figured this way. I was covered as far as possible for the treatment of my family's *known* medical tendencies!" A wise mother.

What is the difference between "medicines" and "first aid"?

Good question.

Most of my peers totally miss the importance of the first five hours after the disaster, when in the case of earthquakes, the need is for *first aid*.

Likewise, they also miss the importance of the next ten days, when the need is for *medicine* and the missing family physician.

Let us recap those statements.

I spend a lot of time in my seminars "telling it like it is." After hearing me, no one can honestly say, "But nobody told me how bad it was going to be." I do just that! I do this not to scare people, but to emphasize the importance of those first vital hours after the first shockwave when the injured will number in the many thousands.

Available emergency aid? Zero. Remember, the professionals are victims, too.

Except for the lucky ones who are in earshot of the grounded fire department and paramedics, the only aid the others can hope for is from us, their fellow citizens.

If you are one of those people who are clueless about even the elementary first aid steps (pressure points, etc.) when encountering a victim, you might as well *walk on by*, saving yourself the trauma and realization of your inability to help and perhaps save a life.

Similarly, nothing is considered or voiced about the citizen conditions in the following ten days after the event. Lack of sanitation, broken sewer pipes, lack of food and water, even the very condition of the stress itself will produce emotional and physical breakdowns leading to known and predictable medical conditions, such as:

—Development of infection needing antibiotics,
—Prophylactic measures to offset possible outbreaks of disease.
—Dysentery and common diarrhea, especially in children.
—Colds, flu, and possible outbreaks of pneumonia,
—The list goes on.

If, as I have said repeatedly, survival of victims in the first *five hours* is dependent on us the citizens, then surely the same rule applies to us the citizens in the ensuing *ten days* and possibly *weeks* after the event, medical wise?

We will have to be totally responsible for our own best interests health-wise, using in most cases good old home remedies and grandma's favorite cures handed down from one generation to the other. I wonder how the pioneers handled this one!

First of all, if you have a medical problem requiring regular medication, now is the time to insure that you have at least a month's supply on hand.

Will all the pharmacies re-open in a month? What if your family doctor is a victim and is not there to give you a refill on your prescription? What steps have the medical fraternity taken to cover this event? Suppose you find another doctor with the office door open. Is he or she likely to continue your medication without ever having seen you before?

You see, we have many areas to cover in the provision of our own needs. Do follow up on this issue if it affects you.

Possibly you could have a notarized statement from your present doctor to pass on to the next M.D. to cover this actuality. Whatever you do, you can be sure that you will not have access for a refill of your regular medications for a long time.

Secondly, if you have a pending surgery, or a condition requiring elective treatment (that is a condition that needs attention but can wait its turn), think about it. I had a case like that, a hernia repair that had to wait. In the meantime, I had a prescription for muscle relaxers and mild pain medications on an "as required" basis. The disaster will not give any warning and your surgery date may be postponed for a very long time.

Thirdly, let us consider what will be the norm. The family is in the backyard doing their thing and someone wakes up to find sickness has struck. . .or that burn on the hand has gotten infected. What can we do? We have only one course open to us. Use our own home remedies, or ask neighbors for one of theirs!

Having completed a preliminary discussion of home remedies, I have to leave this at this time, with the hope that I have been able to stimulate you into some research of your own.

One of life's eternal paradoxes is the fact that these days so many people are into holistic medicine and natural remedies (rising health care costs?) while, conversely, so many other people just have no idea of the existence of such a science. One feels like a pioneer even daring to wander into this subject at all! Hey, if this section reminded you to pack some aspirin and Pepto-Bismol in your stuff I should be happy! A more inclusive study of the home medicine chest is in Chapter 12.

Now finally we come to the fifth section of our survival preparations:

E. Well-Being and Morale

Apart from myself, I know of no one who considers "well-being" and "morale" as part of the survival package! Yet, even in the crudest of war situations, entertaining the troops was always given a high priority, although in the early days I am sure it was because the troops responded by fighting better rather than for any consideration of the state of their minds or psyche!

From my own experience, having suffered from those long weary months in some God-forsaken sand hole or soggy slit trench without any diversion other than the insects in possession of the spot long before my time, this whole subject is of very real importance to me.

In these pages, I am attempting to guide you through a process that will successfully move you from your present comfortable dwelling place to a place beyond the wildest realm of your reality ever to be conceived for the purpose of living—that place being your back yard!

Having provided for all of the eventualities I can think of, I would be remiss if I left you with no creature comforts for your mind and, if it is acceptable to you, your soul. What a strange irony life seems to forever confront us with. For most, the constant attempt to catch up with our own tail leaves us with so little of that precious commodity leisure time that we hardly know what the words mean anymore. For most people, when such a moment does occur, we reach for the "on" switch of the remote.

Now we find ourselves in the backyard. There is no remote, no T.V. even! And, if we have neglected this area, nothing to occupy the amount of time we are going to have to live through. All of a sudden, we have nothing *but* time! Surely we must prepare just as carefully for this eventuality as we did for our other needs.

Using the established format of this manual, let's take a step back and consider the situation: We are at probably E plus 3. Our preparations have paid off and, after a couple of days to "work the kinks out," our system is getting to be routine. Getting up with the sun, starting the fire, smelling the fresh coffee and biscuits (Hey, this camping out is not that bad!) and going through the chores of the day. Listening to the radio (sparingly) and exploring the neighborhood (carefully!) are now complete. By this the third day we are beginning to get a little bored.

Now is the time to open the Well-being and Morale Box. What did we each put in it? Each? Yes each of us. . . all right, back to "Start!" Just as we packed our personal-needs box, so we must now tackle the task of trying to offset the advent of falling morale and depression. If we do not provide for it, a negative situation will arise. We are living, no matter how well we have provided for ourselves, in a most traumatic state. Our life pattern has been interrupted and, no matter how we may have believed we could handle "a couple of weeks' rest," it just isn't happening. Sleep is fitful, at best. And the concern over other family members in different parts of the country is always uppermost. By now the possibility of bickering and lack of tolerance is being felt.

Going back to the beginning, when we were involved in preparation, we hopefully talked amongst ourselves about our personal needs stuff. I am sure that a lot of banter ("You packing that?", etc.) must have occurred. At that time, a good idea is to have a family competition: "All individual members of this family are to attempt to determine what five items they would consider most important prior to being shipwrecked on a desert island." Anything electronic is out! A good-sized suitcase or small footlocker is good for this purpose. Having made the selections, these items would be packed away ready for use on E plus 3 or even sooner. Things like:

—Books of study, not necessarily school work, but that course on art you bought and never had time for? That kind of thing.
—How about a set of oils and some canvas or other material for painting on?
—Clay for modeling? In the original bag the clay keeps for years.
—The book or books you never had time to read?
—Start a diary?
—Puzzles and games?
—Spiritual study materials?

You go from there. I think I have given you enough food for thought! Now go back to the backyard in your mind. What can you do to fill in the time? Now, time is either your enemy or your blessing. You might want to pack one of those self-help books. How about *Making the Most of a Bad Situation*. I'm sure it's out there somewhere!

All of the psychologists I have talked to agree that backyard boredom can be a major problem for us to cope with. We need to:

1. Establish a pattern of living as soon as possible. ROUTINE.
2. We must develop a positive ATTITUDE.
3. Avoid worry in its negative form. As opposed to CONCERN.
4. Be a caretaker to self. Eat and drink REGULARLY.
5. Keep BUSY. Idleness promotes gloom!
6. Be supportive of others. SERVICE TO OTHERS pays off.
7. Hey, you knew it was coming, you prepared. Now SURVIVE!

Yes, we must prepare for the days after just as we prepare for everything else in life. If you are unfortunate enough to lose your house, even after services are restored, you are probably better off making a stand in the backyard than hoping to find a decent shelter. For the first three to six months, the alternatives will be limited. A tent city is probably as good as it will get.

Many years ago, during my research-and-development phase, I developed a unit called an E.S.D.U. (Emergency Survival Dwelling Unit), a self-contained portable shelter that would support a family of four. Funds not forthcoming, it sits in model form. After Hurricane Andrew, my son said to me, "Pity we didn't have the E.S.D.U. developed!" Pity indeed. Perhaps it will be available soon.

Once the aftershocks quit and service is restored, having the refrigerator dragged out and running will make all the difference, trust me!

One thing must be made clear at this time. Employment, as we know it, will not be possible for a long time to come, so your backyard plans will have to be put to a long-term use!

Establishment of survival needs and plans? I think we are covered. Next then;

4. Protection of Survival Needs

Having taken all that time and effort to prepare all of our "need" items, it surely must follow that we have to be very diligent in our steps to protect them. Let's take it one at a time.

First of all comes that footlocker or other container with our personal needs. In the example of the family of four, probably the husband and wife will have packed their needs together in one container, while each of the offspring will have a container of their own. A suitcase, perhaps. Now we have to consider where to put it.

If you have a tool shed or portable building, you are in good shape. It would be nice if our clothes were dry when we needed them! Getting dressed in the backyard in the middle of winter in damp, musty clothes is not fun. Look for a suitable spot outside. Perhaps a handy person could make a low, small building for this purpose. (You can send for plans of my shock-proof storage shed; see Diagram 22.) I also have a lean-to in my yard, built against a wall. It's eight feet long, four feet high, and four feet wide. The ends are closed in. It has a tin roof, and the front is covered with a large tarp that hangs down. This front serves to keep the elements out, while keeping the contents very easy to get to.

I have said previously that most block walls will come down and mine is no exception. However, the ends of my lean to are designed to act as supports for that section of the wall which will safeguard my supplies (see Diagram 23). I have several twenty-five-gallon barrels of water here also.

Built to my own design, this building may "rock" and may even "roll," but it will not break!

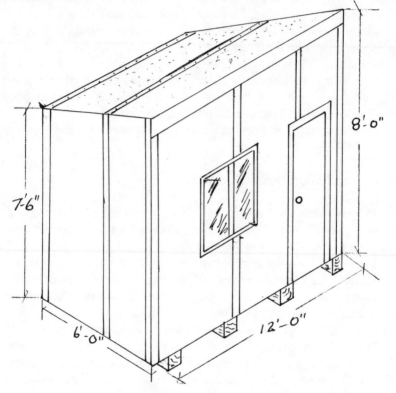

DIAGRAM 22—QUAKE-RESISTANT SURVIVAL SHED

You might consider talking to your neighbor about making a section of the wall between you more secure by building a lean-to on each side of the wall, making that section strong enough to stay up. Then you both would have a safe storage unit.

Now we consider our food supplies. Mine are in amongst other things. I have an eighteen-gallon plastic storage bin that has all my

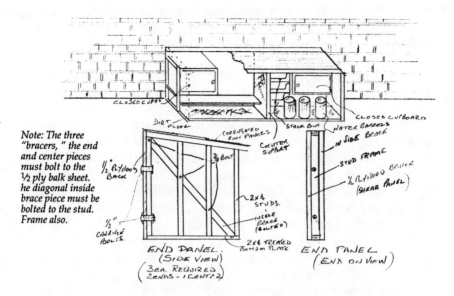

Note: The three "bracers," the end and center pieces must bolt to the ½ ply balk sheet. he diagonal inside brace piece must be bolted to the stud. Frame also.

DIAGRAM 23—LEAN-TO STORAGE SHED AND WALL BRACE

dry supplies that we have talked about, along with our tent, tools, and utensils stored in the lean-to and my shed.

Just outside the back door, under a pile of cement blocks, are the first aid supplies. This, together with the auto first aid as back-up, makes for a very complete set-up. However, I stress once again the need to try to keep your auto supplies for the purpose they were intended. They are Go gear and should be kept as such if possible until the fear of evacuation is past.

Your well-being and morale items may be stored with either the food or the tools. Now, what if you have no shed or lean-to? It is easy for me to say, "Then get going and make some!" Yes, it would be nice, but in the worst scenario, the large lawn and trash bags will have to do. Seal them well. And, in the case of the food and medical supplies, wrap them well with several layers of newspaper before putting them into the plastic bags. Now choose those places that are out of the direct sun—if possible, under thick shrubs or trees. Keep your first aid supplies close to a back door, even if you have to do as I did and make a "burial mound" for them.

Some water and food torpedoes will be buried in the ground, as well that small tube of plastic pipe that has the documents and (hopefully) some money in it.

Protection of the supplies is of vital concern to us at all times.

Even the tools for turning off the services must be protected by hiding or securing them to the adjoining pipes very thoroughly. The same for the water shut-off key or tool.

Prior to the event, the major safety concern for our supplies will be to keep them from the elements. That is why location is so important. After the event, we must be concerned with security of our supplies, facing the unfortunate situation that *we* have taken positive steps for our survival, but what of those *who have not?*

Being cagey and careful to arrange our supplies in a conservative manner will most certainly help the cause. In the period after the quake, the aroma of a simple pot of beans will smell like a feast to those who have no food. We will seem, to others, to be living "high on the hog," which, under the circumstances, we will be. We will not, however, be in a position to support the neighborhood. Perhaps, as we enter our discussions in this next segment, we can pick up some hints or wisdom to help us in this matter.

Now we move on to our next section:

5. Assistance to Neighbors

It seems to me, as we enter this very broad field of "neighbors," I should share with you some of my thoughts on this subject. I shared with you that, on that day way back in 1980, sitting in my car on a deserted road, it came to me that I had a wealth of information that you did not have. This truth has been more than reinforced in the years since. Let me expand on that theme. Under extreme stress, the will to survive knows no bounds. Self-preservation, I have heard it said, is the strongest urge we humans possess. Certainly, for the naive, reactions by those around us at extremely stressful times can be, to put it mildly, somewhat shocking. In my own experience, I have witnessed, both in the civilian population and in the military, people under stress behave like strange, unknown animals at such times. Some of these people I had known for years.

Consider this fact: At the present time (September 1992), over 90 percent of all of us, that includes government, law enforcement and all other branches of public service, and employers and businesses in general, have not, in any way, provided for disaster!

Now before you all jump on my back, step back a moment. Oh, yes. I am aware that many of the agencies I have mentioned are involved almost daily in emergency preparations. Hospitals spend great amounts of money on such exercises. Communications networks are set up. Command posts are at the ready. Yet out on the street, not one black and white police car has a supply of emergency food or water on board (not officially, that is)!

If disaster were to strike at this time, very few factories, large employers, state, county, or federal offices have a plan to aid injured workers or provide for their well-being for a prolonged time. Many officials of the agencies involved in very complicated emergency planning leave to go home each night without a survival kit in their own car!

Consider the larger stores in the shopping plazas and malls. Have you seen, or are you made aware by any indication that these corporate entities have any concept of disaster? Approaching a large store in my own neighborhood recently (no names, but I am sure Sam turned in his grave!) I was told by a messenger (I didn't even get to speak to the manager), "We get all kinds of earthquake information sent down from corporate office." As my wife and I walked around the store and looked up at the rows of heavy items on pallets stored ten feet in the air on those flimsy shelves, we both had sadness in our hearts that these well-meaning people have no concept or—what is worse—no preparations for the aid of the hundreds of people lying injured under all that inventory that should never have been there in the first place.

Now, here we are, preparing for our survival needs and considering our neighborhood and the safety of both our supplies and ourselves. To attempt consideration of this situation without considering the "devil you know" is rather foolish. Having personal experiences under these conditions, it is my duty to expose these facts to you. As a concerned person, you are walking a lonely path. It is the walk of a *responsible* person, concerned not only for *yourself,* but for your *family* and *friends.* Now I have to challenge you. Can you generate a little more concern, and direct it toward your neighbors?

Hold on now! I know you are not your neighbor's keeper! I also realize that he is responsible for his own affairs. But, may I point out to you that:

First, there is safety in numbers.
Second, it helps if all the neighbors around you are prepared
    because it takes the emphasis off you!
Third, and very important, the life your involved neighbor
    saves may be *yours!*

An organized and concerned neighborhood provides both safety and support to each other. Using the principles established in this manual so far, let us put these principles to work in the neighborhood situation. Look at the hazards and safety factors:

—Any physical hazards in your area?
—Chemical plant? Paint or other hazardous site?
—What about the age of the group?
—Retirees?
—Active?
—What about the other end of the scale?
—Young families?
—Many handicapped?
—What is the age of the community?
—Old houses?
—Any wood shake roofs?
—What sort of fences, wood or block?
—Do you have a Neighborhood Watch group? Is it active?

Now we have some stats to go on.

A large number of retirees could mean that included are some of the professions (doctors, nurses, etc.) or some of the trades (contractors, etc.). Organized monthly meetings could be arranged as social gatherings. A monthly newsletter is not hard to achieve to keep the busy family members who cannot attend up to date.

What about the available products in the group? Any campers or motor homes? Tents? How about tools? Most retired or active do-it-yourself types have a good supply of tools. Chain saws will be in demand, as well as labor and skill to construct shelters.

An active Neighborhood Watch group can be a wealth of information. They already know everybody on the street. Organization of medical and safety patrols can easily become a reality.

Consider the open-group attitude so common in Europe. Whole neighborhoods are closely integrated with each other and share common tasks. In this dire emergency situation, we have to consider setting up first aid stations within our own community or block.

Search and rescue of a neighborhood organized beforehand can go into effect within the first hour. Certainly, this kind of help is many hours or even days away otherwise.

Consider also, in such preparations, the familiarity with each other's circumstances. Which are the more vulnerable? Where are the shut-ins? Which mother is alone, being the wife of a fireman or night worker?

Perhaps this approach is not possible in your neighborhood. No matter, you can still make an effort. If all else fails, you must at least try to communicate with those on either side of you. There is still safety in numbers, even if they are small. You and your two neighbors make a block of three. Looking out for each other, you are a lot better off than alone.

Back to our starting point, "assistance of neighbors." Do, by all means, communicate with your neighbor. Share your plans. Perhaps you could go in with each other on bulk purchases of food and supplies (think of the purchasing power of a whole street). In sharing with your neighbors, you may find indications of available skills that can be a benefit to the whole group.

Certainly, after the first shaking stops, you will want to know how your neighbors are—not only their personal safety, but the safety of their houses, which could affect you. An injured neighbor will not be able to turn off services, which could result in a possible explosion. We could say that the three-legged stool of safety, in this case, is comprised of:

—Protection of self,
—Protection of property, and
—Protection of neighbor.

Once again I stress that my way is not the *only* way to go about these issues that I raise. Many of the suggestions that I give may serve only as a starting point for your own thinking. That I stir you to *some action* is my main goal.

Consider then, this whole atmosphere of actual *preparation*, the hands-on actions. Then let us move on to some other aspects just as vital, our *planning* phase.

6. Maintenance of Family Post-Disaster

Having completed the suggested preparations required so far (all that food and water and backyard stuff), it is time to sit back and take a breather!

If we think about it, we obviously come to the point in our meditations when we say something like:

"All right, Smartie, what do I do now? Here I am, in the
backyard. The first shock is over. More are happening, but
my family and I are safe and in one piece. . .now what?"

Good, I am so glad that you are safe. Further, as a result of your involvement in this fascinating subject of survival preparation, you were led to this, the next logical step. "What now?"

You see, survivalists are always asking "What now?" for it is the continual awareness of what comes next that enables the good survivalist to continue to survive. Knowing the future hazards allows for countermeasures to be taken. What does that mean?

It means that, having provided for the disaster itself, we must prepare our family for the *afterwards*, and the possible hazards that will come about, *as a result of the disaster*.

Now it is time to sit down and have a family powwow. In your family, communication may not be the most practiced activity in the world; T.V. and a busy schedule required to keep the wolf from the door sees to that. Perhaps survival may be of sufficient interest to capture the attention!

A good lead-in could be "What is the present school survival scoop?" This should produce some reaction leading to something like "You know, we have to consider our own plans here at home for afterwards. . ."

In seminars, I promote the family survival drill as a means to getting the family involved. This requires the following: One Friday night, let the head of the household (after everyone is asleep) turn off all the services except the gas. That's water, electricity, and the phones. Then go back to bed. Come Saturday morning, wait for the howl to go up!

"Mum! Dad! There's no T.V. and the toilet doesn't work. I went to call my friend to see if it was like that at her house, and the phone is out! What are we going to do?" All this in such a plaintive tone!

Now isn't this an ideal time to introduce the topic of survival? "You know family, this is what it is going to be like after the big quake. And there are some things that we must talk about." Away we go.

The next question that should come to your mind is "What are we going to talk about?" Good, that's *my* lead-in!

There is so much talk today about "getting used to the Big One." (I hate that term. Why avoid saying earthquake? No matter how we hide, it is still a fact of life for us all.) Certain psychologists are advising making a game out of the whole situation. The term "Trekkies" is being replaced, I am told, with "Quakies." These are people who are "into earthquakes," making a hobby of keeping up with statistical data, knowing how many tremors there are a day, where they are, etc. The principle is that the more familiar one becomes the less frightening it is! Ho hum!

As responsible adults, we must always maintain a serious attitude toward disaster, whether it be natural or one we create for ourselves with reckless habits. I want to pass on to all I see the security that comes from not only knowing, but being in a state of preparedness.

In our family, we have to maintain the approach that we have done as much as we can for the event. Now we must prepare for afterwards. First comes the acceptance of the fact that the disaster will come without warning. And what will our actions be at that time?

At home? We know what we will do, having already established evacuation routes and assembly points.

Away from home? Children stay in school until picked up. School is safe. Parents have to decide now whether it will be Go or Stay for them. The rest of the family *must* be aware of this decision.

In the backyard? Stay close to home. Children will have a strong desire to explore the neighborhood. No way. In London, children were injured time and again playing in the rubble of destroyed buildings. All excursions from the family backyard should be as a unit, be it touring the neighborhood or visiting with friends. This kind of safety is important.

We already talked about routines. Establish a chore list and academic or other study times, always aiming to defeat our old enemy, boredom.

We have to consider the condition of health. Family members must be educated to the fact that if they are feeling under the weather, early symptoms must be shared rather than being put off. "But I didn't want to be a bother" is to be discouraged!

Finally, this is a family unit here. Ask for input from all the family members as to how to handle this situation of maintaining the family unit, post-disaster.

Now we have to talk some more about our nemesis, evacuation. We talked about the possibility. Now let us pursue it to a conclusion.

7. Evacuation Plans

First, as always, the preamble. What sort of area do you live in, and in any of the four compass directions, what is around you from a safety point of view?

Here you are, all set up in the backyard. It is E plus 5, and—boom—some arsonist sets a fire somewhere. Or a natural or accidental occurrence takes place. You must know and plan around, now while it is quiet, the location of the safe places.

—Where is open land?

—A large park perhaps?
—A school playing field?
—Any place that will serve as a fire break?

Having decided *where*, you should next plan *how:* "If we have to leave, Mother, you grab some cooking utensils, the very minimum. Billy, get the Go gear out of the car; I'll get the food torpedoes." This kind of action is essential if we are to avoid the situation of sudden evacuation in a panic with nothing. Remember, we planned for this. We can still survive for a while with our emergency supplies. The fire will pass and, hopefully, we can soon return to our own familiar places.

This is a nice little scenario for a fire situation. What about other hazards?

Floods? We must know where the high ground is. Or if we live in flood country, we will now put that rubber boat to use. (Our supplies would have been in the attic wouldn't they?)

A real problem can come from toxic situations. We talked about familiarity with our neighborhood previously and, if you answered positive to this hazard (in other words, you do have a chemical plant nearby), you should be familiar with the safety procedures ahead of time. Go to the plant and ask for advice on safety measures and pamphlets on the type of chemicals that are there and their possible effects on humans.

You will always be told, "There is no danger of a possible leak of any kind. We have so many safety measures and back-up systems for you not to be concerned." Just look the person straight in the eye and, just as assuredly as they were with you, say, "Oh, but I am preparing for my family's survival after a major disaster like the earthquake. We live just a few blocks from you." This should bring the person down to earth and enable an intelligent conversation to ensue. You must know your enemy.

What is the hazardous material?
What is the possible effect on humans?
What can you do to protect your family?

If you are in any area that has a potential for toxic hazard you *must:*

1. Have a gas mask in your kit. If the county or federal agency cannot supply one, go buy one from a military supply store and send them the bill. There are federal laws on the books; ask your congressman.

2. Be aware of the drill required. Put on gas mask, pull down sleeves or put on clothes that cover as much of the skin area as possible (plastic garbage bag?) or, if you do not have a gas mask, cover the mouth with a wet cloth,
3. Seek inside shelter, and
4. Reduce all physical activity to a minimum.

Hopefully there is a breeze or wind to carry the stuff away. Mostly, the danger comes from the chlorine groups that affect the lungs, making a gas mask a must. If you are in any doubt, talk to the local fire department. They are always up-to-date on the local areas and toxic problems.

Of course, our main problem comes from the situation of a fire that produces toxicity as a result of chemical changes brought about by the action of the fire itself.

Toxic problems are downplayed at the present time. However, that does not excuse the alert survivalist from being informed.

Closing remarks to Chapter 4: The Home

I confidently say: "Looks good to me. Looks like I covered all the bases. Think I did a good job without getting too dramatic. As I see it, any reasonable person could find their way to survival preparation using the suggestions. Yep. I feel good."

Before I get too high in the clouds, from my grab-bag of responses on the seminar trail, let me present my ideas of possible reader response to this chapter.

Three examples of reader types:

Type one, very sheltered person.
Type two, skeptic.
Type three, the penny dropped, the light bulb went on!

Type 1:
"Honey! (High-pitched hysterical voice) Look at this awful book written by this terrible man. (Thrusts book under husband's nose) Honey, do you know what he is saying? (Goes on without stopping) He is saying that our house is going to fall down. That all the stuff in the house will be lost. That all my lovely figurines are going to be broken. Why, those figurines have been in my family since Great-Grandma. And that we are going to have to live in the backyard and not be able to

shower. . .(she gasps and takes a breath) and I hate camping. Oh, George, tell me it isn't true? Besides, I saw this special on PBS with this fireman, and *they know,* and he said just lie on your bed and ride it out. And he didn't say anything about living in the backyard. Besides, he said go out and pound the ground and it will make you feel better! So there! (Changes to pleading tone) Honey, we won't have to live like those poor people in Hurricane Andrew country, will we, Dear? I mean we have had lots of earthquakes and we didn't have to do a thing, did we dear?"

Type 2:
Husband (Archie Bunker type):

"Look at this stuff in this book here. What a load of sensationalism. Some fancy 'survivalist' (with a sneer). Bet he never went through a good earthquake. Can't compare bombs with earthquakes. Besides, this house will stand anything. It's built to all the latest codes. Anyway, I put all my stuff in the hall closet just like that fireman on PBS does. If it's good enough for him, it's good enough for me. Besides, he showed all those pictures of all those tall buildings. Said how they swayed and don't come down, and all the plans for first aid and rescue. This guy's full of hot air. Besides, I'll deal with it when it happens like I always do."

Wife:

"Well, I was talking to my friend Elsie, and she knows this woman in Big Bear and she said after the third night of the shaking they all went to the church hall. They were all afraid to go in their houses. And she said that the ceiling came down with the first wave and all their water was in the house and she wouldn't go in no way! Anyway, they only got one paramedic team in the whole town, and anyway they had a lot of them log houses and they all fell down, and anyway. . ."

Husband:
"Shut up!"

Type 3:
(Comes home from work all excited) "Hi Hon. How was your day? Kids all right? Guess what! I heard about this survival manual they are all talking about at work, so I stopped off at the bookstore and got a copy. Boy, I can't wait to read it

all. Makes so much sense from what the guys are saying. We talked to the union man about getting us some first aid stuff on the job, like stretchers and things. . .Well, Love, it pays to be prepared before it happens. I thought I could read it tonight and you read it tomorrow and we could compare notes, talk to the kids and get really prepared. That hurricane stuff could happen here, you know. Besides, I hate the thought of our family having to go and wait around to get some water, and live in an Army tent! Yuk. According to the author, we can all prepare and support ourselves. Oh, and we must get Junior to teach us about first aid. He learned all that in Boy Scouts. I remember when he got his badge."

Why don't you take a moment to identify yourself?

Before we go on, let's spend some time with the considerations of the other two major disaster situations that prominently plague our planet, namely flood and the hurricane/tornado situation.

There is, of course the one positive we have going for us, and that is the fact that both of these natural disasters carry a built-in safety factor. Either visually, seen by the witnesses, or via the media, we get a good early warning. In the case of floods, certain areas are what as known as "prone to flooding," so residents know that as soon as weather conditions are in a certain mode, a flood will be a natural outcome.

Lets talk about this situation first:

Flood

I once lived in "flood country." Not down there in the valley where the whole area disappeared, but up a ways so that I became one of the watchers who daily braved the torrential rains to go down and see "how high it got so far." I remember watching and feeling like King Canute standing there and trying to tell the water "Go back!" as the debris-filled, swollen river pursued its inexorable path.

Since that time, and my journeys into the survival field, I have had time to reflect on those experiences. To my surprise a similar pattern exists for all of these disaster situations.

"Do I go or do I stay?" is still the first question to be decided. In this, the flood situation, there is plenty of history to go on.

Is your house one of those that has been continually flooded in the last few years? Maybe missing a few years for the dry seasons? Does your house flood up to a certain level so that you can remain in it? Or do you have to evacuate?

So many times we see in the flood reports pictures of either:

A. People are sitting or standing on the roof of a multi-story house that is under water beneath them, or

B. They are shown sweeping out the mud and debris from the floor of their house after the floodwaters have subsided!

Usually, interviews with those involved say about the same thing: "Well, we have done it before, so this is nothing new!"

The other scene, of course, is of the square miles of water under which a whole village or town lies submerged!

I always experience the same feelings. "But you could have. . ." But then, I say that all the time! Let's stay positive!

For the Stay group:

If the water comes up over the first floor and basement, you obviously need your Stay gear upstairs in closets or cupboards. The difference is that your backpack will only be for dire emergencies (if the water keeps on coming). Otherwise, you have so much going for you that the "quakies" wish they had.

First, you are not limited to the kind of foods you store (of course a good long shelf-life doesn't hurt) and you do not have to be concerned about breakage, as there are no shockwaves to worry about.

Second, with the provision of a camp cookstove, you are able to provide hot food to order. Which certainly has its advantages over the fire pit.

Third, in my supply planning, I would consider a rubber, inflatable boat to be essential.

And fourth, of course, don't forget the drinking water!

Otherwise, the same principles laid down for other Stay survival groups apply.

For the Go people:

Living in flood country, to me, means to be aware of the historical situation. We talked about this in Chapter 1. In most cases, waiting to leave until the last moment or having people risk their lives to come and rescue you in a small boat in raging water is, to put it mildly, rather irresponsible.

Surely, the better way is to use the time you have (that time when you are witness to the signs of the oncoming flood) to pack the automobile with plenty of supplies for the amount of time it takes for the water to go down (a pre-established fact). This is time that you have that others, in disasters like earthquakes, do not have. It is indeed a blessing, and should be taken advantage of!

First aid and the risk of injury in flood situations is lessened, and the emphasis on first aid kits can also be lessened.

There is a lot of detail work that the experienced "flooder" is familiar with that I am not going to elaborate on here, even if I am charged with staying with the little details! Things like moving valuables upstairs, etc.

If you live in a single-story house, of course, your only hope is the attic for those valuables and hope the roof doesn't get covered with water.

If you are ordered to evacuate, or your common sense tells you to leave, either you have a relative/friend nearby to go and stay with, or you are going to follow the same survival plans as the Go person in Chapter 3. As you drive down the road to safety, believe me, you are going to feel a lot better knowing you have supplies and food in the trunk.

Now for the "winds."

Hurricanes and Tornadoes

Is there much doubt that in the hurricane situation you are going to evacuate when ordered? I sure hope not! In that case, I will not spend time on the Stay group. You are, to all intents and purposes on your own, leaving us to be concerned with the Go crowd.

One feels that, with the amount of time involved, the evacuating vehicles would look like a scene from the *Grapes of Wrath*, with supplies piled high on the roof and the rear loaded down indicating a full trunk. Yet, as we observe each evacuation, it is obvious that this is not the case!

There seems to be this common denominator that applies to all disaster survivors. They are, for the most part, completely unprepared. I am convinced that this stems from the participants being raised in a society that does not require that one fend for one's self! Given a list of "how-tos," the survivors take an attitude of "Gee, why didn't I think of that; it sure makes sense to me!"

The details for the homeowner in the backyard survival mode should serve as a good list of what to provide for.

1. Personal needs,including special medications, etc.

This includes each member of the family (clothes, sleeping bag, toiletries, etc.).

2. Food and water.

This should be for a period of what? At least five days? That is a good rule of thumb for the "quakies," and would serve well in this situation.

3. Protection of property.

Naturally, take all valuables with you, or do as the homeowner does at evacuation time—bury them. They will be there when you return; only you know where they are.

Follow these few simple rules and you should be in better shape.

Now we have to face the return of the hurricane victim to a flat piece of land and a pile of debris. This was the Londoner's situation following an air raid in the 1940s.

You are faced with the stay-or-go decision. Either you can see enough around you to make staying feasible, or there is no chance of making a stay situation work.

What are the determining factors? You will need, to stay:

A. Tools and utensils to both create a shelter and cook the food, and
B. Enough materials and supplies to make staying possible.

It is reasonable to assume that, in the process of evacuation, most of the food and supplies commercially available will have been consumed. Therefore, fresh supplies have to be found when you return to your home.

—Where? Not from the authorities, obviously.
—Whatever is in the stores will be fought for.
—Then, it would seem that, we have to provide for ourselves.

The answer, just as it is for the "quakie," lies in pre- planning. If you have a basement, you are home free. Basements do not blow away. They do, however, suffer effects similar to those of bombing (the phenomenon of the "blast" effect—air suction that will strip an area clean, sucking everything out).

The answer is to construct a cupboard or storage area in a wall or a corner in such a way that there is a smooth surface for the wind to pass over, leaving the contents intact (see Diagram 24). A storm cellar with a steel lid securely locked does the same thing, as do water-proof plastic barrels well-buried.

Note: By removing some wall blocks, a "cache" of any desired size may be constructed. Be sure that the damp-proof integrity of the wall is maintained. A small room is also a consideration.

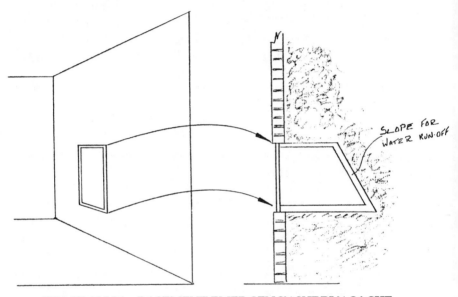

DIAGRAM 24—BASEMENT EMERGENCY SUPPLY CACHE

What to store? See the section on the backyard survival page and follow the procedures there.

Tornadoes, now, are a different breed altogether! Very little warning, spawned in an instant. Very often, the time factor is definitely not on the side of the survivalist! Again, we have to pre-plan.

Why the old-time storm cellar has gone out of vogue, I have no idea. If you do not have one, digging just a mini-cellar with a good strong lid is certainly worth the effort.

After all, what is involved? A cellar of very small capacity, say six feet by six feet by six feet, would be adequate. Personal needs, tools and utensils, food and water, are basically it. First aid and morale supplies are not of such magnitude. Services are quickly restored, and aftershocks are not the threat.

The main thing to remember, and your local builder will help you if required, is to incorporate the basics of hurricane-proofing for a tornado in a below-the-ground type of design. A smooth surface will not create resistance. Allowing for an unobstructed flow of wind as it passes over your storage unit leaves those precious supplies intact.

In Chapter 8, many of the aspects of survival as they apply to mobile home parks, apartments, and condominiums would also apply to the situation of the victims of the wind- and flood-type disasters. Rereading the suggestions for them should help those of you who are affected in a similar manner.

Conclusion? As in all survival considerations, know your enemy, and plan accordingly, well ahead of time!

APPENDIX TO CHAPTER 4

As promised earlier, here is an appendix to go with the food section from backyard survival.

Many times on the lecture platform, I get to where I am "wound up, and running with the ball," especially on this particular topic. "Food and the Backyard Survivalist" is one of my favorites. Often, I look up and young women in the audience tend to have a stunned look on their faces. Reality strikes, and then I realize that I am off track!

I have to remember that I am not only a "hobby" cook. I have, over the years, developed ideas for what would work in the backyard. Looking out into the faces before me, I have to remember that most people today usually have time to use only the microwave! By the time the weekend comes around, using the stove and some pots and pans is, in many cases, a lost art. Then, I also have to remember that I am mainly a vegetarian, and a fussy food buyer, as well.

About this time, as I stand there in front of that type of audience, it occurs to me that, if I were in that audience and faced the prospect of trying to prepare meals out in the backyard, I would probably have the same reaction as I see on the faces before me. . . forget it!

It's not that there is a lack of desire on the part of the would-be survivor. It's just that there is a sad lack of knowledge of even the basics of cooking other than from a pre-packaged item—period!

So obviously, if I am to be your survival guide via these pages, I have to start at square one with a mini-course, as it were, on backyard survival food: its meaning, purpose, and preparation.

Who knows—perhaps a backyard cookbook will be the result! Or, as a bonus, what you learn in this section may serve you in good stead in your kitchen in these, the "normal" times! As to a forthcoming cookbook, it sounds like a good idea, but for the purpose of this appendix, I will keep strictly to basics.

Backyard survival food: its meaning, purpose, and preparation. Let's start right at the beginning.

Meaning

For the inexperienced cook, the very idea of backyard food is enough to strike terror into the heart. Scenes from movies like *Robin Hood*, together with pictures of shipwrecks and such, lead to an image of hunting and stalking. Pictures of people holding raw fish which, having been gutted, is now being cooked on a stick over a smokey fire. . .Yuk. No wonder I see those horrified looks from my audience! In actual fact, it is not like that at all.

Backyard survival food is no different from everyday, "normal" food. The only considerations are that, first, we have no refrigerator, and second, in the main, we have only the supplies that we stored ahead of time. The food itself still has the same meaning. . ."The way to a man's heart is through his stomach," as the old timers used to say. (Do they still say it, I wonder?) There is a whole wealth of logic in that statement that certainly applies to this situation. It is an agreed-upon fact that, with the initial shock that will follow the disaster, any signs of normalcy will be the best counter to that shock factor (food being a most normal commodity, a hot meal will *mean* normalcy in a highly stressful situation).

Looking from another aspect of the *meaning* of backyard survival food, how about admitting that attempting backyard survival *without* food would be meaningless, as survivors of Hurricane Andrew and similar disaster soon found out. For us then, this food is the means for us to be able to survive independently in our backyard for an unknown period of time.

Purpose

We all look at food from different perspectives. Obviously. Why else are there so many books about food? Cutting through all the small talk, survival food *must fulfill the purpose of maintaining the highest level of health and well-being possible*. At once, I can hear all those of you so inclined loudly extolling the virtues of a meal at your favorite fast-food restaurant! Sorry, folks. No can do, but, if you follow the guidelines already set out for you food-wise, you will come out of this experience healthier that you thought possible. During the Second World War in England, only raw, unbleached flour was available. As a result, after the many years before bleached flour returned, stomach ulcers and other intestinal problems had all but disappeared. Sadly, most folks returned to the white loaf!

The purpose of the food we consume as survivors *must* be to maintain our standard of health and, as far as possible, maintain a sense of well-being. A poor diet results in a melancholy and poor attitude in general. Supplying a balanced diet in a regular manner offsets this condition.

Remember, when we were packing away our supplies, I emphasized the planning of the daily meals (breakfast, a mid-day snack, and a full evening meal). Now, from this other end, that planning surely pays off. The purpose of the food then, is to keep us healthy and, as far as possible under the circumstances, happy!

Preparation

Backyard food is prepared just like "normal" food: baked, boiled, or fried. Oh, we can think of all those fancy phrases like broiled, sautéed, or casseroled, but the basics are the same.

Fried means cooked over heat in any open container, usually a frying pan. But, if one is not available, you can still fry even on a flat piece of plain metal. Frying is that act of cooking over a fairly high heat, usually in a quick manner. Pancakes are a good example of food prepared by frying.

Boiled is a pretty well-understood term and refers to putting food into a container of water over heat until the food is cooked. Vegetables and rice are good examples.

Baked food, under backyard conditions, is a challenge. But many foods can be baked in any closed container that will maintain the heat. Baking is used for foods that require maintained heat for rising purposes, as in breads, and for foods that are thick, such as meat roasts. Do not despair—meat (if still available) can be cooked over an open fire.

In the text for setting up the backyard into areas, I talked about fire pits. Remember? Now you can see the reasoning behind it all.

The small, above-ground fire is for fast frying and quick boiling of water for tea or coffee, a pot of rice or just plain "bringing to a boil" before transferring over to the below-ground pit which is for long, slow cooking (those delicious stews that fill the air with scent of the contents of the pot). Careful management of both the fire pits as to heat control will allow even the inexperienced to produce good meals from all those delicious grains and dried fruits. Using the sourdough starter, pancakes and sourdough breads are just around the corner. And, at the end of a long day, there is no rule that says you cannot sit in the dark and dream of better times as you follow those glowing embers into sleep. . .

To conclude, I'd like to add some comments about utensils. I have shared with you that I am an avowed thrift-store junky. In those places one finds all those long-discarded cast-iron and other similar *thick* type cooking vessels. For reasons of economy, they were long ago pensioned off and banished from the modern kitchen. These are ideal for our survival needs. They withstand high heat without burning the food and, once brought to the desired heat, they maintain that heat even when pulled off of the fire somewhat. If you are lucky enough to find a large cast-iron stew pot, one of those huge, two-hands-to-lift type, they make great ovens!

Any last words? Yes. Don't let the concept of backyard survival deter you. After all, spoiling some food in the beginning sure beats standing in line waiting for the Red Cross and a handout! My backyard is more inviting any day than Tent City! Good luck and hang in there!

Now let's move on to Chapter 5. . . .

CHAPTER 5
Schools

The workplace for some

Each school day, all over the country, millions of children of all ages leave their homes and participate in the ritual known by all of us as going to school. Upon entering either the school bus or the school grounds, these children become the responsibility of those who are in charge. Like the adults who enter the work place, these children surrender their protective needs to someone else.

In the case of the adults, it is to the employer. In the case of the children, it is to the staff or faculty who, for reasons mostly beyond their own control, are never able to provide the standards or atmosphere that they, by their own choice, would like to have. I have yet to talk to any member of the educational system, from the principal on down to the janitor, who was satisfied with the status quo.

On the face of it then, we are about to consider survival of the student body with a faculty and staff who are already burdened with a negative atmosphere. Now *we* are going to come along and badger them with survival planning!

Overworked and burdened though they are, the situation is: "If they don't, who will?"

Following the format I have suggested, what is the situation we are planning survival for?

1. In California, mainly earthquake. Other parts of the country? The list is varied, but we can't rule out. . .
2. That unspoken hazard, toxic air pollution. (Since hurricanes, fire and flood allow for plenty of time to evacuate or shut down the schools, we will not concern ourselves with them.)

Basically then, we are preparing for a *sudden* major disaster, and although I specified California, we would do well, I feel, to consider the earthquake problem to be just as likely in other parts of the country. The area around the New Madrid fault, as well as the whole of the New York area, should be included in this. How whimsical to think that the people of California, whom we are struggling to make earthquake-conscious, could well be the spectators to other states who are not so alert to the danger and are therefore less prepared. While I am qualified to handle Section 1 (Earthquake), I hope that those involved would consider a similar approach to the problems of Section 2 (Toxic Pollution) while there is still time. To my way of thinking, a similar approach to both situations could work well.

We could imagine, for example, that the warning sound, be it siren or bell, for Section 2 would be a directive to proceed to a protective sealed room rather than going out of the building into the open. The problem of "How long are they going to be here?" leads directly to "What will they need?" The students will be placed in a similar situation in both cases.

Let us use the precedents already set down. The first one is: "You are on your own for the first few days." Let's now set the scene as it really will be.

One day, the children, as they always do, by private or school transportation (more about that later), will arrive at school. There, when the bell rings, they will proceed to their various classrooms and hopefully become involved with the study of the subjects at hand. Keep that phrase in mind—"Become involved." Much as we may malign the educational system and teachers in general, kids (those of them who care, that is) *do* become involved in the subject at hand.

Now, out of a clear blue sky, to interrupt that involvement, will come the shaking of the ground. As soon as the penny drops, the students will do what they have been taught to do, "tuck and hold" or some such activity. Then, also as they have been taught to do, they all will troop outside, performing the all-too-familiar evacuation pattern. Only this time, it will be different. This time it will be for real!

At this point, many of my friends and I disagree. They say, "Don't be so soft; write it as you know it will be. You've been through it in London. Tell it like it is. Give 'em a good jolt. Write reality, man!" I used to use this technique on the lecture circuit. It seemed to me that all I did was send the minds of the audience wandering off into a daydream of the pain that they conceived might be theirs someday. On the broad face of it, who is to say who will and who will not be a victim?

Logically, my desire to share my knowledge must always be as a survival specialist, not as a recorder of horror. Why throw daggers at my audience? Rather, I prefer to stay on the positive side. This is what will happen. And this is what, it seems to me, we should do to prepare. Along those lines then, where were we?

The students were all outside the building.

This is the point at which I am going to break off and backtrack a little, so hold on to that thought.

"We are on our own" also means "*They* are on their own." Like a ship on the high seas, this school, this campus, and all who are on it, are completely on their own. It follows, then, that we will need to prepare for all of their needs.

—Where will they be? At school.
—What will they do? What they are *taught* to do.
—What will they need? Whatever is needed for their con-
    tinued survival.

A long time ago, I developed a form that I use in school earthquake preparation seminars. Let's work with it.

The columns use the format with which we are now familiar:

"Where will I be?"
"What will I do?"
"What will I need?"

Substituting *they* for *I*, we proceed to explore those columns:

Education Before (Where will they be?)

Just as it was true for me to say, "I don't know your daily *journey*," it is just as true for me to say, "I don't know your *school* and I don't know your classroom." If I give this worksheet to a principal, that person will carry out the work-up for the whole school, including all the personnel on the staff.

Likewise, if the worksheet is before a teacher, that person will do the work-up from the point of view of his own classroom, including the students and possibly teacher aides in the room. For the purpose of this study, I shall be as all-inclusive as possible, looking at the whole picture rather than the individual roles.

All involved must become *survival* conscious. All roles must be not only formulated, but discussed and learned.

The Four School Places

Education Before	Action During	After—What To Do
Where will I be?	What will I do?	What will I need?

FORM 1—EARTHQUAKE SURVIVAL WORKSHEET

a. What is the student enrollment?

b. What is the ratio of adults to students? Include all adults on the campus, as all will be needed.

c. What is the layout of the campus? Make a drawing on paper. If you have a shop on campus, see if you can get them to make a three-dimensional model of the campus.

d. Plan the evacuation routes for all the classrooms, trying to avoid overlapping routes.

e. Decide the location of the first aid station. Be sure you have room for stretcher patients.

f. Plan the assembly points in the safe area.

h. Assign duties and find the weak spots. How many adults have any nursing or first aid background? Any maintenance men on the grounds? What is the status of physical fitness of the faculty? Many near retirement?

The list can go on. You must include communications, cooking, toilet, and sleeping facilities. It is always a pet peeve of mine that, even in schools with a good overall program, the drills are put into effect, the kids go out and practice the routines, then from their position somewhere out in the safe area, they go back to the classroom and carry on with lessons. It never seems to enter anyone's head that, when the real thing comes along, no one will *go back to the classroom.*

The drills should *start* from the point at which they normally stop, taking into account that not only are you on your own, but what you see is what you get. If some students are at P.E. and all their clothes are back in the locker room and the aftershocks are thick and heavy, who is going to risk becoming a casualty by going back inside for clothes?

As part of our planning, we must include in "Education Before" *all* of the aspects of "Where will they be?" A good idea is to sit down and make a chart of the time of day school starts, where the classes are, what time breaks and recesses are (lunch breaks, assemblies, etc.). All aspects of the school day must be covered.

High schools, during changes of classes, are especially vulnerable. It is at that time when the halls are full of milling bodies and mass confusion. Even that point in time must be considered as a time for practice and drills. Forgetting or overlooking the vulnerable times cannot be permitted if we are to cover all the bases. Sometimes there is no "duck, tuck and hold" time available!

So, we have started our overall planning, our bird's eye view as it were. What were the weak spots? What can we do? List *your* problems and have a brain-storming session as a total staff project. Be innovative.

—Any Scouts on campus? They are first-aid trained.
—Do you have a football team? Strong "jocks" make great search-and-rescue candidates!

I raised a lot of eyebrows at one high school when I suggested that suspected gang members be asked to act as campus security during this time of stress! Using *all* resources must be the rule.

This should stimulate the thought processes for this part of the program.

Let's move now to the classroom itself.

Teacher, look at your room. Examine it carefully. Look up. Do the overhead lights run in line with the desks, or transverse to them? I recommended in one second-grade room that rearranging the desks a few feet would allow for lights to fall into the spaces between the desks rather than on them and, in turn, on the students themselves.

—How much glass is there?
—Which way will it fly?

Glass stores energy for as long as it can then, Boom!! It explodes, sending daggers of danger to cut the exposed parts of the body and, yes, often through clothes.

Glass windows should be taped with transparent tape to prevent the menace of slivered glass. In London, we had to use thick, brown, sticky paper. Now, with the clear transparent tape, all windows can be protected without looking ugly.

Is your exit door one of those steel-framed jobs in a steel door-jamb? There is about one-fourth of an inch clearance from door to jamb. A very slight movement of the structure will seal that door shut! How will you get the students out?

Be sure the children know the evacuation drill *exactly*. The way out, the way there; and they should even practice going to their designated spot without the teacher being there (teacher may be a casualty).

Children are the most adaptable creatures on earth. They can roll with the blows and make do remarkably well. I remember seeing (in Italy and the Middle East) orphaned children band together and help to find food and shelter (often by stealing, but at least surviving).

Having witnessed this kind of scene many times, I ask the question, "Is it fair to keep the students in the dark?" I realize all too often when I visit the school campus that, many times, faculty members had not thought through the process of disaster as it is now being understood and as earthquakes occur in different parts of California.

In the classroom, the dialogue has to be something like this:

> "We must be aware that in all earthquakes so far, the first things to fall are those overhead lights. So I want you all to look up and see where the lights are in relation to you. This way, you might need to go under the desk on the right side rather than the left side so that when the lamp falls it will not be on you."

This kind of thinking and action "puts them into the reality" of the situation. The conversation continues:

> "Most likely, that door will not open at quake time. Don't panic! I have this wrecking bar in my desk and we shall all go out through the window."

Neat kind of simulation drill here, don't you think? This is the kind of *thinking action* we need to learn.

There will be casualties. Students are not altogether "out of it." They see movies about earthquake and, bad as the movie may be, at least they are aware that someone may be hurt. Part of "Education Before" must include the discussion of trauma and how it will be handled.

A class must know, for example (and so must you), what is to happen to the injured student lying on the floor when the shaking stops and it is time for the evacuation to start. It is not good policy or procedure to have the class crowd around and attempt first aid then and there. Further aftershocks could endanger the whole room if rapid evacuation is not carried out. The situation could be handled something like this:

> "If there are injured in this classroom, the rest of the class should follow the evacuation plan. As your teacher, I will determine the action to take and, if necessary, I will call the first aid team to come and tend to the injured student. It is important that you all leave as quickly as possible."

Does this sound feasible to you? The students should be aware that, first, you know that there may be casualties and second, and most importantly, that you have a plan to take care of the situation. If there is a doubt in their minds, they will tend to take matters into their own hands and not leave without their injured classmate, meaning:

a. The whole class will be put at risk from potential further aftershocks, and

b. Attempts at first aid by unskilled hands often do more harm than good.

Frequently, when I work with schools, statements similar to the following are made to me by teachers:

"Yes, we do have a great plan on *paper*, but it will be hard to put into action because we do not have the time to practice the drills. For example, I do not know where all the first aid stuff is, and I am on the first aid team!"

There is a tremendous problem to overcome in this regard. Drills are rarely, if ever, carried out to the extent that the important aspects of survival training are brought out. We must take time to go past the "assembly on the field and back to the classroom" stage. There is far more to it than that!

What is the answer? Time must be set aside for non-classroom opportunities for *adult* disaster training. A chance for the faculty to work to "get the bugs out" without student input. Presenting a smooth team effort at disaster time is the best morale builder there is. Evenings, weekends, or whatever it takes. Lives could be at stake! The difference between organization and chaos is too much to gamble on, the aftermath too terrible to risk.

Consider the following facts and use them as a basis to develop *your* school's survival planning:

1. Where is the hospital or first aid point for your injured students?

2. Given the size of your student body, and the expected percentage of casualties, how many injuries can you be expected to sustain?

3. What plans have you made or will make for transportation of injured to the hospital?

4. What type of buildings does your school have? How old are they?

5. What percentage of parents from your school work out of the area and will not pick up their students right away?

6. How many kindergarten and/or special-needs children do you have?

7. Do you have any children on special medications? Any diabetics?

8. Now let's consider the faculty. Any handicapped teachers? How about their special medical needs?

9. Do all teachers have or plan to provide their own survival gear? Finally,

10. You will of course have planned for, or are planning for, food, water, shelter, and toilet needs for at least a five-day period. *Minimum*. Ten days is more realistic.

The facts I have given you to study and consider are meant only to be guidelines, a sort of starting point for discussion. There are special needs and circumstances at every school site. Only you, who are familiar with the peculiarities of your school, can say what they are.

Climate, wind conditions, urban site as opposed to rural, all factors come into play and have to be taken into consideration. As I said at the beginning of this section:

A school is like a ship on the ocean, an island unto itself.

You should, by now, be able to handle the "Education Before" procedures, hopefully enlarging on my suggestions. Now let's move on to:

Action During (What will they do?)

At some time of the school day—and by now we should be ready for *any* time in the school day—*IT* starts. The ground and the buildings begin to sway and jump. There is noise, dust, and confusion. Literally, it seems, all hell has broken loose. The sounds of children screaming fills the air. . .dust and noise and sounds not heard before. . .objects falling. . .glass shattering. . .the teachers' voices calling for calm, assuring that it will be all right. Suddenly, it all stops and only noise *inside* the classroom is heard.

Now the value of the preparations pay off. *The quality of the preparations before, will determine the quality of the survival state afterwards.*

As the dust swirls around through doors and windows, figures can be seen emerging and quickly moving to their designated assembly areas. They are dazed and huddle together. Some groups have a teachers with them, some do not.

In the distance, adults can be seen moving about as quickly as possible, going about their team tasks. Some set up the command post; cries of "over here, need a first aid crew," etc. can be heard. There is a strong smell of gas. Those assigned run to turn off the electric power.

I could go on and paint a word picture of the scene as it will unfold for you. For me, old pictures of my own time return too easily to my consciousness.

I am an earthquake survival specialist. Sharing my knowledge with you, not my horrors, is my task. In the kindest way possible, I have to convey to you all the truth of past disasters as I have *seen* them. As it *was*. Not as you think it *might* be, but as *I know it will be*. We are going to be on our own and must face the facts as they *will* be. Otherwise, *you* will be in a state of "La La Land" and *I* will have failed at my task.

The picture of a disheveled young lady in San Francisco still burns brightly in my brain. She stood in the street, in front of collapsed buildings and screamed to the world at large, "But nobody told me how *bad* it was going to be!"

From that time on, it has been my opening statement, "I am going to tell you how bad it is going to be and, from here on, you will never be able to say, 'but nobody told me.' I am going to tell it like it is."

Whether you listen and accept the facts as I present them is, of course, another matter. It still bothers me that a very small percentage of all who commute each day (many of them long distances) have survival packs in the vehicles with them.

At the end of this chapter is a composite School Disaster Planning Guide. It tells how to set up the Team and briefly outlines the duties of the various responsibilities (first aid, triage, etc.). It should help you to handle this "Action During" phase and answer the question "What will they do?" Again, what *they* will do is largely up to what *you* do in preparation.

Now, as quickly as possible, we must move into the last section of our planning.

Survival Afterwards (What will they need?)

Starting at the point that the whole student body is outside in the open, now we must move into what I term the "living after" mode, or *Camp Out Time!*

Be prepared for adjustments to your plans. The seasons of the year must be taken into account (the cold of winter, the heat of the summer) as well as the time of day, etc.

You have established the state of your buildings:

—Did you have any that were declared "earthquake safe"?
—Did they make it?
—Do you have any structural shelter at all?

It will be dark soon. Now is the time for those responsible to set up the tents or whatever you had planned. The sooner evidence of any kind of routines can be seen by the students, the sooner calm and confidence will begin to appear.

Let's step back and take a bird's eye view of the scene. The shaking stopped a while ago. All the students that are able are out in the open. The adult teams are going about their duties. Reality, in the form of injured people, is an awesome sight to the students who are watching.

Obviously, as soon as possible, we need to get actions started that involve the student body:

1. Organize the students in their groups and, if possible, sit down.
2. Double-check the roll for missing students.
3. Control student pick-ups by parents.
4. Check search-and-rescue operations. Do they need help?
5. Transportation of injured by whatever means possible should be taking place.
6. Building and safety crews will have checked for possible fire hazards, condition of utilities etc.
7. Record and assign volunteers.
8. As soon as possible, start support routines (drinks, snacks, toilets, sleeping arrangements). As the time progresses, staff will become free of duties and can be re-assigned to help these student activities.
9. If personnel is available for the purpose, "stress teams" should go to work at this crucial time.

About now, an assessment as to where you stand should be made:

a. You are prepared, and you have prepared others for the coming aftershocks.

b. The current student-to-adult ratio is established.

c. Off-campus volunteers have been absorbed.

d. Some contact with outside authorities may have been established.

e. On-site injured are comfortable, and a review of their conditions has taken place.

f. All personnel who left to transport injured should be back on site by now.

g. The student body should be re-assessed as to condition and state of mind.

h. The stress team should be out there doing its work, putting to rest rumors, building morale, etc.

i. You have prepared for the fact that there are no lights. As darkness falls, whatever form of emergency lighting you have should be tested now. It is a further aid to the morale of all.

j. Security will now be a priority—not only protection from intruders, but from students wishing to leave, or go "for a look around."

k. Patrol activity around the campus should be established.

All sorts of unforeseen little situations will have popped up and will have been handled (Oh, for the luxury of a "dry run"; a weekend camp-out maybe, when many of the little problems would have come up).

Night will fall and, later, the new day will dawn. E plus 1. And now the task of establishing a routine becomes most important. In my experience, not enough (if any) time is given to the consideration of routines. It is a missing ingredient. But as day two stretches into three, then four, and five, routine becomes more and more vital to survival in an orderly manner. Without it, morale will drop and students will start to leave the campus, mainly for the want of something to do.

In the planning stage, the question must be asked and answered: "What will we do with our time?" You must plan to occupy *all* the time, as any leader worth his or her salt learns early on when planning for a camp-out for the Scouts.

The remarks for the Stay portion of automobile survival in Chapter 3 apply just as much here as they did there. School books and lesson plans must be worked out in the quiet times so that E plus 5 (and even 6) can be handled in an orderly manner.

Now we should move on to the period of time at about E plus 5 or 6:

—Some parents, previously delayed, will have arrived to pick up their students.
—Communications should have been established with law enforcement agencies.
—Many problems will have arisen and been dealt with.
—All injured, by now, will have gone to a treatment center.
—The campus should be functioning well with the shrinking student body.

Now we are going to cross over into the realm of time not mentioned in the usual survival manuals (those put out by the turn-off-the-utilities-and-have-some-food-on-hand people).

By E plus 6, you will have become used to aftershocks, but never comfortable with them. By now, unless there was a good supply of "gray" water, all concerned will look a little dirty. Male staff will have six days' growth of beard, and hygiene will be at a low standard.

With these facts in mind, pay particular attention to these details in the planning stages.

It is essential for the staff to have had survival gear in their automobiles. A minimum of five days was required (see Chapter 3). Remember?

Supplies of cheap mouth wash and aftershave lotion can be stored very easily and are life savers at this time. With a high alcohol content, they make a useful antiseptic.

Close attention must be paid to toilet hygiene for, in this period of time, minor outbreaks of intestinal problems will occur (diarrhea can turn to dysentery overnight).

One of the areas I still struggle with is the uncharted, complex medical issue and all that goes with it. In any normal situation, we are used to and accept that minor health problems will turn up. There will be sore throats, minor ills, and little accidents.

What can we expect under conditions of stress? How many times have we heard a parent say, "My Willie will have an asthma attack if he is under stress!" What about now; what do we do if little Willie *does* have an asthma attack?

Here is another item for pre-planning, it would seem. It is a good idea to be prepared to put into effect some disease-control measures for the control of possible outbreaks of any type of infectious disease. Be it a skin ailment, head lice, or an intestinal virus. Many good pamphlets with such information are available for study prior to setting up these types of controls.

Segregation of those affected and sterilization of drinking vessels and utensils, even to the use of precious water for this top priority, are important.

Chapter 12 will consider, in more detail, some treatments for minor ills, aches, and pains.

In our survival planning preparations, it is important that we deal with disease treatment and control, being especially careful to include the older students in our discussions. Under field conditions, the panic and rumors that may result from control actions can be offset by the informed older students. The idea that a plague has broken out has to be avoided at all cost!

I believe that to be safe we must plan for accepting responsibility for survival of the total student body for a period of at least ten days. Over this period of time, there are bound to be problems that cannot be planned for, such as:

—The conditions of roads around the school site,
—Weather conditions,
—Outbreaks of fire on or near the school site,
—Student hysteria or melancholia,
—Insufficient supplies,
—Staff problems, ill health, etc.
—Air conditions, smoke from fires, etc.
—Vandalism.

These are some of the variables that I can think of. Your own area may have characteristics and problems of a particular nature.

Looking back over this chapter, it becomes apparent that planning for five to ten days of survival is a lot more than putting away some canned food and a few gallons of water!

So we *have* covered all of the bases as far as we know them. We *have* given prominence to student needs primarily. Let us not now forget the adults, and their needs. How will it be if in all the planning for *them,* we forgot about *us?!*

Actually this is a trick question. If you have followed along with the manual so far, you will have your own survival supplies with you in your car. . .if not, shame on you!

We have spent some time with the simple logical procedures necessary for survival planning of the school and student body. Let's re-cap:

—Education before (Where will we be?)
—Action during (What will we do?)

—Survival afterwards (What will we need?)

I urge all faculty to sit down with each other, going step by step over the expected events as I have outlined them and fitting them into *your* school. Take into account factors that I cannot be aware of:

—The age range of your students,
—The economic level of the parents,
—How active is the P.T.A.?
—How involved are the students in campus life (band, sports, etc.)?
—How about classroom volunteers?

A school is made up of many parts. It is not to say that all schools are as active as others. If you find, in your discussions as a faculty, that you seem to have a "tiger by the tail," wonderful! It means that you had a realistic discussion and the true facts were faced head on!

The sad state of affairs at most campuses today is that the student population is at risk and will fail miserably attempting to survive for more than twenty-four hours, given the present approach to survival planning.

This is, I realize, what appears to be a destructive and negative statement. It is not meant to be. However, if I ask *you* to face the facts as they are, surely I would be remiss if *I* did not face the same facts regarding school site preparations as I *know* them to be. The reasoning?

1. FUNDING.

In these times of financial crisis, funding for education is lacking, let alone for disaster preparations. A true list of needs becomes astronomical!

2. OUTSIDE STORAGE.

There is still a reluctance to arrange outside storage. Yet history, past and very recent, clearly demonstrates that inside storage of vital supplies is not practical. Imagine the first aid team having to dig out their supplies before they could tend the injured? Same for food, water, etc.

3. SUPPLIES.

A true inventory to support a small student body (say 400 students) for only five days is mind-boggling unless one has spent some time with a calculator! The word *true* inventory was used purposely. We are all used to the popular lists of needs but so often, for lack of experience, forget, for example, that food requires utensils and paper plates, as well as preparation for consumption. Followed by, of course, proper disposal.

4. FIRST AID.

A true first aid station, with adequate supplies, including stretchers and cots, splints and medical supplies in keeping with expected disaster traumas, is sorely needed.

5. RECORDS.

A good flexible system that can allow for rapid parent pick-up as well as reflect student movement on and off campus (ie: teams of student stretcher-bearers leave campus, and this fact must be recorded to avoid the confusion of them perhaps being declared missing and a search-and-rescue being called).

6.PERSONNEL.

The adult-to-student ratio is, at best, deficient. Face possible adult casualties and it becomes a major problem to be addressed.

7. EVACUATION.

Little, if any, consideration is given to the actual procedure for evacuating injured. How? By what route? To where? Have you actually talked to personnel where you think you should take your wounded?

8. COMMUNICATIONS.

On-campus and off-campus contact must be provided for.

9. SECURITY.

For students, staff, and supplies.

10.TRAINING.

Workshops to provide basic knowledge of search and rescue, first aid, and fire fighting. We glibly prepare plans for disaster by assigning staff to the various teams, expecting them to be instantly familiar with duties unknown to them. How many, for instance, would be aware of the right way to enter a destroyed building on a rescue mission, avoiding further collapse of the building?

11. TOILETS.

If the luxury of chemical toilets is available, how wonderful! For the less fortunate, training in the adoption of primitive methods must be undertaken. In our pre-planning, this aspect of survival must be faced and dealt with. Parent co-operation would help.

12. PRACTICE.

The dry-run approach. Just to go out and go through the motions is better than a paper routine.

Faced with these almost insurmountable odds, what are our options? We can, of course, say, if only privately, "What an order; I can't go through with it!" or "Well, let the chips fall where they may. We'll muddle through somehow. We always do!" or how about "Turn it over to the school board; it's their job!"

Excuses. Excuses. Yes, we could pass the buck, but we won't, will we? For out there are our students, looking to us to show the way. They will survive. There is no doubt about that. The question is, in what physical and emotional shape? Scarred for life emotionally? Forced to act as I have seen children in other parts of the world, fighting each other for food and water, searching the ruins of what was once their home, not knowing where their parents are, and, even worse, being at the mercy of the environment. "It's a jungle out there" was never more appropriate.

Tell me "It can't happen here." All well and good. What if it *did?* Everything else has happened here in the recent past, it seems. Gambling with the odds is for the individual. Now we consider the hundreds of lives that are our responsibility. History must not record that we gambled in the hope that the problem would not be that bad.

These are the negatives. Now let's look to the positive side. What *can* we do?

1. First, by an emergency meeting, all parents and school board should convene to face (in a *positive* manner) the situation as it exists and decide what to do about getting it to where it should be.

2. At this meeting, let's tell it like it is (400 students to survive on their own for only five days will require a minimum of 2000 gallons of water. That's one gallon of water each per day). Expecting a 10-percent casualty rate, of which 50 percent will not be ambulatory, we will need at least twenty stretchers and twenty cots. (Go

on down the lists, including toilet paper.)

3. To offset the poor adult-to-student ratio, a strong volunteer force of stay-at-home folks must be recruited.

4. Fundraising must be undertaken. Each year, marching bands from towns large and small are seen at the Pasadena Rose Parade. Each year, their proud achievements for raising the large sums of money for uniforms, instruments, travel, and accommodations are publicly proclaimed. If fundraisers can work for one school project, why not another?

5. We must explore the possibilities of a share-and-care plan. For parents who travel out of the area and have no hope of getting home for many days, designated neighbors or relatives could be nominated to shelter the children of such parents until the parents return.

6. A further extension of share-and-care could be the using of close-in residences as shelters for children whose homes are distant (a sort of buddy system in which students accompany classmates home until their own parents can pick them up).

We must all do as much as we can to alleviate the present situation of planning for survival of large numbers of students and all the inherent problems. Any step that reduces the numbers reduces the problems.

Conclusions then? Include as many people as possible when planning for survival. Especially include student input.

This, except for the loose ends that we have not encountered yet, concludes this chapter. There are however, a couple of these loose ends that bother me:

1. Travel to and from school in the school bus.

In the general scheme of things, responsibility for students on the school bus rests with the driver and the transportation agency. I have yet to find any agency that has adequately faced this issue.

Question: "In the event of a disaster, what is your action?"

Driver: "I pull over to the side of the road and get on the radio."

Further questions are pointless and embarrassing to the driver. It is obvious that this is a very vulnerable situation.

Provision for treatment of injured, as well as a clearly defined policy as to what actions are to be taken for various situations, have to be mandatory. In my own experience, this is not the case. School buses, at the moment, are the weak link in the chain, exposing students to an unnecessary grave hazard. What is required?

First, disaster-level medical and first aid supplies must be carried on all school buses. Adequate supplies are vital.

Secondly, a clear policy must be established as to the procedure regarding injured passengers. Waiting at the roadside for help that is not forthcoming is not acceptable.

Furthermore, having children of the same age and grade level on a bus is not good policy if the result is that the only responsible person on the bus is the driver. We must face the possibility of injured children needing urgent medical care, which cannot be provided because there is no one to look after the rest of the children if the driver is the only one who can leave with the injured.

Obviously, older students must travel with younger ones, or teams of parent volunteers must accompany buses in the country and on long distance runs. All responsible teachers and parents must face and correct this issue.

2. The injury-from-glass issue.

The report published by the government after the San Fernando earthquake of February 9, 1971, emphasized:

"Steps must be taken to reduce the hazard of flying glass and
the resultant injuries from same."

Repeatedly, I bring up this issue at school seminars. Despite the fact that after each minor earthquake, flying glass figures prominently in the reports, no action is taken to tape windows to avoid and eliminate this hazard.

How comforting in London during the period of the bombing, to sit near the window in a restaurant and see the criss-cross of tape across the glass and be comfortable in the knowledge that one's eyes and face were safe from the hazard of flying glass!

3. Apathy.

I am concerned that many well-meaning people in the educational scene are lulled into a false sense of security because they have put away some food and hold a few drills. They feel that they are ready. This sense of security is passed on to students.

I have stressed realism throughout this text, so there seems no point in continuing to belabor the issue. Disaster strikes with a sudden impact for which we can *never* be fully ready. We can, however, be *prepared,* providing we accept the reality of the situation. The reality is "You really are on your own." Each one of us is in the same boat, from the highest to the lowest. Period.

4. Communication.
Sadly lacking is dialogue between all concerned. We seem to avoid the real issues of the whole disaster scene. Is it that the total picture is too much for us to comprehend? Or are we so insulated as to believe that the authorities will always be there to rescue us from real harm? A good example of an exercise in communication:

> The student body is assembled on the playing field. The drill is over and they are all preparing to go back to class. The principal steps up to the mike on the platform and says, "We are going to do something different today, students. The names of all the students whose parents will pick them up right after the earthquake will be called. They all live locally. As your name is called you may return to your classroom. Those of you who remain will be the ones who, with the teachers, will be here for some time. Camping out as it were (a murmur goes up from the crowd). What I would like you to do, is to turn around and meet those around you. Get to know each other. We are all going to share a unique experience."

This is an example of realistic communication.

5. Supplies.
One of my many concerns is the failure of people to properly calculate the amount of supplies that is required to sustain a large group of people for a period of time. Let us use the round figure of 100 and a period of five days.

Water:
1 Gallon per day for 5 days = 500 gals.

Food:
500 each, breakfast, lunch and dinner—that's 1500 meals!

Soft goods:
1500 plates, cups or glasses, plus "eating irons."

Toiletries:
How much toilet paper a week does your child use? A full roll? Half a roll? For a hundred then, 100 rolls throwing some in for emergencies?

General supplies:
Lanterns, flashlights, batteries, medical supplies, and medications, etc.

6. Credibility.
Finally, we have to face the general credibility of our efforts. At a large public earthquake seminar put on by the local Sheriff's Department, a woman with a child came up to my station. The child was asking all sorts of intelligent questions about the school scene. The mother interrupted with, "Honey, don't worry about it. As soon as the earthquake stops, mummy will jump in the car and come down and get you!" Looking at the woman, I realized that she *believed* what she had just said. I hoped the child was more in touch with reality!

On a radio talk show that I was invited to, the host began his interview with the remark, "Are you one of those doom and gloomers?"

Until the general public, and parents in particular, are truly convinced that survival planning on the school campus is really necessary, we do not have the credibility to ensure a 100-percent effort on everyone's part.

My only hope as the crusader is to try to stimulate your drives so that you, in turn, may get as fired up as I am regarding survival planning.

After the fact will be too late.

I briefly mentioned the inclusion of students in the school's disaster planning activity—especially, one feels, at the junior-high and high school level. We have poster and essay competitions for all sorts of other life-threatening situations; why not earthquake survival? We could produce some innovative results!

How do we keep our high school and junior high students on campus? Our greatest challenge, it seems to me, is going to be to find the answer or answers. I am sure there are many different solutions to the question. Involving them in the process could at least be a step in the right direction.

One final note. Chapter 4, which deals with Homes, discusses Backyard Survival. In that section will be found all sorts of information which will be helpful in the activities required in the school camp-out phase, with many useful techniques, including how to make a screened backyard toilet, underground storage of food, and other helpful hints.

In finishing this chapter, searching for some final words (pearls of wisdom?), the only thoughts that come to mind are thoughts of the reality of the whole scene. That of several hundred students and their teachers surviving the most awful disaster any of us will ever see. Thoughts of London inspire me to say:

It is possible; you will survive.

Sound preparations will determine your condition afterwards!

Practice makes perfect!

On the following pages is an appendix to this chapter. It is a basic school disaster plan for elementary and junior high/high schools. I include it that you may either review your own school plans or initiate some, incorporating the principles suggested.

After we look at the Disaster Plan, we will move on to our next point of concern: workers in locations other than schools, facing their problems in Chapter 6, The Workplace.

Appendix to Chapter 5

Standard Disaster Plan
for Elementary/Junior High/High School

The purpose of this plan shall be to present, in as concise a manner as possible, a step-by-step procedure that all concerned may study, practice, and, at the appropriate time, execute with utmost efficiency. This plan focuses on elementary through high school ages. Factors which are peculiar to college and other residential situations are discussed in Chapter 9.

From the outset, let it be understood and agreed upon that these procedures have been developed as a means of handling a disaster of the utmost magnitude (no pun intended), an earthquake of 8.3 or greater with an intensity unknown in our times.

One feels that preparations, as undertaken here, are somewhat similar to parenthood; you learn as you go and remain optimistic for the outcome!

Facts. All of the "experts" on the subject agree on certain aspects. The following are pertinent to the school setting:

1. All buildings that were not constructed to include earthquake codes may suffer severe damage.

2. All communications of the normal nature will be lost.

3. Utilities will be lost due to destruction of service lines coming in to the school, and/or the service within the school itself will be interrupted due to damage.

4. Travel of any kind by normal means will be greatly restricted. Access to and from the school site may be difficult or impossible.

5. Public services (police, fire, paramedics, etc.) will not be available for an unknown period of time.

6. Parents who travel some distance will not be expected to

return for an undetermined time (see Travel Survey in Chapter 3).

7. Needed supplies not at hand will be difficult to procure. This will include supplies for the school staff of a personal nature (special meds, etc.).

8. All responsibility for the safety and well-being of the school in toto will rest with the school personnel. No outside help can be expected for many hours, possibly even days.

Conclusion? We are on our own. The next logical step then seems very obvious: preparations must be undertaken *before* disaster strikes. All concerned must not only be aware of their own roles, but also be familiar with the duties of the rest of the staff. Our challenge is clear. By all means possible, we must produce and effect a plan of action with which *all* concerned are familiar.

How very simple to say, yet how complicated when one views the broad picture. The plan must aim for simplicity and action and is divided into three sections:

Education Before
Action During
Survival Procedures After

Education Before

Student awareness cannot be over emphasized. We should start with the basic questions:

—*Where will I be?*
—*What will I do?*
—*What will I need?*

Classroom preparation should be at the discretion of the individual teachers. Action to be taken during the quake can be practiced as often as needed, along with discussion of the evacuation procedures. The younger grades may require greater emphasis on certain aspects of the evacuation procedures than the older, more self-reliant students.

Staff awareness of the overall situation, as well as the basic plan itself, is most important. Training sessions must be held so that *all* are familiar with the basic details and must include the initial actions required to ensure, as far as possible, campus safety and security.

Combined student and staff training is required so that, in the *vital first thirty minutes* after the quake, actions are as close to rote as possible.

At the proper time students should arrive at their assembly areas unassisted and maintain a quiet demeanor, leaving the staff to swing into their roles as quickly as possible.

Action During

It is not possible to visualize the actual earthquake itself in any clear detail. Obviously the site of the epicenter, the intensity of the quake itself, the effects on the school site as a whole, coupled with the effect on given areas of the school site, are all factors that cannot be pre-determined.

During the actual time of shaking and jolting, the actions already practiced should come into being automatically, as will the instincts of self-preservation. (Obviously, the practice drills as well as the understanding of possible events pay off at this time of reality.) "Duck, tuck, and hang on" seems to be the universally accepted norm for this time. Let us accept this as the only "action during" we will take.

As soon as the shaking stops, we automatically enter the most important phase (see Diagram 25):

Survival Procedures After

1. All mobile students will, at once, evacuate to their assigned assembly area using the designated route given.

2. All staff will swing into assigned duties of:

—Command post set-up/communications start-up,
—Search and rescue,
—Triage and first aid center set-up,
—Clerical controls and security procedures, and
—Building safety-procedures actions.

These first actions will bring us to the point that:

—All classrooms are evacuated,
—All injured are cleared from buildings and taken to the first aid area,
—Clerical controls are set up,
—Perimeters are secured, and site safety is secured (utilities shut off where required).

The situation may now be assessed from the command post and strategy established. Casualties are known and further actions for medical services can be determined; assessment of building damages are known; and, clerical controls being in effect, early student release can be undertaken.

Now we are able to move into Phase Two of Survival Procedures After, which first involves reassigning staff to secondary duties, with the emphasis now shifting to the support functions to maintain the status quo and to prepare for the continuance of safety and security of the situation. Completed tasks allow for a shifting of duties; the completion of search and rescue, and the establishment of the injured in a central point lead to the release of staff concerned with these duties.

Now we must place emphasis on other areas. Primarily, the energy of all staff be directed to student morale and organization. Decisions will be made at this time to compensate for possible staff injuries or demands in specific areas that would produce an undesirable, unbalanced situation requiring a shift in staff concentration (i.e., a class being without adult guidance, a fire, heavy casualties in certain areas).

Once student attitude is established, long-range activities must be undertaken. These will include preparation for camping out as a unit. Obviously, food and sanitation will be high on the priority list, as we proceed into what is to become our normal-for-now routine.

Let us now review our situation:

—The quake has happened,
—All classrooms are evacuated,
—The injured are centrally located,
—The command post is fully functional,
—Clerical procedures are functioning,
—Students are being released in an orderly fashion, and
—Staff personnel are taking up secondary duties.

It is time now to establish of routines that will support a camp-out situation. Obviously, the success of the situation will depend on the

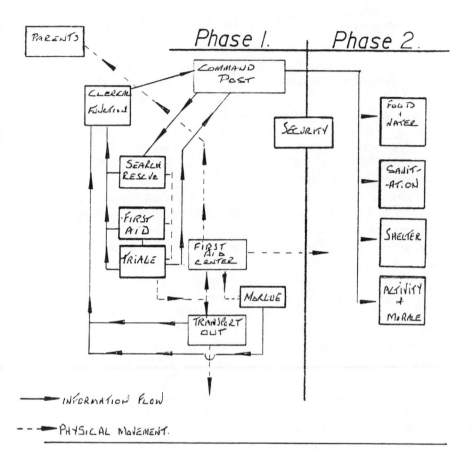

**DIAGRAM 25—BASIC DISASTER PLAN
FOR EDUCATIONAL FACILITIES**

quality of the preparations taken beforehand, as will the decisions agreed to in the initial planning stages (the type of toilet procedures, food and water availability, volunteer involvement, as well as good old down-home ingenuity). All the efforts put in at the beginning pay out at the moment of truth.

Now that we have a feel for the overall scenario for which we are planning, at this point we will break away from the sequence of events to focus in more detail on each assignment. There will of necessity be repetition in much of this discussion, because the assignments are integrated and and in many cases taking place simultaneously. I suggest that in the planning stage those involved lay out on a large surface descriptions of all assignments and visualize and study their integration.

Phase 1 Activities
The initial assignments are limited to:

—*Command Post and Commander,*
—*Search and Rescue,*
—*First Aid,*
—*Clerical Command,*
—*Security.*

Phase 2 Activities
When initial activities are complete and the situation is stabilized, reassignments are made to Phase 2 Activities:

—*Food and Water,*
—*Sanitation,*
—*Camp-out Comfort.*

COMMAND POST SET-UP, WITH COMMUNICATIONS

As part of our planning, the physical command post will have been designed, built, and stored in "kit" form outside. The communications walkie-talkie and base unit must also be secured outside. The "uniforms" for the various section leaders should be in the same area. For ease of identification, different-colored hard hats should be used for section leaders so they can be recognized in the uproar, dust, and confusion.

The object is to enable the commander and section leaders to drop what they are doing and go to the designated command post and take up both their identities and their duties. This is a *vital* component of the survival plan!

As soon as the shaking stops, the maintenance personnel shall take the prepared table set-up to the appointed command post. This will be a pre-planned unit. Secure the walkie-talkie units, setting up the home base at the command post. (The importance of regular testing of these units is obvious. Batteries must remain fresh!)

As soon as the commander of operations arrives, the communications units for field use shall be handed out to section leaders as they arrive. There should be one unit for each of the following:

—Search and rescue section leader,
—First aid section leader,
—Security section leader, and
—Clerical records clerk.

While the command post is being established, students should be evacuating their classrooms for the assembly area.

The clerical staff will set up the student record file, separating those files of the known "parents out of the area" from "parents who will pick up."

As soon as possible, the command leader will establish contact with field section leaders and begin recording reports on the prepared School Site Plan. This site plan will enable the command leader to note (probably with colored map pins) conditions as they develop, making note of the "hot spots" as they are reported.

Other details, such as reports from security as to when parents arrive to pick up students, will be recorded with other pertinent information as it comes in.

In addition to the reception of incoming information, it is also the duty of the commander to see to the *Checklist of Vital Actions*. Such a checklist will have been compiled earlier, and will include all items considered vital and/or threatening to safety, such as the shut-down of electricity or other utilities.

This checklist will also verify action for areas already designated as high priority, such as the possibility of students trapped in known high-risk rooms (the computer room, for example). Rescue of those faculty/students known to be physically handicapped will also be handled at this time. These actions should also include the interaction between the commander, the first aid crew, and the triage unit.

It goes without saying that the decorum and attitude of the commander will set the standard for the morale of the staff as they carry out their duties and conditions unfold. Aftershocks may occur almost from the start of the first quiet period after the main shock wave has passed. Above all, we may expect much noise and panic from the students as they encounter the sight, for the first time, of injured fellow students or staff. The reality that this is really "the big one" is the first challenge to all concerned. Certainly, the quality of the command center performance activities will be the crucial factor in overall effective action. *Prior preparation will be the key to success!*

We cannot overemphasize the urgency of calmly and efficiently establishing the command center. Consider the situation in which these actions are taking place: noise, confusion, panic. The very coming into being of the command post can be the stabilizing factor that restores confidence. We need to be able to exclaim, "Wow! Thank goodness someone has a handle on this thing!"

SEARCH AND RESCUE, FIRST AID, TRIAGE

It is not practical to separate these groups from an organizational standpoint. They are all closely related in on-the-job performance. An integrated overview is in order. Later, we will focus on each group individually.

Let us take an imaginary birds-eye view of the school scene as it appears just after quake time. . . after the shaking has stopped. Some buildings are damaged. The sound of pounding on doors may be heard as students attempt to exit in an orderly manner. Some students are already leaving their rooms for the assembly area. The command post set-up is being carried out to its site, and section leaders for the groups we have discussed are coming out into the open putting on their identity hats and arm bands. *At this point it becomes clear that those involved must have an understanding of procedure, or they will not know where to start!* Practice sessions are mandatory. (Input from experts in the field would help. Direction from higher authority should be automatic but, so far, is not forthcoming—remember, you are on your own to implement this plan.)

Going back to our birds-eye view, it's obvious that a disorganized search-and-rescue team would instinctively rush to the spot that looks the worst. Then, having dealt with that situation, rush off to the next one. . .and so on. Finally, when all seems to have quieted down, the realization that half the classrooms have not been attended to might strike home as word is passed that students are trapped in a room not visited. This disorganization and chaos can be avoided by firmly establishing procedure ahead of time. Additionally, it is imperative that you establish beforehand the simple coordination of effort between the search-and-rescue group and the first aid crew.

Let's imagine the teams in action:

Search and rescue obviously is the first on the scene. Entering a building, they accomplish a rescue. The victim is removed to the outside of the building and the first aid team moves in. . .search and rescue then moves on to the next site and the first aid team follows. . .this sounds like a nice, well-orchestrated event. Will this happen in our situation? It could, but it's dependent on much practice and rehearsal.

The scenario we went through was the action of an experienced team of professionals who have worked together for a long time. In the atmosphere of a school disaster, there are many pitfalls to be avoided. Let's go over the scene again as it would be if we had a situation of first-time effort (as it will be in most cases). Search-and-rescue (probably two, maybe at most three people) enter the class-room and effect a rescue pulling a student out into the open. The first aid crew (again probably at most two, perhaps only one person) moves in to attend to the victim. The rescue crew moves in, also offering advice and help. Now all three or four (in some cases many more) people are gathered around the victim, and in time all help to carry the injured person over to the first aid area.

What are we learning?

From the outset, it is very obvious that unless guidelines are established, the duties of the search-and-rescue and first aid people can well overlap, leading to delays in applying effort where it is needed.

Secondly, it should be established that search-and-rescue should begin at a defined starting point in order that the whole site may be assessed as quickly as possible.

In some instances, a badly damaged classroom may require that all available personnel be called for assistance. Does all search and rescue then stop at that point? Obviously not. Leaving *one* person behind, the rest go on with the procedure of search, so that, as quickly as possible, the whole school site has had a total search, and an early report can be made to the command post.

Various scenarios could be worked up providing a variety of examples of search-and-rescue/first aid situations. This is more the purpose of rehearsals and drills than of this text, but at least we now have opened the door to what will hopefully be spirited and realistic discussion.

As we conclude the integrated overview of search and rescue and first aid, it seems fitting to comment that the terms we are using seem to roll off the tongue so easily. Yet, in actual fact, we are attempting to imitate a very highly specialized group of people. It is very difficult, without actual on-the-job training, to convey to a group of teachers (no matter how dedicated) what is actually involved in the hands-on carrying out of the duties required. The very unfamiliarity of the situation itself is, at first, traumatic. Search and rescue sounds simple. But who among us has ever done it? So, too, with first aid...

Another aspect that must be mentioned is the availability of actual people. The ratio of adults to students is shrinking all the time! These factors must be taken into account in the preliminary planning stages:

—How many of the staff have any training?
—What about physical health and strength?
—How many volunteers are available?
—How long will it take for volunteers to arrive on the site?
—How about the use of students, especially those who are Scouts and have training in first aid already?

Addressing these questions and reaching conclusions will at once highlight the strengths and, of course, the weaknesses of *your* situation.

Finally, there are some decisions that must be made before we can go on with the execution of our search-and-rescue/first aid plan:

1. Should we choose the search-and-notate method where one person with the walkie-talkie races around the complete site calling in to the command post and the command post then dispatches personnel? This system is recommended when there is extensive building damage, allowing for action at the worst sites first.

2. Victims must be pulled clear of buildings. Obviously, the danger of aftershocks must be considered. Should the triage person accompany the search and rescue team, or wait to be called?

3. When first aid is rendered, who will transport the injured to the first aid site? If total on-site injuries are light, the first aid team may transport. If, however, there is a heavy call for their services, their time would be too valuable, and transport should be left to others.

4. The injured are all in the first aid area. It is obvious that some have serious injuries and require advanced medical attention. How? Where to? By whom?

We cannot leave this discussion without consideration of the sleeper in the text, namely *Triage.* Webster's describes Triage as "sorting out those who need urgent treatment, those who need little treatment, and those for whom treatment is too late." What an awful concept! The phrase "It's a lousy job but somebody has to do it" springs to mind. Corny as it seems, this is the position we are in. Perhaps not in as dramatic a situation, but, none the less, the injured should be screened so that scant resources can be best utilized.

We have spent some time in this overview. We have done so because the *first thirty minutes* is totally focused on securing the safety and well-being of all persons (both students and faculty). Now that we have seen how the operations of search and rescue, first aid, and triage are integrated, we will go on now to briefly look at each individually.

SEARCH AND RESCUE

Slogan? "As long as I know *what* to do, I *can* search and rescue."

The first consideration to be addressed is the question "how many people are available?" A team leader and as many hands as possible are required. In actual fact, perhaps one or two are all that are available from the outset. Maybe strong senior students could be primed and ready ahead of time, developed through the planning stages.

As soon as the shaking stops, the team leader should assemble the team and put into operation the plan that is agreed upon.

Either a rapid search and report by a single individual, followed by action as required by the team, or the hot-spot-to-hot-spot-by-a-whole-team approach will be used.

The aim is to search, to report as quickly as possible on those buildings that are clear, and to clear in as safe a manner as possible those buildings that are not. Policy will have to be determined to establish procedure. The norm should be that search-and-rescue *rescues* (pulls the victims clear of the structure, reports "structure clear," and moves on to next area) and first aid *administers first aid*.

Prior training is helpful, but in day-to-day reality it is a forlorn hope to imagine that career teachers have time to spend learning the ins and outs of search and rescue! Common sense will prevail in most situations. Training, if it is to be undertaken at all, should have the emphasis placed on the "rescue" aspect rather than the "search." Extracting a victim from a building without further injury is a greater skill to learn than how to get into the building in the first place.

A basic knowledge of first aid is very beneficial but, in the scheme of things, search and rescue's primary concern is to locate and retrieve victims, taking them to a place of safety where the proper first aid may be administered. Remember that it is so easy for the duties of search and rescue and first aid to overlap, an undesirable situation.

When the operation of search and rescue is complete, the team reports to the command post for a new assignment. Usually, this team will take up such duties as setting up shelters, assisting with a food station, etc.

In conclusion, let me stress to you that your prior planning pays off in the on-the-spot decision-making process. Considerations of the time of day, for example, forewarn of the necessity of speed in clearing buildings ("It will soon be dark; let's get the lights set up. We still have X buildings to go!").

FIRST AID AND TRIAGE

Closely linked to the rescue effort comes the first aid group. For a moment, let us spend some time on research:

—What is the current student enrollment?
—What is the ratio of adults to students (all adults, including cooks, clerical workers, etc.) on campus?
—What is the grade span of this campus?
—What is the percentage of the lower grades and the higher grades? Number of "special needs" students?

Against the background of this knowledge, let us ask these questions:

—What is the percentage of casualties we can expect on our campus?
—Using the facts already expressed, how many very young casualties may we expect?
—Finally, how many first aid supplies do we have, and is it adequate for the figures we have just developed?

Now we can evaluate the size and format of the first aid team and how we will operate under disaster conditions.

Obviously, the ideal situation is one in which the team leader, with several assistants, is operating from the onset. If this is not the case, a team leader, acting more as an administrator and advisor, would recruit volunteers and direct them to places of need.

Adequate supplies must be on hand from the start. The type of supplies must also be established beforehand. Kits with an excess of

Band-Aids, for example, are of no use for the conditions. Ace-type bandages and material for splints and compresses are more appropriate.

In considering supplies, stretchers will be in very high demand. If they are not available, the knowledge of how to develop substitutes for handling the injured will be needed.

As soon as the shaking stops, team leaders and individuals will report to the command center, don their identifying gear, secure first aid kits, and follow the established routines as to direction and emphasis. Simultaneously, the triage persons will establish their operations.

An ideal situation would be for a retired doctor, living in the neighborhood, to volunteer to come in and be the triage person. That is the skill level one would hope for. If such a person is not available, the staff person with the most depth of medical expertise is the one required for this position. A nurse or former nurse or Army medic is desirable.

Above all, the triage person must be able to distinguish between a serious injury and one that only looks bad. Cuts from flying glass often fit the latter category—lots of blood, but little there after clean-up. Like the boxer at the end of the round with a nasty looking gash over the eye. . .some work with the sponge and a little salve, and he looks like a new man.

It is important to include this fact in our Education Before presentations. Children adapt well when they know what to expect, but tend to panic in the unknown situation.

The triage person has a very difficult duty: not only to guide the rest of the teams and the command post, but also to work without the aid of the normal, on-site equipment and supplies that are usually available (no medications for pain, no I.V.'s, no medical doctor on hand), surely a most difficult position to be in, but a vital position to be sure.

Let us, once again, step back and take a bird's-eye view of the probable situation:

The shaking has stopped. The command post is set up and in operation. The triage person is out in the field with the rescue first aid teams, directing operations. Soon, the triage area starts to have casualties brought in. The first go-round is complete and the triage person can return to the triage area.

Decisions must now be made as to the dispersal of any seriously injured, comatose, or near-comatose victims who must be transported as quickly as possible. Questions arise as to conditions of the roads around the school site. Is it possible to transport part of the way by vehicle? Have we clearly established where our serious injuries are to be taken?

May we send out a student as a scout to give us an on-the-spot evaluation of conditions at our possible destinations? Too bad if you transport a serious injury to an already backed-up facility!

If there are serious injuries, can we reach some agency on the radios? Perhaps a helicopter is in the area?

Is there sufficient shelter for the injured? Shelter requirements are part of the triage person's responsibility, as are making these requirements known to the commander and maintaining the well-being of casualties.

In our pre-planning and brainstorming sessions, the triage person will be the one to supply the vital information as to medical requirements, types of supplies we should aim for, and where and how to store these vital supplies. The triage person will have the experience so necessary in the planning stages.

For most of us, this whole situation of injuries (words like "critical," etc.) are totally foreign and somewhat frightening. Having an experienced ex-Army medic or surgery nurse on the team can make such a difference.

Plan for the worst when injuries strike; the whole first-aid/search-and-rescue scene is a very trying situation at disaster time.

The duties of the triage person may be summarized as follows:

—To, as quickly as possible, identify a serious injury.
—To render or supervise the most efficient first aid.
—To organize transportation as quickly as possible.
—In the case of instant fatality or gradual fatality, to supervise transfer of the corpse to a selected area.
— To be in close touch with the command post at all times, keeping the commander aware of the current situation.

CLERICAL CONTROLS

The clerical procedures and routines to be put into effect at the time of a major disaster should be well established prior to disaster time. Incorporating the requirements of both the local school boards and higher education authorities is an absolute must. The card system, a manual accounting for each individual, is already in existence in many public school systems; this kind of system is mandatory for the clerical controls that are essential in the aftermath of disaster.

As soon as the shaking stops, the clerical person or team will proceed with the records to the command center, setting up a work station. As soon as the evacuations are underway, reports of student location will begin to be relayed to the clerical records control. At the elementary school command post, the ebb and flow of students is easy to control. If needless risks are to be avoided by search and rescue teams, student whereabouts becomes critical information. It's important that we know the absentee list, those who were not in school that day, so that the reason for absence of students from the assembly area can easily be determined.

The flow of information back and forth can be easily imagined as the teams in the field begin to function. Missing students are located and noted as "injured," "recovered," "not injured," etc.

Soon after the shaking has stopped, we must be prepared for elementary school parents to arrive to pick up their students. At this time, the established procedures will swing into effect.

One problem that can be foreseen is the situation of excited parents being impatient for student release while the records are being set up. From the outset, the command center must establish the firm rules that are to be followed for student release. Communication with parents must be established *beforehand* as to the procedures that are to be followed:

1. Parents *must* report to the command center to secure student release.
2. Record cards must be updated and signed before student release can be obtained.
3. A runner system of student release should be used. Once release is confirmed *a student runner should be used to go to the assembly area to physically contact and conduct the student to the command center.* If parents rush to the assembly area and take students away, circumventing the record-keeping function, chaos will result.
4. Students must be aware that they are not to leave the assembly area and run to meet the parents as soon as they see them. The importance of the clerical function cannot be stressed highly enough.
5. For any student who leaves the grounds for any reason, be it as a runner, a scout, or as an injured victim, the records *must* be updated to reflect the student movement.

It becomes quite clear that, through all the confusion of the disaster event and its handling by school personnel, out-of-control parents can be almost as large a disaster as the event itself. The Education Before action, most definitely, must include emphasis on this point. Reasonable parents can and must be educated to support the recording process. Just as importantly, students also need to understand their responsibilities.

Back-up System

What if the recording function fails? We have, thus far, outlined the plans for action in the firm knowledge and belief that "all systems are go," while in other areas functions will be performed regardless of the difficulties. In this, the vital area of clerical function and student records, we are introducing elements and people that are outside of our firm control. Horror stories abound of the circumstances surrounding the event of parents picking up children. We must expect the unexpected!

Some simple system needs to be developed that will enable a student to leave the grounds, even if the clerical function has not been followed. What are we trying to control here? Here's an example: a parent rushes into the area looking for the student. Once spotted, the parent rushes to the place and, taking the student by the hand, exits the area daring anyone to stop the exit! How can we control this activity? One idea comes to mind.

Each student has a small token, something like a lapel button pinned to the outer garment. As the parent exits with the student, the token or button is taken off and given to the security guard. At a future time, a runner takes these tokens or buttons and gives them to the clerical person, who can then update the records.

The seriousness of the clerical responsibilities cannot be overemphasized; there are many recorded instances of people risking their lives entering a damaged building in search of a missing student, only to find the student had already left the grounds! A back-up system eliminates this situation.

During the bombing in London, establishing the occupants of a building was always the most difficult task. We learned *not* to enter a building unless we were sure there was a possible victim inside. Too many lives were lost on "wild goose chases."

I hope I have been able to highlight the importance of the clerical function and record-keeping in general. I feel sure that keener minds than mine can solve the problems even more efficiently.

A point to remember: never give up hope for a missing person. Books could be written of the stories of those who were missing and turned up safe days later. In a different place than they were thought to be. . .? Who cares how!

SECURITY

Coupled with the clerical function is the security system. Depending on the number of people involved, this can be a very simple or a very complicated affair. An outline of the objectives should be understood at this point:

1. To secure the perimeter, as far as possible, providing a monitoring system for entry and exit.

2. To ensure the safety of the school population during the time past sunset.

3. To ensure, as far as possible, that all students leaving the grounds are with authorized people.

In addition to these basic functions, security personnel may be utilized as part the general support team. Always, the number of people available is the criterion.

We need to highlight the problems that are sure to be encountered. The period we are preparing for will be a very stressful time. In the heat of the moment, human emotions will be very close to the surface. It must always be the aim of all security personnel to present a calming, reasonable attitude. ("As you can understand, if students are not properly recorded when they leave we may spend time looking for them" is more calming to a distraught parent than "Well, those are the rules and there are no exceptions.")

Experienced personnel in the security field know the appropriate approach in various difficult situations encountered in everyday life. However, at the time of disaster, inexperienced people may find themselves trying to handle a situation for which they are not trained. The time of Education Before can be used to emphasize these types of situations.

This is a stressful time! Under the pressure of the moment, a parent may be militant and impatient (in many cases, understandably so). Consider a possible scenario. A local parent is out shopping. The quake hits and the parent is involved in the mess at a supermarket. Canned goods are all over the floor, dust and noise abound, screaming voices and total confusion prevail. By some miracle, the parent sees daylight streaming through a crack in a wall and clambers out. The thought hits. . .my child! One look around and it is clear that the roads are impassable. Running. . .crawling. . .walking and totally out of breath, the parent arrives at the school to find the gate barred by security: "What's your name?" No wonder there is a potential for anger at the gate!

We must, first of all, accept that by merely even considering disaster preparedness, we place ourselves in an approximate 4 percent minority of Californians. Even slight consideration of the other 96 percent will expose some of the security problem. Priorities will include:

1. Protection of vital supplies (both of food and medicines).

2. Protection of survival equipment (clothes, tents, blankets, etc.).

3. Protection of persons.

4. Protection from animals.

Within this framework are many grey areas that are the by-products of our society today. Addicts of all kind will be on the hunt for their own particular product. Many other segments of the masses will be let loose in many frightening ways, with which I am sure the sociologists are far more in tune than I!

In our Education Before training and procedures, we must stress the importance of this aspect of security for both male and female security personnel. Strong students (the athletes perhaps) should be organized to assist the uniformed security forces, especially in the patrol aspect of this work.

I ask all concerned to listen to a word from the wise, as it were: It is truly going to be a jungle out there, and especially vulnerable are going to be any organized group that appears to have an abundance of any kind of supplies!

In actuality, this preparedness may not be necessary, but why take chances? Logically, where else will looters turn after the wrecked stores have been picked clean?

Hunger and thirst will affect us all at the same level, producing a *need.* How the need is satisfied will depend on. . .

PHASE TWO ACTIVITIES

Having completed the assignments that are necessary for Phase One activities (roughly the first two hours of the disaster), we may now move into Phase Two: the "what happens now?" period.

Let us repeat a version of what we've said so often in our discussion: *All Phase Two activity depends on prior action and prior planning.*

These second-phase activities really begin when the commander determines that the overall situation is calm enough to allow for people to be released back to their normal duties (teachers return to their home group, cooks back to the kitchen area, etc.).

As we discussed earlier, Phase Two activities are involved in the furtherance of the support of the remaining campus population and the provision of their future needs. These will be:

—Food and water,
—Sanitation, and
—Shelter and Camp-out activities.

First come *food and water.* How much food and what kind will have to have been planned for ahead of time. Likewise, the amount of water and type of storage will also have to have been considered.

The first question confronting the commander at this time will be "What do we have to work with?" Questions that may arise would be, for example:

—How did the kitchen stand up?
—Do we have any utilities?
—Are the food storage areas safe?
—Were any supplies lost?

Taking up our bird's-eye view posture, what is the situation? The shaking has stopped. The teams have completed their initial assignments. The primary shock wave of emotion has passed, and now the students are entering the restless phase.

Now is an ideal time for some activity to develop in the food and water department! In our training sessions, brainstorming will have taken place as to the actions to be taken to handle the situation now before us.

At the elementary school level, parents who are going to will have picked up their students. For the remainder, the inescapable fact stares them in the face: no matter what happens next, first we have to prepare to stay where we are for the foreseeable future! This includes shelter, food and drink, and sanitation, not necessarily in that order!

In the main, the elementary school student, as far as possible, will be provided for. At the high school level, one feels that a great deal of the burden could be shared by the students themselves. All car owners should have a minimum of five days' food and water supplies as part of their own emergency planning. How the rest of the problem is handled depends on a number of variables:

—Funding,
—Student enthusiasm,
—Faculty support,
—Ingenuity, and
—Safe storage.

I would start with the present staff of food providers. After all, if you get the cook out of the kitchen full of enthusiasm, a good time might be had by all. Remembering the wizardry of some Army cooks I encountered in the field on combat duty fills me with hope! We could, in the pre-planning stages, challenge the cooks with: "You know, the greatest challenge will be to provide food from the back of a chuck wagon, just as the pioneers did. Got any ideas of what we can do now? To prepare for that day, as it were?" It isn't hard to imagine scenarios from the humorous to the dramatic as a result of that approach. Still, we have to start somewhere!

I had a thought as I wrote these words. What about having the student body build a real "chuck wagon?" It could stand there on campus, in a protected area and, when required, the sourdough pot could be started and pancakes-to-order could be a reality in short order! (No pun intended!)

All joking aside, once the challenge is presented to the student body, I have no doubt that a successful (if unorthodox) approach and solution will be forthcoming, and the campus turned into a multi-colored tent community!

SANITATION

There is much debate, and this writer has strong feelings, about just *how, when,* and *where* the sanitation problem should be handled.

Ideally, sufficient portable toilets will be available and may be so arranged as to enable students to function as normally as possible. Should this not be the case (and it probably won't be) other alternatives will have been researched and agreed upon. Now is the time for these plans to be activated.

To expand a little on this subject and to provide some food for thought and discussion, let us consider some facts:

1. At some time after the quake, those students who will be picked up will have left. The remainder will have already experienced the need for a "potty break," but usually the stress of the moment overrides the first urge.

2. Need overcoming stress, something has to be done. As a stop-gap measure, if the buildings are still standing the existing bathrooms may be pressed into service. If the water supply is still on (if it were turned off early on merely as a precaution, turning it back on under controlled conditions might not be a bad idea), the only problem will be fear of aftershocks causing damage to the structure and the occupants while it is in use.

3. If there is no water supply the use of existing facilities cannot be allowed.

4. As always, in a large population hygiene becomes a number-one concern in the conditions created by disaster.

The problem is magnified when the danger of infections, which can spread rapidly under these conditions, is taken into account, making the *method* of sanitation very important.

Consideration of these factors needs to dominate any planning sessions. With the input from available literature, as well as the ability to provide chemical toilets, hopefully the problems surrounding this situation can be minimized. One thing for sure: no amount of avoidance of the problem will ease the situation. This is a fact that must be faced and, while we are at it, let us also remember the needs of the poor overworked staff at this time. For me, properly constructed and controlled earth toilets are still highly acceptable.

CAMP-OUT ACTIVITIES

Now we are in the final phase of our disaster planning. No matter what the hour of day the earthquake happens to strike, tired minds and bodies will require rest. True, there may not be much prolonged sleep, but rest there must be.

It always seems sad to me, when I read all the manuals put out by various "experts" and school authorities, how the main emphasis is always placed in the wrong area.

"The best laid plans of mice and men gang oft to go awry" is the truest quotation for this situation that could ever be.

Of course, we must plan our search and rescue, our command functions, etc. Our attempt to handle the inevitable must never be weakened. But, we must also accept that the predominance of unknowns in the equation regarding pre-planning make positive conclusions very difficult to establish.

That there *will* be an earthquake is of little doubt.

That there *will* be casualties is also of little doubt.

Somehow, even with all of the variables that could come into play, there is no doubt that the situation *will* be handled. Heroism will prevail. . .

But in retrospect, we may say, "If only I had known, I could have done a better job."

When we move past the immediate time of the quake itself, we come to that period most ignored, yet most stable in its predictability. . .camp-out time—that time when all the initial noise and confusion is past, day is fading into night, and certain actions must now take place.

Most of us who have spent time in Scouts and similar camp-out activities will have a pretty good idea of the approaches to this problem. Community involvement. . .implementation of the "buddy" system. . .utilization of all available skills at hand. . .all make for a successful approach to this very neglected situation. Some details for consideration?

A. Establishment of *organization* as quickly as possible is mandatory to offset post-quake shock.

B. Food and a drink, no matter how small, is the fastest way to establish morale (a fact known to every general and army cook who ever existed)!

C. Self-sufficiency is the establishment of a sense of self-control. It follows that the more the students are able to do for themselves, the better. If each student had their own sleeping bag, how simple life would be at this time!

D. Individual nurture packets should be mandatory. These contain the personal items that students put together themselves, containing information regarding family members (local and out of state), photographs of family members, and little, precious items we all seem to gain comfort from at times of stress.

E. As far as possible, and within the framework of school and parental cooperation, individual survival packs are also the ideal to be aimed for, be it knapsacks, sports bags, or other containers, as long as the package can be grabbed on the way out the classroom. (I have had it said to me in the past, "But it will make the classroom so *untidy*.")

F. Provision for protection from the elements must be considered in this camp-out phase. Protection from the damp of the ground at night, plus protection from the hot sun, cold wind, or rain of the season is the foundation of maintenance of well-being.

G. Activities to support the situation should be well thought-out ahead of time. Left to their own devices, older students will take off during the night, or even during the day, if not occupied. Also, in our pre-planning we will have covered the security aspect. "It's a jungle out there" is a good place to start.

Here we are, with possibly several hundred students all clustered in a safe place, all waiting for some sign that the end of the world is not about to happen. At this point, most of the planning manuals end their text! Conclusion?

There is still a great deal of the educational process to be undertaken. A closer relationship between the parents and the school fraternity must be developed. Community involvement must be analyzed right at the beginning of any disaster planning and considerations. So often, those involved have a mistaken concept of what the community has to offer.

Have you both realized and *accepted* that there will be no police, fire, or paramedic personnel to come dashing down the street with sirens wailing?

As you develop your survival plans, "Check it out" is a great way to start! "Our nearest first aid delivery point will be So and So hospital." Good. Now go to that particular facility and check out *their* reaction to your ideas. You may find all sorts of problems you may have to face.

1. It may not be a trauma center, in the true sense of the word. (Emergency? Yes. Heavy trauma? No.) Find out where they send *their* heavy trauma cases now. Taking your victims *directly* to the proper place may well save lives!

2. Your chosen nearest facility may not be a good choice for several other reasons. Lack of capacity, heavy demands from a close, highly populated community? These are but a few of the problems you would do well to check out beforehand.

A close study of your own facility is required before, sitting in the room you are in at the present time, you make decisions to put the first aid over there, the tent area over there, and so on.

Out in the open, you are advised to "check it out" as you go. Does the wind blow in a certain direction? Might not be ideal for a first aid area! Is there a nice "dip" on the grounds, adding to the shelter factor? Might make a good place for the toilets! This is the kind of thinking to develop in the planning phase. *Reality will not be denied!*

One example comes to mind at the high school and college level. There is no doubt that strong, healthy young adults will not be content to "sit around here!" Going home will be a call as strong as that to any homing pigeon! How do we face this issue?

Well, obviously we can say, "Hey, go for it!" and watch as individuals take off in their various directions. Or. . .we can say, "Now hold on there! Knowing what's out there, prudence dictates a *plan.* Let us determine who is going where and make up some teams." Isn't this a more safe and sane approach?

Couple this kind of thinking with a deeper involvement of the board of education, school administrators, city fathers and town councils and, hopefully, some action may be forthcoming from those who will not stir unless activated!

Bringing some of the pertinent issues that have yet to be faced into the open so that solutions may be developed and responsibilities faced is the aim of all of us involved in this situation. The more grease that can be added to the wheel now can only help to silence the howl of "afterwards," which, of course, will be very loud, and also very late!.

Working together, we should develop a firmer grasp of not only the disaster situation itself, but, more importantly, the desperately needed solutions!

STUDENT SURVIVAL KITS

Just as I believe it is true that reasonableness prevails amongst reasonable people, it is also true that creative thought is stimulated by creative input.

It is my sincere hope that this manual falls into the creative input bracket and that, at this point in the text, those involved with the "school scene" will hopefully, by now, have some creative thoughts of their own!

One thing that stands out to me as I study the text is the stark reality of the shrinking statistic of the adult-to-student ratio and all that it entails. Surely the very numbers of the dependent population should make us recognize the enormity of the problem. Anything that can reduce the burden of dependency from the shoulders of the providers will ease the problems of those first critical few hours.

One of the measures that can help in this regard is the portable survival kit that can easily be assembled at home and carried daily by the students, including the pre-school groups.

Obviously, the size and scope will vary according to the influences that prevail at each individual school site. Basically, the goal will always be the same: to establish as far as possible the independence of the student for the first few hours while the staff is in the process of "getting it all together."

Unlike the auto kit, where a backpack was recommended, in this instance a simple sports bag will suffice. This is easy to take on the school bus, as well as being handy to tuck under the desk. The kit should provide:

1. Personal needs.
>   Change of underwear and tee shirt, etc.
>   Several pairs of socks.
>   Sweat suit or sleep suit.

2. Toiletries.
>   Towel and washcloth.
>   Toothbrush and toothpaste.
>   Roll toilet paper in a ziplock bag.
>   Comb and hairbrush if used.

3. Simple foods and water.
>   Small, 8-oz plastic container of powdered foods and drinks
>   easily mixed with water (Protein powders, fruit powders with

high mineral content).
    Beef jerky, dried fruits, and other foods in this category.
    At least a 1 gal. canteen of water.
    Folding utensil kit.

4. Nurture packet.

This consists of all pertinent data about the student and his/her family and includes photos and out-of-state phone numbers, any medical info, etc.

5. Sleeping blanket.

Directions follow for the construction of a simple sleeping bag made from a blanket. The size of the blanket will depend on the age of the student.

Any special medications that the student normally requires, such as allergy or asthmatic medications, must be available. In most cases, medications are kept by the school nurse and given by her to conform to the doctor's requirements. (Behavioral medications fall into this category, also.) On no account should these type of medications be given to the student to carry in this type of survival gear.

In the case of the pre-school grades, while the contents of the bag may follow a similar pattern, the contents will be tailored more in keeping with these younger students. (A teddy bear was included in the sample pack made up by my wife and me for a Head Start group we were training.) The aim is the same for all student levels. . .reduce the dependency factor as far as possible.

Although we have discussed the needs of both student and adult in this chapter, we now move on to The Workplace, Chapter 6, even though we realize that you teachers are already there!

Basic Sleepsack

Materials Needed:
—Blanket (twin-sized for 3-6 yrs.; full-sized for 7-9 yrs.;queen-sized for 10-14 yrs.; and king-sized for 15 yrs.-adult)
—Needle and spool of button thread or sewing machine

Directions:
1. Fold blanket in half widthwise (See fig. 1).
2. Stitch together the 3 unattached sides (See fig. 2).

3. Fold sewn blanket in half lengthwise (See fig. 3).
4. Stitch together across the bottom and up two-thirds of the side of the blanket (See fig. 4). Leave the top one-third of the side and all of the top open for easy access. (Double-stitching along all areas provide extra reinforcement for those seams and increase overall durability.)

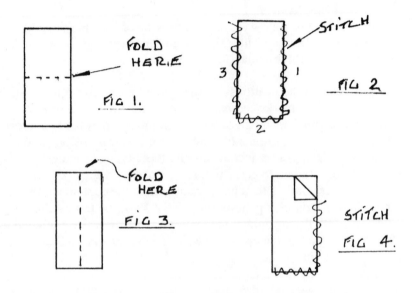

DIRECTIONS FOR MAKING BASIC SLEEPSACK

CHAPTER 6
The Workplace

Like homes, workplaces come in all different shapes and sizes. All, however, have one thing in common. Once we enter them, we are no longer in control of our own survival safety. We are at the mercy of our employers, be they corporations or small businesses. If we are self-employed, that is a different matter. The ball then lands squarely in *our* court!

Over the years, at every opportunity I have had, the subject of worker safety has been given my best shot. Think about it. You go into work each day. As a practicing survivor following along with this manual, you have your survival kit in your car and your home is well on the way to being ready; now, facing the devil you do know (Remember the first rule of survival? Know your enemy!), you are about to face the hazards of your workplace.

If you work in a school, you are ahead of the game. Plans for the students' survival must include you. In other work situations, however, the position must be considered differently. Let's take our by-now-familiar overview.

For the purpose of study, we will refer primarily to employment locations are that are located in the more populous areas in the cities and busy shopping centers. Your task will be to adapt our discussion to *your* employment situation, whether it be a large major plant which has its own grounds and is, in fact, almost a little city of its own or a business in a suburban or rural environment.

Each day, millions of us place ourselves in the hands of our employers, whether they be large factories, banks, schools, or small offices. The employers become our guardians, for want of a better word.

In the large-employer situation, a union or management team is usually involved, placing the actual employer at a distance. The employer becomes a figurehead. In the case of the small business, the employer often is a friend, or becomes one over the process of time. Perhaps you are an employer yourself, or are self-employed, in which cases these remarks will apply to you in reverse, as it were.

Whenever I stand outside a factory or tall office building, my mind always wanders off into "earthquake and survival." Questions pour through my mind:

—What procedures are planned for that place in the event of a disaster that should occur during working hours?
—If there is a union to represent the workers, has an item been placed on the agenda to cover this event with management?
—How much first-aid supplies do they have?
—How many trained first-aid people do they have?
—From a logistics point of view, how many casualties do they expect to have? Leading to,
—Any evacuation/survival plans?
—Any provision for a first aid/triage unit?
—Any supplies of blankets/stretchers for the wounded?
—Plans for "afterwards"? Or do they all go sleep in the street?
—Finally, but by no means all the last that should be asked: What is the state of the buildings? (More about that later!)

I can just hear the response as I have heard it before as I raised these issues: "What do you think this is, wartime?"

My answer is always, "Yes it is. War for the survival of the injured and for their safety. They will possibly die if plans for their needs are not met now!"

This is a family survival manual. Each day, one or both primary family members are placed into a hazardous situation because these issues are not raised. *You are on your own!* Learn that phrase (You should know it by now!) and, above all, accept its consequences. Each day, millions of us go to work and place our well-being and, in the event of catastrophe, our lives on the line without a thought of "What if?" To me, that is a gamble. And good survivalists don't gamble.

We know by now that, in the event of a major disaster, there will be no paramedics, no ambulances, and no public services as we know them now. It must follow that, as a worker, I am responsible for *me*. No one else is taking that responsibility from me. I must know *now* what my chances are and how I can best provide for my own safety. What are the prospects for you in the time of crunch? To answer that question, we must answer other questions, questions about *your* work situation.

Remember the traveler's quiz we took earlier? Here's one for the workplace. A hazard assessment chart. I cannot cover every job situation, but you should be able to place yourself pretty closely by using the category that most suits your own situation.

A word of warning: Most of us, going to work on a morning following a big trembler of the day before, experience a slight uneasiness that comes from knowing our workplace. It's that sub-conscious survival instinct that is saying, "I don't like this!" Completing this quiz will "dot the I's and cross the T's" of that uneasiness. Perhaps you are one of those who daily scream down the freeway at seventy-plus miles an hour and think nothing of it, until you witness a high-speed accident. That same survival voice says, "Hadn't we better slow down?"

To me, good survival comes from facing the *true* hazards of our daily lives as they become clear to us, either from what we hear or what we see. The action we take as a result of this insight is, of course, up to us.

Facing our realities, let's do the following quiz.

WORK HAZARD CHART

Location

Downtown urban area	☐	Hospital	☐
Suburban city	☐	Transportation	☐
Thick commercial area	☐	Self-employed	☐
High buildings	☐		
Narrow streets	☐	Number of Co-Workers:	
Large office	☐		
Small office	☐	1-10	☐
Supermarke	☐	10-20	☐
Small store	☐	20-50	☐
Bank	☐	50-100	☐
Insurance office	☐	100-500	☐
Doctor's office	☐	500-1000	☐
High-rise	☐		
Large single-story	☐		
Mall	☐		
Government office	☐		

It should not be too difficult to assess your job hazards. The object here is not to scare you, but to face your realities and to learn what to do about them. Obviously, if you park your car in a concrete sandwich (a multi-level parking structure) every day, it is reasonable to assume that Mother Nature might eat it for lunch one day! You, knowing this fact, and accepting it, would be well-advised to carry your Go gear with you to the place of work.

Further evaluation of your answers will lead to further insights. Mostly, I want to point out that this kind of process does not, in any way, lead to remarkable fact-finding, but rather the illumination of facts that are already known—circumstances which, in most cases, we knew but "swept under the rug," an attitude which leads, of course, to the I'll-deal-with-it-when-it-happens outlook.

Perhaps you might want to copy this quiz and share it at the workplace. At least it could be the catalyst that results in the development of some survival awareness, especially on the part of management. Who knows? Some actual planning may develop!

Any group of twenty or more workers without a disaster plan seems to me to be engaging in an extreme gamble for all concerned. I could, at this point, go off into a long discussion of who is responsible, but I choose to postpone that issue for Chapter 11.

No union at your place of work? Be your own. Talk it up with co-workers. Ask the questions yourselves.

At many businesses that I go to, like a company with many branches (banks come to mind), the local managers themselves organize their own survival plans and ask for direction. Whether this is company policy or not is not my concern. When I go in at a very early hour, I know that these workers are here on their own time, as I am. To be able to give only a short pitch is good enough for me. At least they are facing the enemy now!

Organize together if you can. The ideal is always "One for all, and all for one," especially in a large plant where survival of self includes protection of others, but if this concept is not feasible, organize yourself as an individual. The priorities are the same. Remember our survival stool?

—Where will I be?
—What will I do?
—What will I need?

There are so many possible combinations attached to the first leg of the stool that I could easily get bogged down in detail. Staying logical, and still using the stool concept, our priorities are involved in protection of self, followed by protection of property. So let's follow the three-legged stool format. First comes:

Where Will You Be?

I like the approach of considering the likely places you could be at quake time and, as far as possible, preparing survival plans for each place. The result is a confident feeling of being ready. Having given *thought* to the situation, you are starting an action *process!* At work you could possibly be:

A. At your work station or desk,
B. In the bathroom,
C. Taking a coffee or lunch break. This could be in a provided place, outside, or at your work station,
D. In an unfamiliar place (going on an errand within the work building, going on an interview, going out to lunch, things like this) that would put you on the stairs, in an elevator, or in a place not part of your usual path or daily routine, or
E. Entering or leaving the building.

These are the five the most likely places. Remember that you can only be in one place at one time. Let's consider each place separately.

A. Work Station or Desk (Your work space)
What's it like? Have you ever stopped and taken *a good look around you*? Could you write an essay and describe your work space *in detail*?
Just as I asked you in to consider the details of your journey from an earthquake point of view in Chapter 3, I ask you now to do the same thing regarding your work space. Be honest in your examination!

—Are there hazards?
—A lot of glass?
—Overhead lights?

Be aware that we are not trying to find *faults,* we are looking for the *hazards!* I'm asking you to do those *simple* things we have been told to do many times (i.e., secure book shelves to the wall, tape windows to prevent flying glass injuries, this kind of action). Look at your work space as though for the first time.

Do you work with machinery? Are there hazards attached to that kind of machinery? Does it contain liquids or chemicals that could spill? Perhaps your safe action is to move away rather then toward your work tools. Always, we must be aware of where safety lies.

It is negative to say "This is a dangerous position" without continuing with the positive "Where is the safe alternative?"

A case in point: I was giving a talk at a county office facility. Rows of desks were placed in front of large floor-to-ceiling windows that were painted to make them opaque.

As soon as my remarks about windows and glass had sunk in, the talk turned to what could be done about those windows. The kneeholes of the desks were open; to dive under the desks would have been futile since flying glass would have injured those attempting to shelter under the desks. I pointed this out to the employees.

As we brainstormed this situation, the consensus was to "run for the door, out of the way" thus being out of the line of fire, as it were, when the shaking started.

My suggestion was to have the open holes covered with plywood, thus making them safe. At the same time, I was able to point out that there is often another solution to make an unsafe situation *safe*, rather than find an alternative safe *situation*. (Remember our discussion about the home? If the couch from which you watch T.V. leaves your back to a window, going to sit in another room has not made the first room safe; covering the window with clear tape will.)

So taping windows, perhaps moving the work station a few feet, and securing objects all serve to remove possible hazards and make an unsafe location safe. We are always looking for the *hazards,* thus creating a safer environment, even if *total* safety is not possible.

Another rule about your work station or place is "Always be aware of another way out!" Become familiar with your immediate surroundings as well as the building in general. So often we are so totally involved with our daily tasks that we are not really sure of what is across the hall. We need to increase our awareness to include these details.

There may be other problems that you cannot solve for yourself, such as being in a high-rise building. Most of these buildings have all of the alternate exits clearly marked on floor plans and posted throughout the building. Become familiar with these routes. They may save your life in an emergency situation created by smoke or debris, etc. Don't be caught in a situation similar to looking at the first aid manual after you encounter a severe wound; it's a bit too late then to try to find your way out!

B. At the bathroom

Bathrooms are, in the main, a safe place to be. Due to the nature of the construction requirements, bathrooms have a number of extras not found in other rooms: extra blocking to help keep pipes in place, tiles on the walls and floors (set in grout and cement-like compositions) serving to add strength to the walls.

It was a standing joke in London to see, in the rubble of a building, the toilet standing free and proud, usually accompanied by at least one wall. I always made a mental note to head for the "john" at the appropriate time!

Another plus is that the bathroom has little or no window glass to worry about. Take a good look around at your potty place. Look at it from a new perspective. Seek out the possible hazards if the quake should come while you are in there.

In survival planning discussions at the staff level, some emphasis must be placed on bathroom safety, for want of a better term. Bathrooms are notorious for having little or no way out. When there is a window, it is usually high up over the alley or busy street. In commercial buildings, if there is no window, an exhaust fan takes its place. People in the bathroom can easily be overlooked and, if the door is jammed, people could be left behind.

If you are planning strictly for your own survival at the workplace, be sure that you use the bathroom on a buddy-system basis. Let a friend know when you go to the bathroom. In the event of an emergency, *someone* will know where you are.

C. Coffee or Lunch Break

Do you have a cafeteria or lunchroom? Or do you eat at your desk? Or perhaps outside? Consider break time, individual to you, as a place you might be at quake time.

Just as you are not familiar with my day, I am not familiar with yours. For this subject of the "break" then, I can only generalize. Consider your situation:

—Is your lunchroom large or small?
—Many tables and chairs like a restaurant?
—Where are the exits?
—How strong are the tables?
—Look up; what sort of lighting is used? Which way do they run?

I always look up at lights. The industrial kind with its big starter will weigh almost thirty pounds. Well-lighted cafeterias have dozens of them, all held up by lengths of thin chain or wires. Always be aware of what is over your head waiting to come down.

Consider the counter configuration. Does it have long rows of entrees sitting in hot water waiting to be selected? At the end of the counter, are there separate coffee stations with urns of hot coffee? As you sit and eat your meal, take a moment to look around and pick out the hazard spots. That counter would not be a good candidate for a "cave," not with all that hot water and food in trays. Also, stay away from the coffee station. Those urns will fall down.

What is the design of the room? A large auditorium with pillars supporting the ceiling? Where is your shelter? Under the table? How strong is it? Next the windows. How big? Any drapes or blinds? Do you sit near them?

All these countermeasures (no pun intended) to a hazard are necessary for the alert survivalist. Always the age-old question "Which way is out?" must be foremost in our thoughts.

Finally our last likely place to be in at work:

D. Unfamiliar places

By unfamiliar places, I mean places you don't go very often. We are creatures of habit. We do most familiar things by rote. We go in the same door, leave by the same route, go to our workplace and stay there. Usually, the only time we move from our work spot is for a coffee break or a potty stop.

Let's say that, for some reason, you have to go to the boss's office on the fifth floor. You work on the second floor. Is the layout exactly the same? Are you sure? Where are the stairs from the boss's office? Where are they from yours? Turn the same way out of his door as yours?

Being survival conscious means being aware even at those moments when we are off guard and in unfamiliar surroundings. Those strange places will get us every time!

So what's the bottom line of "Where will I be?" I think we could sum it up with one word, *familiarity.* It is essential that we be absolutely familiar with the places we work—so familiar that we could motivate in the dust and confusion of an earthquake.

Now we move on to some *action.* All this time we have been *planning.* Now we do!

What Will You Do?

Now we consider action in a building, as we did in the school.

There are some rules to follow:

—Be aware of hazards.
—Know where the glass is.

Why do I keep harping on glass? Because glass does not stand up in earthquakes. It not only shatters, it flies with great velocity. Glass cuts, badly. Glass cuts bleed, profusely. We want to avoid this hazard. Avoid glass. Know where it is.

—Be aware of what is up.

Ducking and tucking is one thing; not looking up first is stupid. Know what is above you wherever you are.

What can we *do?* Obviously we need a shelter to get under: a desk or a table, that big bookcase. Be sure that the object can stand the weight of the object you are avoiding!

Go back to the house section and study the Law of Caves. Apply the same principles in this situation. The shaking starts. What are you going to do?

Being familiar with the question (After all you have gone over this a dozen times, right?), you are going to head for cover from your hazard. You know what to expect—rumbling, the floor rolling, stuff crashing down, dust and noise everywhere, glass exploding and shattering across the room. . .you choke and cough and cover you mouth. . .

Now it all stops and, for a split second, it is perfectly still.

Then all hell breaks loose as everyone, at the same time, "comes back down to earth." You are aware of cries from injured people and the swirling dust, but, most of all, you are aware of your desire to get out!

Stay calm. Do not rush for the exits as soon as the shaking stops. Everyone else will be trying to get out, too. Be aware of all exits and use the one not commonly used—an uncommon way out, as it were.

Most likely, when the first shaking stops, you will want to take stock of your surroundings. Be mindful of the aftershocks that are to come. That bookcase that almost broke free of the restraints most certainly will next time. That fixture just hanging on one chain will most surely not survive another shockwave.

Is getting out my highest priority right now? If I am in a safe place, is where I am going worth the hazardous journey there?

Most companies, of any size, should hold drills. If not, hold some of your own during break and lunch times. Practice some "What-will-I-dos" for each of the five places you might be. Go to them and look around, then go through the drills.

"Here's the cafeteria. I'll dive under the table or, if I'm over there, I'll dive under the window. That way the glass will go over me. At the counter, am I? I'll get on the floor and roll away from that hot counter!"

Get the idea? Don't pooh-pooh it. If you practice, in your mind you are programmed. If not, you will freeze up mentally and most likely do nothing as a piece of glass slashes your face.

Perhaps you find yourself in a position where evacuation is called for. Using your chosen exit, *stop* before you rush outside! Be cautious! Look for hazards of falling masonry. Does your workplace have one of those fancy facades? They are notorious for falling down very close to the building. If danger is *present* and *seen* before you exit, don't go on. Backtrack and use an alternate way out. We researched all this, remember? The object of all that research and practice was to give you the confidence that will prevent a panic. This is a prime example:

"Stuff falling down all over the place, looks like a wall is going. . .got to get out. Let's see, where am I? Oh, yes. In the west hallway. The door is at the north end. Here I am. There's the door and I am outta here!!! Whoops, wait a minute, gotta be cautious. Whoa, look at that whole chunk of masonry hanging over the doorway! Let's see, the nearest other exit without going back into. . ."

Get the message? Think survival. Be ready! Summary then:

—Where will you be? Somewhere at work.
—What will you do? What you have trained yourself to do.
—What will you need? That's next.

What Will You Need?

Always, at this point in the text, no matter the chapter, I have to stop and get hypothetical. Not knowing your answers to the quiz, I have no idea as to your particular circumstance, so I have to generalize. You are either in or out of the building (If your company has a survival plan you must go with it unless your own safety is in jeopardy) and the shaking has stopped.

Now, you are already aware of your decision process. (Your Go-or-Stay decision from Chapter 3, remember?) This will now dictate your course of action.

If you are a Go type, you will want to locate your supplies and do just that! Remember, of course, that your action is being dictated by the environment you are in. A dangerous situation will require a faster Go. A safe situation would allow more time for preparation. Time of day, etc., are all factors. We talked about that in the other chapters.

If you are of the Stay group, you still have one more decision to make: whether to stay here at the workplace, go out there with your automobile, or, if circumstance warrant, find a place away from the vehicle, in a safer environment.

Now can you see how pre-disaster planning is so vital? For example, here is this large company that employs a high percentage of female employees (an insurance company, for example). After the quake, the building is in great shape, but the office is in a downtown high-rise and most of the workers travel in from the suburbs (some over an hour's drive). With no provision or planning for this inevitable situation, what happens now?

The lights are off. It is late afternoon on a winter day. Daylight is fading fast. What do all these people do? I could spend many pages on that situation! So what do you *need?*

It depends on which type you are:

1. The Go type.

Get your gear, change your clothes and *go,* giving thanks for your own energies and planning. Think about Chapter 3 and be careful!

2. Part of the Stay brigade.

You will need to make an immediate assessment as to the safety of the building. It will be either safe or unsafe. If safe, put into effect the plans that accommodate the living together of both sexes. You will need:

1. A change of comfortable clothing.
2. A supply of your personal toiletries and any special medications.
3. Sleeping gear, include a sleeping bag and pillow. An air mattress would be great.
4. Morale and well-being materials.

Group requirements include:

—First aid supplies sufficient for the size of the group.
—First aid personnel trained for triage duties.
—Water sufficient for the group.
—Food likewise.
—Toilet facilities. Except for rare instances, chemical inside toilets are a *must*.
—Cooking and food equipment.
—Eating and drinking requirements.
—Communications, at least a radio.

These are the basics for a group of workers who are required to stay as a group. As you can visualize, if you have not planned in advance, you are indeed in a sorry state, to put it mildly.

As an interesting aside, let me tell you about a report in the newspaper recently (September 1992). This concerned a survey done as a project by a large newspaper. The survey questioned two groups (both in California):

1. The scientists and workers at the Seismic Facilities, and
2. Fire, police, and paramedics.

Now here are the startling survey results. Those in the first group, the scientists and workers involved in everyday activities associated with the earth and all its daily activities, had survival supplies *in their cars, at the workplace, and at their homes!*

The second group, those who are out amongst the public every day, expressed a fatalistic I'll-deal-with-it-when-it-happens approach.

Now, reviewing our progress so far at the workplace, what is your opinion? Yes, I agree; it's time to get organized.

We can easily see that, for those who stay at the job site for a given period of time (and I stick to my ten days as a minimum), there are a lot of issues to be discussed, issues that will involve the actual location itself. The style of building and how much natural light is available will be factors in our planning for afterwards.

Now, what of those who are in the Stay group, but whose building does not make it? A very difficult situation indeed.

In the pre-planning stage, the question of "building condition" will have come up. Such things as the age of the building, its design, the very location itself will, or at least should, have pinpointed a weak situation to be allowed for in countermeasures.

What are the alternatives?

First, we should look at the possibility of outside storage for our supplies. A smaller out-building, storage shed, or garage, perhaps. If there are some outside areas (gardens, lawns, etc.), look for possible sites for a portable building.

Supposing, by location alone, our workplace has little chance of survival? A small building in a forest of high-rises or other structures that pose a danger? We might have to consider splitting the supplies amongst the workers to be stored in their cars.

If we doubt our building's integrity, what are the chances of a camp-out situation on the company grounds? In that case, purchase of several individual tents or a large, circus-type tent capable of holding the staff seems to be an option. If company grounds are not available, then certainly the local area must be explored for safe locations for the staff to go. Where is the nearest open land? A park perhaps? (Remember my saying those same words in Chapter 4? But then, isn't a group of workers like family?)

The bottom line is that all workers will fall into either the Go or the Stay category. Having to stay means not sleeping in the street. Having to stay without any planning beforehand is too much of a disaster for even me to contemplate! Given the present state of readiness in the workplace, that is exactly what we are facing. . .*a disaster* upon a disaster (no humor intended).

Before we leave our discussion of the workplace, we must, unpleasant as it is, cover another most important area: first aid. Like schools, the majority of companies, especially non-manufacturing types, are very poor when it comes to first aid. After all, how many traumas occur in the computer room? The example of the large insurance company comes to mind. Civil services and county offices also fit this group. A cut finger? Reach in the drawer and pull out a Band-Aid!

In the aftermath of disaster, this will not do. Several dozen workers will need more than Band-Aids! This, then, is the workplace:

—Be it ever so humble it's where I earn my bread,
—Be it ever so mighty its needs must still be fed!

Disaster knows no boundaries and observes no status symbols. In the workplace we are indeed at risk. But there is still time to provide solutions for the *known* problems.

Now, what about a hazardous plant? Say a paint factory in full operation at quake time? Would not survival preparations include a shut-down procedure? In the interests of public safety, we cannot just run off and leave things to chance.

Or can we? Will we?

Now, before we leave the workplace, what about the other side of the coin? The employer. Are you an employer?

—Who is responsible for worker safety?
—In the aftermath, can the employee sue his employer? ("You did not provide for me!")
—Or can the employer hold the employee responsible? ("You did not show responsibility. You ran off and left the pot boiling!")

Ideally, all those in a given workplace will work together to plan for the preservation of life. One thing that stood out so clearly in London during the bombing was that early medical service was essential for the continued survival of the victim. We *must* be prepared.

"You are on your own" does *not* have to prevail at the workplace. Sure, there are budget problems, political problems, and a host of other ramifications. Even so, one feels that determined people can overcome all obstacles, if the outcome justifies the means. I can think of no greater justification for concerted action than life itself!

Now let's go on to the next area outside our control, those other places in Chapter 7.

CHAPTER 7
Other Places

The Stores and Those Errands

Of the four places we can be at the time of an earthquake, we can pretty well establish, using logic and studying our daily habits, where we are *most* likely to be at a given hour of the day. "Other places" was last on our list and, in most cases, that's where it is—last on the list! ("Got to remember to pick up some milk on the way home!" or "Don't forget you have the dentist this afternoon!")

We are most vulnerable while at these other places. At most other times, our whereabouts are known to the rest of the family, even without a lot of communication. We all know that Dad is at work from nine to five (or whatever the hours are). We know the children are at school, and that Mum works part-time from ten till three at the store. Under normal conditions, like the planets revolving around the sun, all keep their place. . .until someone breaks the routine! Then, we are indeed on our own, in more ways than one. Consider the following little scenario:

Betty is at work and her girlfriend calls. "Hi Bets. Cindy here. Say, you remember that recipe that we talked about? Do you think if we had lunch you could give it to me? I'll buy!"

They arrange to meet and all goes well. Betty gives Cindy the recipe, and, after a short meal heads back to the office. On the way back to her office, Cindy has a slight fender bender. Knowing she is going to be late, she calls the office to explain. Her boss says, "Say, it's quiet this afternoon and you sound shook up; why not take the rest of the afternoon off?"

The accident report goes faster than she thought and, since it is early, Cindy decides to stop off at the mall, which is just two off-ramps away. Besides, when the going gets tough, the tough go shopping!

Cindy's husband gets off a little early and calls her office to see if she would like a dinner date. Hearing that she has had an accident he is frantic. . .

You can write your own end to this little playlet. There are at least four endings that I can think of!

The point is that, in the area of the other places, we often flit from place to place and are not aware of either time or location. From our family's point of view, we might as well have dropped off the planet!

The concern regarding other places is that, in the main, we are so preoccupied with the activities we are engaged in that we are not consciously aware of our surroundings. Unless we develop a "survival" method of thinking, we can end up in the wrong place at the wrong time when disaster hits.

Let me expand on that a little by sharing my own attitudes on this other-places thing.

First of all, I am always "survival conscious" of my surroundings. Entering a strange building, I at once establish the basics:

"What's up above?" Danger of falling objects.

"Where are the exits?" Other than the door I came in.

"How large is the roof span?" Meaning what are the chances of a cave-in?

"How many stories?" This combined with the age of the building may keep me out, period!

I always ask myself, "If the earthquake happened now, where and how many are my hazards?" As a result, I have established a set of loose rules that I follow. They go something like this:

1. Always establish a safe parking spot for your car, even if this means walking a little farther than you would like. If the spot up front is close to a hazard for my vehicle, I don't park there.

2. Always try to use the same supermarket and the same stores. These places have passed my own set of rules:

—They are of simple layout; I can find my way around in the dark.

—The management leaves the layout alone; it's not changed around every other week.

—The counters are strong and will provide good "caves."

—The building has steel-beam construction that I can see

with my own eyes. I can see what is up there; I don't have to wonder about what is behind that false ceiling.

—They have rear exits with which I am familiar. The manager may not know I know, but I do! This means that, first, I can find my way back there in the dark, and second, that I will not have to compete with all the other customers to exit the building.

3. Avoid malls or large stores on the weekend. Monday, those same stores are empty; you can shop in half the time and have the safe spots to yourself.

"Other places" and our three-legged stool of survival? Same principles, same format, so:

Where Will You Be?

By now, you will have realized that we can no longer say "Where will I be?" and get a definitive answer like "at work," "at home," etc. These other places cover a lot of ground! Ever call a friend's house and be greeted with, "Now let me see. They said they were going to the store, but then they might have gone to. . ."? We have all had this experience! So it is important to realize that we now are dealing with *spontaneous* situations, events that occur on the run, as it were.

Because we pay so little attention to these types of seemingly unimportant little journeys, we can easily be caught in an unprepared position. And you know by now that good survivalists are *never* caught unprepared! Considering all the factors involved, is it possible to familiarize ourselves and therefore prepare for even the "other places"? Why not?

I have condensed the vulnerable other places into nine possibilities. Remember, you can only be in one place at a time!

The NINE List

1. At the stores.

This can be the supermarket, a small specialty store off the beaten track, a giant mall containing stores on many levels, those mega builders' supply houses (a favorite of the do-it-yourselfers). I also include the post office, the bank, and the D.M.V. in this category. These are the most frequent, routine places we go and, due to our working habits, it seems we all hit these places at the same time. This first section, then, could be called "popular places."

2. Specialty businesses or facilities.
Beauty salon, health club, work-out place, this kind of thing.

3. Somewhere by appointment.
Doctor's office, dentist, lawyer's, getting the car fixed, etc.

4. Night school or special training center other than a job.

5. Hospital.
Either visiting or as a patient.
6. Visiting.
Friends, neighbors, short-term or stay-over.

7. A night out.
Going out on the town may include a long drive, dinner and a show, formal or informal, alone or with a group.

8. A sports event.
At a large stadium for a professional event or in a smaller setting for the local school team.

9. Vacation time.
Could be at a popular resort, away in the country, at the beach with family, etc.

These are the nine categories that I feel are the most suitable, covering the basic life situations for those of us who are "average." Obviously, there are a whole variety of other places that would be included for with those who have special life styles. Even so, they could all fit, from a survival point of view, into one of these categories.

Our reactions must, as far as possible, be standardized for each of these situations. No, I am not going to ask you to learn nine routines! That would be asking too much and encourage the response "I'll deal with that when it happens!" (Which I could understand.) No, learning a set course of action is not the object. Life and situations are too complex for that.

What is expected is that, with a few pointers, you will develop survival habits that will swing into play instinctively. Good old habits; they control our lives! (But that is another study!)

Study of the nine situations leads to a summary:

—Most are "in" somewhere and involve heavy concentrations of people.
—Two could be "outdoors," but still in an organized facility (like a stadium).
—All involve large or small buildings and/or a house-like atmosphere.
—A hospital.

Can we be more specific? Let's try. How about:

The SEVEN List

1. In a very crowded place (everyday).
2. In a quiet place (once in a while).
3. In a large building, or
4. In a small building.
5. In a complex such as hotel, hospital, federal building, etc. (rarely).
6. In the open air, such as lake, beach, country, etc. (sometimes).
7. A house-like setting, such as professional offices.

Do you notice a pattern beginning to emerge?

The FIVE List

1. Large crowds in a large building.
2. Small crowds in a small building.
3. A well-organized large environment.
4. House setting, very quiet.
5. Open air.

Which leads us to:

The THREE List

1. Things we do almost every day.
2. Special events, maybe once in a while.
3. Things most of us do rarely.

Our original NINE locations are consolidated to SEVEN, which, in turn, are condensed to FIVE. These FIVE, then, are reduced to

THREE very important factors: things we do everyday, things we do once in a while, and things we do rarely. To go one step further with this process, we learn that:

—Actions for everyday activity must be learned by *rote,* a learned habit.
—Actions we do once in a while need to have a well-thought out plan of action.
—Actions we do rarely can be given some thought, too, but can be dealt with at the time. I am sure that this is the only time I will agree with the I'll-deal-with-it-when-it-happens crowd! (It just shows how even a good survivalist must learn to be flexible!)

So, you will be in one of nine places. You are *most likely* be in a large crowded store, for these are things we do almost every day. This will account for Number 1 on the NINE list, Numbers 1 and 3 of the SEVEN list, and Number 1 of the FIVE list. First then the. . .

Large, Crowded Store

Supermarkets, department stores, builders' supply places, those giant drug emporiums, electronic stores, etc.—a brief list is sufficient for you to get the picture. We are considering here the type of place where a lot of people are all intent on doing the same thing at the same time, and then getting the heck outta there!

Most of the buildings conform to a singular design; they are intent on seeing how wide a span can be achieved between four walls! Looking up, one is confronted with a varying pattern of lighting fixtures (not intended for the survivalist's eyes!). Another standard feature of these kinds of stores are the rows of shelves that make up the aisles that we all walk down, pushing shopping carts (or "buggies," as they used to be called) of various designs. These display shelves are worth a moment's study. Some are fixtures, very solid in their design; others are the "erector set" type that are constantly being taken down and put up again with the intent, it seems, of confusing the shopper.

To our advantage is the fact that there have to be delivery doors in back somewhere. Not so encouraging are the "cattle barriers" that we all have to pass through to comply to the electronic surveillance needs. Rapid exit? Forget it!

Picturing yourself in a large store during a quake must make it very obvious, now that you are a little more quake-conscious than you were before, that certain places are more hazardous to your health *during* a quake than others. What is even more significant is that certain areas are even more hazardous from the *"after quake"* aspect. Examples? A single-story house on an acre of land would certainly be in less danger from aftershocks than would a narrow, sky-scraper-lined street in the middle of a downtown business district. The former is relatively safe, whilst the latter is fraught with danger. Similarly, that quiet house on one acre is a safer risk at the actual time of the initial jolt than the busy supermarket.

Put the quake itself *and* the aftershocks that will follow into the same time frame, and it's clear that a large store is not the best place in the world to be at quake time. That's why you won't read about it in survival manuals! We have to go about our daily business and, unlike others in flood or atmospheric situations, we will have no warning. We cannot, however, just shrug off the situation.

In the text, so far, two facts stand out very clearly. First, there is a great difference between the danger from the *primary* shock wave and danger from the series of *secondary* shocks. In the first case, we are at the mercy of nature and our location at the time. In the second case, however, we are very much in control of our own destiny. We are in control of what we *do,* and what we have already *done* in the form of preparedness.

Second, we must recognize when we are in a vulnerable situation over which we have no control, either during or after the quake itself. For the most part, there has been *no attempt to face this issue* by those in charge of the facilities we happen to frequent (public transportation, shopping centers, government offices, hospitals, and, of course, our places of work). We are at the mercy of their state of readiness (or non-readiness). If they play it loose, then there is little hope for prolonged survival.

Facing these facts helps us to at least attempt some act of responsibility for ourselves. We must never forget, for even a moment, that our priorities are still the same no matter what:

—Protection of self,
—Protection of possessions, and
—Survival afterwards.

Let's go now to our second most likely place to be in at quake time:

Small Quiet Stores

This covers Number 1 on the NINE list, Numbers 2 and 4 on the

SEVEN list, and Number 2 on the FIVE list. These smaller stores are either miniatures of the big stores or they are patterned after the old "Ma and Pa" stores so familiar when I was a kid. They are usually quite narrow and have a single front entrance, with a back door "back there somewhere." Usually, they are not crowded, a fact which is relevant to our concerns and which may be significant to prospects of survival. The structure of the smaller store is usually quite strong, as they were normally well-designed and have often endured for a period of time with different owners.

Although some of the smaller stores can be quite wide, this is the exception rather than the rule. From our survivalist's point of view, the smaller stores usually have good, strong counters.

Into this small-crowd, small-building situation could be fit Numbers 2 and 3 on the NINE list and, in some cases, Number 4 on the FIVE list. Number 2 represents those specialty boutiques and similar establishments such as florists, cleaners, etc., while Number 3 represents places usually attended by appointment and can be in either a small building or a large office structure.

Having looked at these places which we frequent regularly, let's now consider some of the less frequented places we may be.

Large, Well-organized Environment

This category includes Numbers 4, 5, 7, and possibly 9 on the NINE list, Number 5 on the SEVEN list, and Number 3 on the FIVE list. "Large, *well-organized environment*" refers to organization from a *business* point of view, not *survival* organization! Of all places, these *should* be earthquake safety-conscious, but it is our experience, unfortunately, that they are not. Let's hope time may change this situation.

Hotels, hospitals, federal buildings, and the like are what we are describing here. We go to them infrequently and, when we do, our "space" is well defined. Through posted signs, we are directed to parts of the building that we are supposed visit. Usually, these are multi-storied affairs using elevators for transportation.

Sporting Events, Open-air Functions, and (of course) Vacations

This category includes Numbers 8 and 9 on the NINE list, Number 6 on the SEVEN list, and Number 5 on the FIVE list.

Vacations and sporting events overlap all the sections because they can take place in every conceivable type of location.

Sporting events, for example, can come under the heading Large, Well-organized Environment, as they often use very large, (hopefully) well-organized facilities and/or stadiums. (Crowd control is always great, but is there thought for disaster?)

Similarly, a night on the town, with or without friends, may use a hotel-type building, as would some vacations.

Now we come to our last area:

House-like Setting

Number 6 on the NINE List and Numbers 7 and 4 on the other lists can be located in a house-like setting. It is very interesting how much we can be involved in this kind of situation. Of course, visiting friends is the classic. But what about the many doctors, dentists, and other professionals who do business this way? Or the times we go for a meeting in a friend's house? We are often placed in a situation of being in "a house." Large or small, plain or fancy, it is still a house and we must consider it in our survival plans.

Now, on to the second leg of our survival stool. This is where I always say a quiet "Oh, dear!" for it is such a tough section to write and, of course, even tougher to be in.

What Will You Do?

Welfare of self; safety of possessions; now what?

How can we fit these goals into such a hazardous situation? How, indeed, if we find ourselves in *the most hazardous* situation possible, like the large busy supermarket?

First, I encourage you to develop a "survival sense." I don't know how else to describe it. We spend time talking about "Where will I be?" This is a planning stage, then we go on to "What will I do?" This is an action stage. But, in between there somewhere is an abstract stage of consideration. It is this consideration that is so hard to define.

You have heard it said, "So and so's are born, not made." These statements usually refer to people talented in an area of the arts, business, or sports. I believe this is also true of survivalists of all kinds. Some seem to catch on right away, intuitively, and take to the situation like a duck to water.

We must try to develop this intuition, for it is the key to the assessment of a situation. What sort of building is it? Does it have a huge roof span with very few support pillars? (Oh, I know they are all to code, but they still come down!) Take into consideration the width of the aisle, the distance to the exits, and the stacked height of the shelves. Consider the hazards that you see around you. It may mean your survival.

If your favorite store has very few or difficult exits and looks to be tough to get out of, change stores and reduce your hazards.

What will you do?

Suddenly the shaking starts, the floor bucks and tremors. You have a nasty feeling in your stomach that this is it. . .and you are right. Things start to fall off the shelves, there are loud, unexplained bangs (cases breaking away from the walls, structures breaking), and the sound of breaking glass. Soon, panicked screams begin, more stuff comes off shelves and, about now, the lights will go off and you are in the dark. (No point in my continuing; the shaking will stop.)

What will you do?

First of all, accept that you are not going to be able to move away from where you are. The shaking floor will not let you! If you have not planned what to do, that's exactly what you will do—nothing!

What must you prepare to do?

Now that sounds better. Now, in the quiet, let us go over a few drills. Our survival considerations, as it were. While walking around the store, pretend you have to take cover. Here, where you are. Now, over there. Here at the produce section. Now, over there at the bakery section and there by meats. Notice that each has a different environment.

Some sections have high shelves, some have low. Some are arranged in long lines, some in squares. Some areas have items that will fall and cause injury, others—hey, a loaf of bread isn't that dangerous, is it?

Remember the Law of Caving? "All items are trying always to return to Mother Earth." How an item will fall to earth, if released, depends on whether another item stops it or part of it by being in its path on the way down? Remember?

As you go around the stores in this the quiet time, think about all these considerations. Make a game up for your family or friend. Call it, "If It Happened *Now!* " and take the defensive action. Yes, right there in the store. Oh, you don't have to actually get down on the floor, but you can sort of shimmy into the shelves a little. Look up every so often to get an idea of what is up there from different parts of the store.

Now, shall we do it all over again? Again and again, in every store and place you are in. The same rule applies to small buildings.

How about in the doctor's waiting room? What sort of building is it? A quiet house, a small office? A large medical complex? Use an elevator? Where are the stairs?

Say you are sitting in the beautician's chair. How nice to have someone working on your hair; isn't it relaxing? What is that right in front of you there? A large store window? Oh, dear! All that is between you and all that glass is air! Bring yourself to say, "Sally, I know you think I am weird, but could I sit in that last chair back there rather than this one by the window?"

Many other small-building situations are of a different nature. The cleaners would be a good example of one of them. This type of business, and others of a similar environment, are types of places that we enter only partially. The entry and the small area we occupy are only a fraction of the whole building. Our survival actions are concerned only with that part we are in.

The cleaners, the printers, and many other small businesses have similarities. One enters from the front, through a door that usually stands open, into a narrow space in front of a counter. We at once notice that, at our back, there is a large store-front window that takes up the whole wall. The person behind the counter is in great shape; all he has to do is duck. That leaves us in between the counter and a sheet of glass. Not good.

Present building codes normally specify a required height from the floor to the bottom of a window as a non-glass area. This space, usually a minimum of two feet, will make a safe place for you to throw yourself so that the glass goes *over* you, not into you. You now have a vital piece of new information. If this was not part of your previous considerations, afterwards you could have been saying "I wish I had thought of that!" as you nursed all your stitches.

Are we ready to venture into the large supermarket again? Now, as the shaking starts you have an awareness. You start to go down there, in front of that counter, like an old pro! See the importance of being familiar with "your" store? Have it figured out. There are three basic steps for you to follow. You will have figured them out in your own practices.

First, look for the sites of those caves. At the base of some counters there is a "back slope" to allow people to stand close to the counter without stubbing their toes. Try, if possible, to make it to one of these cave sights when the shaking starts. Adopt the crouch and cover technique. Crouch down as far into a shelter as possible, make a ball of your body and cover your head with your arms. As soon as the tremor stops, be prepared for all the dust and noise we have already talked about.

Second, *do not panic!* You knew what it was going to be like. You were prepared. The lights may be out. So what; you know the way out. Take stock of your situation. It will not matter that there is panic and confusion; you are not panicked. Look at the way to your exit—is it clear? If not, look for your alternate. Are you hurt or cut? Try to stop the bleeding, or support the limb if you have a contusion or break. Now, in a calm and orderly manner. . .

Execute Step Three. Exit the building. *If no one else went out ahead of you, stop at the doorway before you go out.* This is so important. Stores are notorious for having fancy facades and over-hangs. Most of these will come down. How sad to get out of the building and fall victim to a hanging structure that is waiting to fall as you attempt your exit. If others are leaving unhindered ahead of you, you know it must be safe.

Now let us go back to our original NINE List at the beginning of the chapter and see what we have covered in our general discussion of "What Will I Do?"

1. *At the stores. Did that.*

2. *Specialty businesses, hairdresser, etc. Did that.*

3. *Somewhere by appointment (doctor etc.). Did that.*

4. *Night school or special training. Let's put it in with large buildings and. . .*

5. *Hospitals.*
There is a group of locations (Number 3 of the FIVE List) that I describe as a "well-organized, large environment." I made the remarks then—and they bear repeating now—that, by *well-organized*, I refer to the inner workings of these facilities. Typically, hospitals are well drilled on emergency procedures (most of them unrealistic), yet have made no plans for the evacuation or care of the patients should the hospital (by some completely overlooked cir-cumstance) be included on Mother Nature's list of places to be destroyed! In hospitals, as in the rest of the public services, there is a pie-in-the-sky attitude that all the wheels will turn as always. Somehow, the fact that police, fire, and rescue vehicles will be as immobile as the rest of us has not yet registered.

6. *Visiting.*

"Friends, neighbors, short-term or stay-over" was the way we described this situation in our original list. You know, it's a funny thing. We in California (and across the country as we are now finding out) sit on this time bomb about to explode at any moment, and yet, for various reasons, we are mostly lulled into a sense of a completely false It-can't-possibly-be-that-bad attitude. Even when we do take precautions and prepare, we have our unguarded times, when, due to the circumstances of the moment, problems of *any* kind are left far behind.

Visiting is one of those times. Just to consider visiting is to conjure up fond thoughts of good times and fun! Going to a friend's house, making that trip to see the loved ones far or near, all are the quintessence of the "good life."

"Earthquakes? Catastrophe? What are you, some kind of killjoy? Come on!" But we are survivors, and survivors are always looking for hazards, remember? So use the same principles when visiting: "Where is the way out?" etc. You know the routine.

7. *A Night Out.*

This one really sweetened the pot! Oh, the grim reality of being a survivalist! Does it always have to be grim and serious? Of course not! *The quality of life after depends on the quality of the preparations taken before*, remember? Taking those preparations and covering all the bases is what this manual is all about.

It was necessary for me to give you that little preamble introducing this section primarily to underscore that there is no time that we can forget to be ready. We must not leave any chinks in our armor of self-defense. We, as serious survivors, cannot afford the dubious luxury of being "lulled."

I consider "Visiting" and "A Night Out" to be situations in which we are almost as vulnerable as when we are "At the Stores." Once again let's take an overview:

Wife: "Hi Hon. Dave and Ann called. They have tickets for
    a concert. They want us to go with them. Their treat!"
Husband: "Gee, that's nice. Where is it?"
Wife: "Long Beach, I think."
Husband: "When is it?"
Wife: "This weekend."
Husband: "Can we get a sitter?"
Wife: "No problem."
Husband: "Sounds good; let's do it!"

Anything wrong with that little scene? Of course not. It happens somewhere every day. Then what's my point? Why put that scene in this text at all? Now I am going to re-write the script and then tell me what you think.

Wife: "Hi, Hon. Dave and Ann called. They have tickets for a concert. They want us to go with them. Their treat."

Husband: "Gee that's nice. Where is it?"

Wife: "Long Beach, I think."

Husband: "Long Beach! Holy smoke, when is it?"

Wife: "This weekend. Why, what's the matter?"

Husband: "What's the matter? Several things. Honey, Long Beach is over an hour's drive from here—"

Wife: "Honey, it's the weekend. We don't have to get up and, besides, since when has an hour's drive stopped us?"

Husband: "Hey, hold on a minute. Are you forgetting all we have been talking about and planning for Earthquake?"

Wife: "Come on, ease up. This is a free trip and, besides, I can get Marge to sit the kids for us. I don't see what's so big about a little trip to a concert!"

Husband: "Sounds great when you put it that way. But I am concerned. I've got this funny feeling of 'what if' in my gut. You know Long Beach is too far for us to walk home from. Marge would have to take care of the children for at least a week, perhaps longer if we can't get across town without a hassle. We'd have to invite them to all stay at our house. I know they are not prepared and I don't see why our kids should have to suffer. Another thing— we would have to take our car; I know Dave and Ann have no car kit in theirs and God knows I've talked to them enough!"

Wife: "Are you crazy? I'm not having Marge and her lot in my house! But you are right; they are not prepared in any way for a disaster. We talked about it and I know she wants to, but it's George. You know him, one of these I'll-deal-with-it-when-it-happens guys—"

Husband: "Yea, and he'll be over here in a flash when it hits and he needs water!"

Wife: "Oh dear. I know you are right, but why do we have to go through all this? Can't we go out without worrying about how far it is, or whether the folks we're with have a car kit, and what about the children and when will it all happen. What if we are doing all this worrying for nothing?"

I could write several answers for the husband to end this script, as I am sure you could. "Hey, we carry auto insurance, don't we?" could be one of them!

It is my fond dream that this conversation would never happen. The wife would have automatically answered all her husband's questions when the offer was made initially. His concerns would have been her concerns. The issues faced here are issues that are very real, but are not faced today by too many of us. Perhaps, in the future, the percentages may change.

Now, I hope that my opening remarks to this section make more sense, for even the most careful of us can be caught napping. Especially for a free concert!

Only two places are under our own control, remember? Home and the auto. At all other times we are vulnerable. Acceptance? As Shakespeare would say, "Ah, there's the rub!"

Do be aware of the Visiting and the Night Out situations; these can be a real bummer, especially considering walking home in formal clothes. . .

8. *A Sports Event.*

During the 1989 World Series, a minor earthquake hit the San Francisco area just as the game was about to begin at Candlestick Park. Millions of dollars in damage was done to structures in the area. (Remember the pictures of the Nimitz Freeway and the Bay Bridge?) The Commissioner of Baseball postponed that evening's game and allowed it to be played in the same stadium the next week. The logic used was that it was good for morale! Not to mention that the city stood to lose a tremendous amount of money if the game had been moved. I believe this was a moral tragedy because once again the public was lulled into a false sense of security, and an ideal chance to "get real" was lost.

The game was played and there were no major tragedies. (Had there been, what it would have done for morale is up for speculation!) In the light of the investigations which followed, it was discovered that had there been one more major shock wave, the Bay Bridge would have come down (two-inch bolts were sheared like match sticks!) and the stadium damage would have been much more extensive.

In light of this information, knowing the potential for aftershocks resulting in massive stadium damage and spectator injuries, the question arises: On what basis did the Commissioner reached his decision to risk all those lives? Was he one of the It-can't-happen-here brigade?

Fortunately, the aftershocks and injuries did not happen; however, but a lot was learned. We must take advantage of this positive learning situation. Let's consider the "sporting event" in more detail.

Sports events are held in one of two places, as a general rule, although there always are exceptions: in a large outdoor stadium (the Coliseum or Dodger Stadium, for example) or in a closed arena (such as the Forum or one of the large auditoriums). The former are open air, while the later are enclosed structures. From a survival point of view, what is our action and attitude?

Obviously, two different sets of circumstances confront us: the covered building has a whole mass of roof structure to be concerned about, while the open air stadium does not.

Remember our old friend the Law of Caving? That's about all we have going for us here. Facing the fact that the roof will, most likely, cave in (as it did at an empty U.C.L.A. structure recently), your protection is the very seat or bleachers you sit on. The action is to crouch down into the row of seats and ride it out, adopting the duck-and-tuck position.

At the open-air stadium, we have no concern about a falling roof. Some covered stands maybe, but a massive roof? No. As soon as the shaking starts, I have no doubt that everybody will duck and cover. It's a natural instinct and there's nothing wrong with that! "Participating in our own survival" is what the shrinks are wont to say.

Now we have to get serious! Prepare for when the shaking stops. Let's put the scene into perspective. We are at a stadium, closed or open, with 16,000-plus at a hockey or basketball game or up to 100,000 at a football game! We know that it took an awful long time just to get in and get to our seats. And the last thing you want to do once in your seat is to ask yourself, "If it happened now what would I do?" You probably would freak out! Yet, in actual fact, that is the point that I have taken you to in this text: that point in time when you are in your seat and the shaking has stopped. . .

Time to get serious, remember?

As the shaking stops do not rush for the exits!

Sporting events have a long history of negative consequences of panic and a mad rush to the exits. The statistics related to this desire-to-get-out rush are staggering.

In this, the cold light of day (as it were), it is my self- appointed task to try to program you into a built-in set of safety rules. One of the most important, both here and in all the hazards we have faced together so far in print, is that the panic of the attempted exit is the most severe challenge we face.

All basic instincts of survival are urging us to get out, but the screaming mass of humanity must be our incentive not to do so. How can we put it in a logical way that will drive the point home? To me, the very sequence of *getting in* is the best deterrent I know to offset a desire to break the system in *getting out!*

For financial purposes alone (certainly not for safety), all gangways, aisles, and stairs at sports stadiums are steep and narrow; ideal for a missed step and a masses-of-humanity-falling- down-on-top-of-each-other incident!

RAPID, SAFE EXITS ARE NOT POSSIBLE!

Acceptance of this fact is the first rule of survival when the shaking stops. Period. Repeat:

RAPID SAFE EXITS ARE NOT POSSIBLE!

If there is any owner or manager of a stadium *anywhere* who would like to challenge this statement, then I challenge you: Without any pre-arrangements, just cold turkey, the next time your stadium or what-have-you is packed to the rafters (without warning mind you), have the public address system yell "FIRE" in a very excited voice!

There is not one sane person anywhere who would take up this challenge. The risk of the consequences in loss of life and serious injury is too great. I know it, and you know it!

All my readers must now accept the fact that sports stadiums were not designed with rapid exits in mind. We, as survivalists, must accept and act accordingly. *Stay put.* In the open stadium situation, I would head in, towards the playing field rather than attempt to get out. That can come later. At least in all that open space the building will not fall on me.

In either closed or open stadiums, be assured that the attendants and ushers are trained in crowd control and the smooth exit of patrons in the sections for which they are responsible. The process, however, is a necessarily slow one and depends on the cooperation of all concerned. One person pushing from the rear, one person slipping and falling, and panic will result. Our first rule of survival, protection of self, still applies, and staying put supports that rule.

Remember how I always ask you to be aware of your journey, your atmosphere, the where-you-are type of thing? Now I ask you to consider that situation again. Not content with planning for our actions inside the stadium/arena and how to best get out safely, we now have to look further ahead and plan for what is out there after we get out. In most of the stadiums I am familiar with (and, being a hockey fan, the Forum comes to mind) I always think, "Wow! At least, if I make it out of here, this vast outside is safe! Just acres of parking space for me to move away from danger."

As for some of the auditoriums in crowded, downtown environments, try to have at least some familiarity with which are the best streets to use to safely leave the area.

Summary? I can only think of a parody statement:

Be cool, Man!

Now to our last place, Vacation Time. If ever there was oil for troubled waters as a writer (survival-wise), it is in the change from sports events to vacations!

9. *Vacation time.*

Whether we are considering a day, a week, or a month-long vacation, like everything else we have talked about so far, vacations come in all shapes and sizes. Vacation time can cause us to be in any of the locations that we have already discussed.

Hotels, popular for vacations, fall into the well-organized group and, due to strict codes, are well prepared for fire and other such events. Concerning an earthquake, however, there is a blank space. Plans for evacuation from upper floors and communications needs, in general, are sadly lacking. Ever book into a hotel or large motel and have the desk clerk mention earthquake emergency procedures?

What is your idea of a vacation? Are you one of the weekend outdoor junkies? Can't wait to get home, hitch up the boat or camper, and *go?*

Are you thinking, "I cannot think of a better place to be when the earthquake happens at a favorite outdoor spot with the family. Here I am, with all my supplies and no stress. I just have to ride it out where I am."

Dream on, dreamer!

Seriously, you will, as a conscientious survivor, have considered the golden rule of survival before you left: "If it happens now, what will I do?" Of course you did! We have come along way together!

How do we go about this?

Let's go back to other situations. First, how many days to plan for? We agreed to at least ten. Next, where are we? Remote area? Busy resort-type place? Same deal. Do I go or do I stay? Then plan accordingly.

If I am going to a remote area where there is plenty of water and no food, my task is to load the old jalopy with as much food as I can ahead of time. At a busy resort, I would use a different strategy, making sure I had several backpacks so that, when disaster hits, I am ready to evacuate. There is no point in staying around with all those other folks who don't have supplies. Most likely, I will be able to drive if I am in an area away from the disaster zone. This type of area is affected by the *effects* (lack of supplies and power, etc.), rather than the *cause*. Being a survivor, I would have already prepared for this. The people visiting Big Bear in June 1992 found this out firsthand.

Conclusion?

Vacation is a happy, restful time. Go prepared to survive supply-wise. Go prepared to stay away from home for a long time!

I began this chapter by saying that we are probably at our most vulnerable while we are at "Other Places." The auto must be given top priority. It has to have our survival supplies in it, and we *must* develop a "survival sense" if we are to successfully pass through this stressful time of our lives.

Now we must move on to our next area of concern: Chapter 8, Apartments, Mobile Homes and Condominiums.

Oh, Boy!

CHAPTER 8
Apartments, Mobile Home Parks, and Condominiums

If I were asked to summarize this chapter heading from a survivalist point of view, how would I answer? An excellent question. Since I asked it myself, I can't duck it, can I? The answer can be expressed in one word:

Collectivism!

For us, as free Americans, what an unfamiliar and unaccepted word this is! Can it be expressed another way, I wonder?

Friendly? No, too *singular.*

Organized? No, too *structured.*

What about "voluntarist?" Ah, now we are getting close. But isn't it always the same few who do the majority of the work? Yes, but it's better than nothing!

What about, "United we stand, divided we fall?"

Now that's a real truth! For if ever a *united* effort was needed, it is now!

In the light of reality, what *is* the real situation? I am sad to say that, in the majority of situations, a well-worn phrase is in keeping with the times. That phrase is "You're on your own, pal!" We Americans do not do well with collectivism!

Let's carry out the first step that I hope you are familiar with by now. The first step in good survivalism? "Know your enemy!" Right, let's do it!

From a survival point of view, apartments, mobile home parks, and condominiums (with few exceptions), have similar unsatisfactory and negative conditions. (For a while,"they" will be used as a descriptive of the trio.) The negatives are:

1. They house a very high concentration of people per square foot, so survival measures pose some unique problems.

226

2. Rapid evacuation from damaged buildings is very difficult.

3. They are constructed or arranged in clusters, making accessibility difficult.

4. They are, for the most part, made of very flimsy construction, especially mobile homes. As for apartments, the higher they go, the worse they get. High-rise structures designed to be such are, of course, the exception to the rule. As for the safety of "stick" construction—Yuk.

5. First aid and rescue at disaster time is very difficult to comprehend.

6. Fire hazard is very high.

7. Survival needs after a disaster pose many problems. (Where to keep supplies etc.)

8. Unless there is a good amount of open space, they are not capable of supporting the housed population within their own property limits. (We provide for the automobile in our planning, but not for the safety of people in a disaster?)

9. Official codes and by-laws are weak or non-existent regarding owner/manager responsibilities—turning off services, providing first aid supplies (realistic, please), fire prevention measures, etc.

Now, if we review what I have just written, it will become quite obvious that most of the problems require a *group* effort to provide a desirable solution. For example, first aid and rescue, fire safety, food and water supplies, protection of self can all be very successfully planned and executed *as a group*.

The shape, size, layout, and design of the structure, we cannot change. The major problems that concern the people *can* be handled. Again the operative word here is *group!* Striving to get tenant-owner cooperation is essential for a successful effort. As we learned in our considerations of the neighborhood, we can provide for each other as a group on a higher level of service than we can individually. Just as the P.T.A. can be a driving force behind student safety, tenant organizations can provide tremendous energy to this problem.

Here are survival questions we must answer, individually or as a group:

1. Where is your apartment located in the building? Does it have an outside balcony?
2. How many stairways does the building have? How far from the nearest stairway are you?
3. Does the building have basement parking? Carports?
4. If carports, is the roof supported by wood or steel beams?
5. Do *you* park in the street, underground, or in a carport?
6. Does the complex/mobile home park have a quadrangle or a set of open spaces?
7. How far is open land from you? Park or recreation area? Sports field?
8. Where will you keep your survival supplies?
9. Who will shut down the services?

To avoid complication as much as possible, I am going to continue talking to you as an individual. I am sure you can figure out the fine line between individual and group effort! I may throw in a few asides here and there, just to satisfy myself that I am not de-emphasizing certain points. Let's go over the points 1-9 from the list above:

1. *Location.*

—Just where is your apartment located in the building?
—Are you on the ground floor?
—Upstairs?
—How high?

These questions are asked to focus your thoughts on *how* you will get out when you *have* to.

An outside balcony, if it is still there, would make an excellent point from which to hang a rope; as an alternative, pick the easiest window for this purpose *now*. Getting out of the unit is your first priority.

In a mobile home, you have to consider the layout from the same point of view. If the unit rolls or is shaken off the stands, you must determine how you will get out from the lowest point. (Wrecking bars should be kept in easily accessible places throughout your mobile home.)

2. *Stairways.*

It is very important to be familiar with the stairways both inside and outside the unit. You must always consider stairs as if they are not going to be there; in this way you are put into the position of finding the next set! It is always good to have a back-up (back to the apartment and down the rope!). We talked about ropes in the home section; the guidelines set down there apply here.

3, 4, and 5. *Parking and Carports.*

By now, we have all realized the importance of the vehicle as a "survival pod." If you park in one of those underground parking places, aren't you placing your supplies at risk? A good idea is to start developing the habit of bringing your Go gear into the unit with you at night. Most condominiums have inside parking. Inspect yours. Is it under the unit? Does it have a clear roof space so that no building (or part of one) is likely to fall on it?

Carports, in the main, are safe as long as they have a good steel-frame construction. Here again, we have to consider yours in relation to what is *up;* what is likely to fall on it?

Where do *you* park your car? If it stands in the clear, leaving your supplies in it is an asset. One thing less to worry about. Once you are clear and in the open, it is something you know you can count on. What if your present parking puts the vehicle in jeopardy?

We have agreed on the importance of our supplies and the necessity to keep them safe. You have no yard in which to put your family's supplies. Oh, I realize that many of you condo owners do have small yards to call your own, but, as close as it is to the buildings, you are not going to stay in it through the turmoil of aftershocks. So we are back to the original question; alternate parking must be found if you are parking dangerously at present. Where? Now, that is a question that may require ingenuity to answer!

—Rent space on a neighborhood driveway?
—Ditto a restaurant/market parking lot? Just at night when the business is closed?
—Rent some empty land?

This is the kind of thinking you are going to have to develop to solve the problems. Oh, yes, you are going to be a trend-setter (in which case, drop me a line or come for a visit and we will set trends together; we might be able to get some city ordinances changed!). Believe me, the inconvenience to you now will pay huge dividends later.

6 and 7. *Open spaces.*

The condominium complex in which I once lived was one of those that boasted a "park-like" setting, with wide open areas of lawns and tennis courts. I had already earmarked my camping spot. My tent was a good as pitched! I always thought, however, "What will I say to the eight hundred other residents who were not interested in survival preparations?"

Fortunately, I moved!

If you are an apartment or mobile home dweller, open space is a very high priority. Open space on your own property is good; but if it is not available, the nearest open area is likely to become your home for a while.

How great it would be if, as a result of the efforts of the group, individual or circus-type tents had been purchased to provide living space for the survivors. Those gated community condominiums are well-suited for this approach as they already have a good, secure environment.

All this talk about open land and camping out may seem far-fetched now, in the quiet time, but the facts must be faced:

A. Only a small amount of damage in a vital area like an entry way, or a stairwell will make the whole apartment block not safely inhabitable, and

B. There are not going to be any services on in the units anyway, be it condo, mobile home, or apartment!

Some alternative will *have* to be found. A nearby relative who lives in a house? A friend in the neighborhood also in a house?

Nothing could be more demoralizing than a tumbled-down apartment complex and you sitting on the rubble! Of course, if you wait long enough, the Army may find a place to put a Tent City up for you. That may sound cold, but it is a fact. Please face it and act now to offset this situation. The victims of Hurricane Andrew did not have this opportunity.

Picture the scene. You are asleep with your family and the first tremor starts. As it goes on, you are aware that, without a doubt, this is the big one. Putting your feet into those stout shoes you keep by the bed, grabbing the flashlight on the nightstand, and gathering the family, you somehow get out into the open.

Now what?

I would challenge you to *Survive I Dare You, the Earthquake Awaits* (The title of my first survival manual). Using the knowledge you have so far gained from *this* manual, accept the challenge of "thought-walking" yourself through your own situation, one with which you are far more familiar than I. Using the guidelines of the questions so far, I know that you can solve your problems in this area. Oh, yes. Just as it is true to say "You are on your own!" it is also true to turn the coin over and say "You don't *have* to be on your own." Raise some hell with the owner/manager of the units. Emphasize the problems. Make them participants!

8. *Survival Supplies.* We have covered this topic in the preceding paragraphs.

9. *Services.*
It always bothers me whenever I see those rows of gas meters and electric service panels lined up on the walls of apartment complexes. Thirty units, thirty services. Which one is yours? It is doubtful if many people even know where the service panels and meters are for their own service. Mobile home owners do; they are under their noses! Going back to the evacuation scene depicted in the previous paragraphs, can you imagine, in all that confusion, each of the tenants going over and cutting off the services?

It's reasonable to ask, "If we are going to lose the services, why bother to turn them off?" The answer to that question is that, due to the quirks of the damage sights, some water and gas may be on for quite a while, while others may go in the first minutes. Even if most people are aware and conscious of the danger involved, what if just one unit is left with the gas on?

Who shuts down the services?

Main shut offs for all residences in this group are always very large. Water mains are usually pipes of up to six inches in diameter, with huge valves. As with schools, it has been my experience that:

A. Either the whereabouts of the key for the security lock is missing, or
B. The shut-off tools are in "somebody else's" care, or
C. The valve(s) are so "frozen" that they are immovable.

In the roads and pathways of these types of facilities, especially mobile home parks, are strategically placed water shut-off valves. Access is via an iron cover of one of various sizes, usually flush with the road surface. A good layer of rust usually seals this lid so securely that several soakings of oil are required to free it. In fact, often repairs to the blacktop have partially covered this lid, requiring a clean-out job to put it back in service. (Boy, you sure learn a lot running a maintenance company!)

These areas for consideration and many others come to light as the tenant/owner groups get going.

It is important to take note of the fact that as a member of this general group, you are dependent on others, in some respects, for your possible survival. What are these areas of dependency?

1. Who will turn off the services? We have just discussed this first area of dependency. Apartments and condos have miles of pipes and wire in the walls. Fire and explosion risks are much higher in them than in houses.

If a fire results in loss of your belongings and the fire was a result of neglect, do you have redress from the neglectful person? A good legal issue here, it would seem to me.

2. Are all concerned aware of the evacuation procedures?

Do you even have procedures for evacuation? If not, why not? Obviously, if a panic situation develops and the exits are blocked, risks that could be avoided could occur.

3. Are there alternate methods of getting out of the building provided? Fire escape or such?

4. Is there any provision for search and rescue other than hoping for a 911 response?

Remember—you could be a victim!

These are four vital areas in which you are dependent. You cannot do it all for yourself, any more than you can turn off thirty or more services. Even if it is for the safety of all!

So it becomes increasingly obvious that tenant cooperation of some kind is necessary; a vehicle for such cooperation might be a homeowner's association.

Frequent meetings are needed to establish both procedures and utilization of possible skills in the groups. Responsibilities can and must be established. Drills and testing of equipment is also a must. Rolled up fire hose, for example, may be found to be dried out and useless when needed. Also, fire extinguishers are placed in buildings in a number sufficient to satisfy a minimum code requirement; doubling up never hurts!

It is not necessary here to go into deep detail. Rather, it is important to highlight the possibilities of topics to discuss and problems to forestall. Your own instinct for survival should lead to strong and positive action to handle problems that do, and will, exist at the time of the initial tremor.

What Will You Do?

Let us briefly run over the *action* part of your survival procedures once again. First, prepare to get out of the apartment, making sure you are familiar with alternate routes. Prepare to get out of the window via a knotted rope to the ground if necessary. The rope should be knotted every two feet to prevent you from descending too fast and burning your hands. Allow for the length taken up by these knots as you calculate the distance to the ground. Check it out! Too bad at the time of need to find the rope is too short.

After the quake, secure the rope and get out fast. Send an adult out first to steady the rope on the ground (if that is not possible, then send an older child) and, if necessary, piggy-back the children down. In a high-rise situation, you are limited by your height from the ground and the physical ability of the family members.

Next order of business? Get clear of the area. Move into the open as quickly as possible. Due to the extremely high voltage lines which run into apartment and condo complexes, the danger of fire and explosion is very high. Mobile home parks are also very high fire risks in the first two hours. We must also consider that the first few aftershocks are going to cause further damage as the buildings settle down with the movement of the earth.

Once you consider it safe, return to your survival gear. As discussed, you will have stored it somewhere safe. Change into sensible clothes and move to your pre-determined place of safety.

A carport constructed with steel posts and beams, as we've seen, makes for a very strong and secure structure. If the surrounding building did not collapse onto it, you may consider this a good survival pad.

Finally, I am going to generalize a little. As a rule, apartments, condominiums and mobile home parks fall into two distinct categories:

—They occupy a serene country-like atmosphere and are rural and rustic, or
—They are squeezed into the most confined space allowed by law.

In the former situation, you will have no problem in evacuating to a safe area for that let's-see-if-it-is-going-to-blow-up period. Two hours is safe; three is better.

In the latter situation, you have more to be concerned about. If your location is in a densely populated area, you are likely to find yourself in a heavily devastated place (mountains of rubble, inaccessible roads, injured people all around). Until you have witnessed such a sight, you have no idea of the feeling of utter helplessness that will be felt at this time.

It must be accepted that areas of extreme devastation are also areas of extreme hazard. Such areas should be avoided at all costs. If you live in such an area, you must leave it as quickly and as safely as possible. Great loss of life and injury occur *after* the major tremor in such heavily devastated places.

Be aware of the hazards of fallen wires. As a rule, when climbing over rubble, apart from the need for balance, *touch nothing*. Never pull anything out of the way; go around it. A live high-tension wire may be buried not far from where you are, just waiting for a path through which to ground itself. Touching a stake or pole may make you "it"!

You need to evaluate your choice of shelter—that secure steel carport, for example—in the context of its surrounding area. A good strong shelter in a built-up area can quickly become a cave in a mountain of debris. Safe as it may seem, secure as you may feel, shelter in the midst of a heavy concentration of debris can become a death trap in the event of fire or explosion. Even a visible path of escape may not save you; having to clamber over mountains of debris is a slow and tiring process, and one can easily be overtaken by a fast-moving fire and perish.

Over-dramatized? The answer lies with the earthquake itself. 8.9 or 9.8—who knows? This is not a manual of prediction, but of survival. Putting your head in the sand will not help you survive. Facing the worst that can happen, and facing it now, can and will enable you to be prepared to avoid simple hazards.

Always, the rule of survival is "know the hazards!"

Just as if you lived in a house, go outside and look at your condo, apartment, or mobile home. Ask yourself the same questions the homeowner asked:

—If the earthquake happened now, what would I do?
—Which is the safe direction to head toward?
—Which is the way to avoid?

Survival for all in this group is obviously a great challenge. Who has the best chance? The condo owner with some control over the management/maintenance staff? The mobile home park with a club house and the ability to organize outside, living in tents, etc. (as many have already done)? Or the apartment dweller in a built-up area? Who can say?

One thing is for sure: *all of them face the number one challenge. . .getting out after the first shock wave has subsided.* Then, in that vital first two hours, "the quality of the survival is equal to the quality of the preparations." Never will that statement be more apropos!

In your own mobile home park, condominium complex, or apartment units, what is the total population? Do you know? You could be shocked! Even amazed. the answer to this question may serve to alert you to the magnitude of your problem. Five or six hundred people hitting the streets at the same time can be quite an event! During a disaster, it becomes a problem of an even greater complexity. Minimizing these complexities is, indeed, a challenge.

Conclusion? Obviously, danger is increased in heavily populated areas. What can we do? The situation is already part of our daily lives, and deteriorating further, as developers are allowed to crowd more and more people into smaller and smaller confines.

From the survivalist point of view, developing and maintaining a positive attitude is the first requirement. Next, a thorough knowledge of the total atmosphere of one's surroundings (inside, outside, and the adjoining few blocks) provides a confident outlook at "crunch" time. Finally, using all available energy, promoting group participation to its *fullest* potential, is the only hope for aid at the citizen level possible under these circumstances at this time.

Disaster is, at best, a nightmare. *Unplanned* disaster is the worst of all situations, for it is a *hopeless* nightmare. As far as I know, the only cure for a nightmare, is to wake up!

For all you Chapter 8'ers, the alarm is ringing. *Please,* don't turn it off!

Let's move on now to a look at Colleges and Residential Facilities.

CHAPTER 9
Colleges and Residential Facilities

Throughout California, there must be at least one-half to three-quarters of a million people who are residents of established institutions: institutes of learning, our college campuses, the many medical facilities other than hospitals, sanitariums, treatment facilities, religious seminaries and camps.

These facilities have a single common denominator; they house, in circumstances similar to those of apartments or condominiums, a population of both sexes who, at present, are not prepared for the onset of a sudden disaster.

My two daughters are college students on two different campuses and represent both ends of the spectrum of this problem. On the one hand, there is Justine at Mount St. Mary's University. Close to Santa Monica and the Bel Air community, the school is in a heavily populated residential area near the heart of L.A. Catrina, on the other hand, is at far-away California Lutheran University in Thousand Oaks. One lives on top of a low mountain in a compact community housed in older buildings, while the other is located on very flat land on a sprawling, relatively modern campus. Vastly different locales, though they share problems common to all the facilities that fall under this chapter heading.

Following the format we've been using, we ask the first question: where will they be? As I see it, in one of only four places:

—In the residence rooms at times other than classes or treatment times, or sleeping, studying, etc.;
—In the organized areas at class or treatment periods; this would include physical education, group therapy, etc.;
—Mealtimes on-campus or in-facility; or
—Off-campus or out-of-facility.

Funny, we strike the old four-places situation again, and since we can only be at one place at a time. . .

Obviously, the population members who fit in the last category (off-campus) fit into the "Other Places" group of Chapter 7, the Travel group of Chapter 3, or in the Workplace setting of Chapter 6.

Agreeing that a common situation may exist may seem an acceptable program to pursue. Indeed, it is not possible to avoid repetition in this type of study for the very same reason that our daily habit patterns are a repetition of similar events. This whole area of residential facilities, however, has a unique set of circumstances that I feel *must* be individually addressed. Now let's look at possible environments of residential facilities through these examples:

—The UCLA Campus in Westwood, CA, with a huge population of on-campus residents housed in multi-level or high-rise buildings of up to ten stories; and, on the other hand, small groups of people living in a variety of situations and housing configurations.
—An Alcohol/Drug Rehab unit in rural Acton, CA. Mostly in small buildings.
—Masters College, again in rural surroundings, but a large campus.
—Many sanatoriums and treatment units in downtown or heavily residential areas.

All right, you may say, what is so unique about this situation? Don't they all fit into some section of the manual already covered? I don't think so. Let us consider a little further.

1. All of the categories included in this chapter have a common denominator. They are what we may term an isolated group. Isolated in thought, in actual physical presence, and in *location*. All totally wrapped up in either their studies or their concentration of their own particular problems ("out of this world," as it were). To be successful, they must *be!*

2. Underscoring the fact that we are concerned with residential facilities, none of the people we are considering live in walking distance of home. To the contrary, many are from out of state and, in many of cases, from foreign countries.

3. All of these people, without exception, are totally *dependent* on their particular bureaucracy for their *complete* welfare.

4. Due to the nature of the beast, as it were, all of these people have an economic boundary. Oh, sure, we are all familiar with a fellow student who was the product of a rich family and drove a ritzy sports car. Likewise, in many treatment facilities, there are members of very influential and elitist groups; but these are the exception rather than the rule. Most of us, when we were in this situation, were struggling much of the time to make ends meet. The budget does not allow for even a to-go backpack, let alone survival supplies.

Now we come to the first question that most don't like to ask and fewer like to face: "Who is responsible?"

Consider my own case. All of my friends and family are aware that I am a survival "nut." Each of my daughters has her own car kit and each is fully aware of what is involved with the coming disaster. Yet, here I sit, writing my manuscript, in the full knowledge that my offspring are in the hands of a system that is totally unprepared to cater to even their most basic needs. (Are you taking notes, you others in my situation?)

The disaster happens. What is to be, will be, regarding building collapse, injuries, etc. Then we face the questions that I have emphasized over and over again in this text:

—What happens during the first vital hour?
—What happens during the following five hours when there should be planned actions for survival?
—Then what about the next ten days or weeks? At residential facilities, this question has the complication of those out-of-state and out-of-country students.

Such a lot of scary negatives for all of us involved to have to face, but face them we must. Probably, the first reaction might be, "But there is no budget." This is often the first line of defense for the what-can-*I*-do crowd. I wonder what will be their defense *afterwards?* Where does the responsibility lie? Does the private facility, school, or rehabilitation unit, having taken the tutorial fees that include residence, have a responsibility to provide even the most basic services of, say, first aid? And, if publicly funded, what arrangements have been made to protect and provide for the off-spring of the taxpayers providing the funding? Does the present government requirement that all schools, etc., have a disaster plan also apply to colleges and similar residential facilities? Especially those supported by public funding?

Let's suppose that all of the these questions have negative answers. Now that I have pointed out the facts, can I expect some actions to be taken regarding these matters?

Having expressed the negatives, it is only fair that some positive actions should be outlined. Back to the three-legged survival stool:

Where will you be?
What will you do?
What will you need?

First, where will they be? We already talked about that. The four likely places and the situations presented in other parts of the manual are comparable to the classroom, therapy group, dining room, and other such situations. This being the case, the next two legs can be combined.

"What will they do?" and "What will they need?" can addressed simultaneously.

Now, let's put the situation into focus. At some moment of the twenty-four hours, the earthquake will happen. Avoiding an exploration of where the residents will be, let us put ourselves directly into the post-quake setting. What will be the *actions* and *needs* of that time?

First, obviously, comes the question "Which is the way out?" This question is especially imperative at night; residents must take into account the layout of the building or dorm, the floor they are on at the time, the time of day (those stout slippers and flashlight *are* by the bed?). At other times of day, the situation would be similar to situations already mentioned in other chapters—the dining room, classroom, group therapy room, and so on.

Next, obviously, come first aid, search, and rescue. These are followed by:

—Triage and dispersal of injured. Where to? How? These actions involve supplies and equipment.
—Shelter and food for the survivors.
—Programs for the continuance of studies.
—Planned group evacuations of student/residents to their own homes.

At this point, please refer back to Diagram 25, Basic Disaster Plan for Educational Facilities, which is appropriate for residential facilities also. Additionally, there are some points unique to college residential situations.

The challenge of record-keeping on the college campus is, indeed, a mighty one. First of all, it is obvious that the time of the disaster itself is critical to the recording function. At bed time, all residents are in a central location. On many campuses, R.A.s are aware of who is in and out of the dorm. During a busy day, however, with much campus travel by these same dorm residents, their whereabouts at disaster time is sometimes a matter of where they "should have been," like it would be on a high school campus. After the power is off, the records are not readily available, and even if the students are following their routines those routines become a matter of speculation.

Once the shocks hit and buildings start to collapse, who is in what building becomes vitally important, especially if injured are not to be neglected for lack of this information. What is the answer?

1. Each building must have a designated Reporting Point.
2. Each instructor, R.A., or person in charge must be responsible for knowing and keeping a current record of attendees. This includes sports, musical and even dining room staff.
3. All campus personnel *must* be issued a simple button-type I.D. (name and student number are all that is required).
4. The central clerical team will have a simple, alphabetized manual system so that as personnel, students, and staff report to the designated reporting point, they can be quickly identified and tabulated (Jones, Mabel, # 6731, Resident Cook. Safe, Injured, etc.).
5. Students must be made aware of the importance of this clerical function.

To simplify the system, just placing the I.D. button in a box, thus freeing the wearer to report for duty, enables the clerical unit to complete tabulations "on the fly," as it were.

Instructors will report to the reporting point in a similar manner, if the time of day warrants this action. Knowledge of how many were in the building allows for the use of simple math to deduct the number of actual occupants from the attendance sheets to determine the "missing" figure to be searched for.

The college campus, the seat of higher learning, has access to faculty, senior, and post-graduate students, who can easily compute the expected casualties given the information as to the age of the buildings, location of the campus, size of the student body, and age levels of the students and faculty. The resultant computations will reveal to the uninitiated a startling set of statistics!

The action to be taken needs to be refined and adapted from the material throughout this manual, honing the plans to suit individual facility circumstances. My main concern, in this area of our discussion, is that *something be done!* At the moment, we sit on a major catastrophe that is *bound* to happen. Picture umpteen thousand stunned students looking at the rubble that was once their dorm and wondering, "What do we do now?" And a just-as-stunned faculty, viewing the same situation, wondering,

A. What do *we* do now?
B. Where are all the records?
C. Do we go or do we stay? What *can* we do? How do we decide?

I think of the small group of residents of a drug rehabilitation program all huddled together as they also wonder, "What now?" No telephone, no public services, no food and water, no organization. . .the list is long.

Faculty, students, and parents, the ball is in *your* court. There is still time. The energy exists to do something now, but it needs to be directed in the proper directions. All residential facilities exist as independent little communities or, in some cases, very large minor cities. As such, they are going to have to survive! *Independently.*

Just as the public schools have to face their problems, so, on a larger scale, must residential facilities. It is a plus factor that most of the college situations have a larger population of non-teaching staff (the maintenance workers, food workers and a whole crew of others who are assets in the disaster situation).

On the other side of that coin, a disorganized group is of little value at disaster time, no matter how large. In fact, to the contrary, confusion is its bedfellow.

It would seem fairly obvious that one of the first requirements is an awareness and understanding of the problem. Centers of learning are abstract in their focus. The word "disaster" does not find companionship with Plato or Pasteur! It is my dream that, at a future time, there may be a degree called Bachelors in Disaster and Survival Planning, perhaps to be followed by post-graduate work leading to a doctorate. As with other sciences, surely people such as I should have to have a credential of some kind!

Now back to reality!

The problems on a college campus are large but not insurmountable. Considering the present state of non-action, however, the situation could become desperate should disaster strike. It seems especially tragic that, of all places, colleges should be in this position. How can the very center of future influence be so unmindful of present-day needs? Especially their own!

Back to the positive approach. The residential facility having achieved a level of awareness, it should follow that an action team should be formed. As for schools in general, use the Disaster Plan in Chapter 5 to plan for:

—Command Post and Records.
—Communications.
—Search and Rescue.
—Triage and Disbursement.
—Fire and Safety.
—Food and Shelter.
—Personal Needs and Hygiene.
—Security.

Taking into account the age of the students, programs encouraging personal survival preparations should be the catalyst for the overall survival program. Students should be responsible for their own travel survival needs. It is true that 96 percent of all who travel have no supplies with them, but surely prodding our college residents to equip the vehicle for disaster will, in itself, stir some thoughts regarding campus safety. To all the residential facilities, I say, "Time is short. Action is required and you are indeed your own keeper. The sanctity of the campus has always been your prerogative. Now, be the forerunner of new ideas and approaches for us, the rest of society!"

Where the demarcation line of responsibility falls is not for me to determine. Accountability finds its own level, I believe.

Now I feel a little more at peace. A problem shared is a problem halved, it is said.

Now on to Chapter 10, Public Transportation.

CHAPTER 10
Public Transportation

Many years ago, when I lived in Toronto, Canada, I used the public transportation system for over two years. That bus became a familiar, dependable friend, always there for me each morning. In the winter, I was spared the process of having to go and wake my poor frozen car from its reverie. Instead, the great iron beast was there, plowing its way through the slush in the winter and cooling me off in the summer.

During that time I became familiar with the travelers, who, I came to realize, are a breed unto themselves. Rather than soliloquize on the variety of types that were my companions, it is more to the point that I concentrate on the two basic types of traveler. On the one hand, there are the like-to-visit types, who just have the greatest time getting to know everybody. The type you miss if they are not there one day. ("Wonder where old Martha is today?") On the other hand, there are those who sit and, by look and posture, demand to be left alone. One may travel for a month and have no idea who they are or what they do.

What has all this got to do with family survival? Quite a bit. Let me elaborate. To me, as a student of disaster situations, travel on public transportation presents a most difficult challenge. Limited as we are space-wise, we have to face all of the trials and difficulties that confront the rest of the travelers. Driver or driven, as the earthquake announces its dreaded presence we all face the same decision-making process. Having survived the first shock wave, do I go or do I stay?

California travelers may differ from their counterparts elsewhere, for they are usually not travelers by choice. And, as soon as they are able, join the ranks of the rest of us, sweating it out on the freeways and all that that scenario entails. As a result, most commuters on the public transportation system seem to share a strong bond, developing a spirit of sharing with each other on their twice-daily journeys. It is that underlying spirit of sharing that, I believe, is the key to survival under these extreme conditions.

Unfortunately, I also believe that the chance of getting this information to these travelers is slim. Most of them have enough burden paying the fare. Survival manual purchases? Not likely! In the hopes that one day there may be a "pamphlet for travelers," I will continue undaunted.

Again, I believe that travelers' spirit of sharing will be the key to survival under these conditions. Acts of sharing and communicating are vital to survival. Sharing with each other in the present time allows for sharing during the stress time, both verbally and materially. Communicating with each other, as a continuum of present habit, will stabilize the stressful situation and, in the immediate period following the quake itself, could be the single most important factor separating survival from panic.

As travelers on public transportation, we face difficulties peculiar to the situation, but *not* peculiar to the overall survival scene. We have already, or should have by now, learned lessons that apply to this situation. They are:

Lesson 1

Always be aware of your position in space! Where are you? Our daily journeys are familiar to us. We know the route by heart. But do we sit daydreaming most of the time? Always be aware of where you are on the journey. If a sudden interruption occurs, you are better able to estimate your chances if you know where you are.

Knowing your daily journey, you will have learned its hazards and, hopefully, its advantages. At the time of decision, this is vital knowledge. Your actions are dictated by that knowledge.

Like the motorist, you must assess your journey first from its hazard point of view. The Traveler's Survey will help you to do this. Knowing your daily journey, could you make it home on foot if you had to? What would be the point of no return for you?

Lesson 2

Face your possibilities and limitations now, while all is calm, thus lessening stress at decision-making time:

Looking out the window, you know where you are. You are aware. "Yes, I *can* make it from here" or "Well, I *knew* this was a stay point; oh, well." Face the fact that: "One day, on this journey, the quake may hit. If it does, this bus/tram/train may be hit by falling debris. If it does, what are my chances for survival? My best actions?"

Remember and re-read the Law of Caving in earlier chapters. Which way are the exits? Do I crouch between the seat or head for the aisle?

The confidence that results from "knowing the enemy" cannot be over-emphasized.

Lesson 3

Be calm. You are prepared for the worst. Your knowledge has forewarned you of your possible predicament. Share this with the others you normally talk to. The worst thing you can do is panic. Panic causes you to be a menace, not only to yourself, but to those around you. (The very fact that you are reading this material is, in itself, part of your survival preparation, and will help you to avoid panic.)

Stay in the positive mode at all times. "This is the worst part of the journey; the hazard factor is high in this built-up area. But I made it so far. Now, which is the safe way out of this mess. . .that's right over there; I remember looking at the map." or "Boy, am I lucky, stuck out here in the sticks! That stretch that I always enjoyed with all the trees and grass that I never had time to look at. Now, here I am, in a safe place. . ."

Hang on to this positive attitude. Survival is for those who dare!

Lesson 4

Be prepared. Can you, as a traveler, carry survival supplies? The answer is a very positive *yes*. There are on the market several types of sports bags and backpacks. Carrying one of these will not make you look out of place. If you normally carry a purse with your personal stuff (wallet, make up, etc.), look down the list of Go items and modify it to accommodate both what you carry now and what you can carry in your pack. Something like this:

First, carry your vital items (money, driver's license, credit cards, etc.) in one of those waist wallets or "fanny packs." If you have to evacuate with nothing else you are in good shape with the irreplace-ables!

Second, do wear good stout shoes that you can walk in to travel. All right, so they are hot; loosen them for now, but have them ready to tighten fast! This will save you having to carry heavy shoes in your pack. Then, if you have to leave with nothing else, at least you can travel in some comfort. Carry the fancy pumps in the pack and change at the workplace. This is a very worthwhile change of habit.

Third, put your survival pack together. Decide on the type (I recommend a light backpack you can stuff under the seat). From the list for the auto, I suggest you take:

1. Several pairs of socks. A must.
2. Underwear and T-shirts. Also musts.
3. A towel and dry wash cloth in plastic bag. Definitely.
4. At least two or three large lawn and trash bags. They take up so little room and are worth their weight in gold as ponchos, protection while sleeping in the bus, etc.
5. Pocket radio and batteries. Leave in the original packing so it is fresh when you need it.
6. A roll of toilet paper in a zip-lock bag.
7. Plastic bottle of mouthwash.
8. Plastic drinking vessel.
9. Metal knife, fork, and spoon.
10. Flat box of baby wipes.
11. Metal magna-type flashlight.
12. First aid packet.
13. Address book with all personal info.
14. Large zip-lock bag with the on-the-go foods. (Beef jerky, trail mix, dried fruit, nuts raisins, etc.)
15. Your choice of vitamins, food supplements, protein tablets, malt tablets, granola bars.
16. Little packets of tea, coffee, soups, etc. Stuff them down the pack.
17. Wrapped "Chewies"—chewing gum, hard candies etc.
18. Powdered juices (orange, lime, etc.).
19. Canteen of water.

In the outside pocket put:
1. Travel tooth brush, comb, and folding hair brush.
2. Deodorant, foot powder, dry skin creme.
3. Any special medications.
4. Feminine needs (if appropriate).

These items are discussed in Chapter 3 (Travel and the Automobile); please refer back to that discussion for details. This little kit is easy to pack and will enable you to be self-supporting for a short time. You must use your own judgment to decide just how to adapt what I have recommended, making it suitable for your own use. Some criteria come to mind.

If your journey is mainly downtown, you will want to travel light so that, in a mobile state, you can move out of a danger area as fast as possible. On the other hand, if you are a suburban or partially-rural traveler, you may want to add to your kit a small, compact cooking stove and a folding canteen. There are several excellent products on the market that are both light and portable.

In the middle of your journey one day, the quake will hit. There will be turmoil and noise and panic. Talk it up with fellow travelers. What are their reactions? Are they positive? Do they believe, as you do, that survival is not only possible, but easy to accommodate? The reaction and feelings expressed by your fellow travelers will give you a very good indication of how they will react under the stress of the situation at quake time. Also, you will have a strong indication as to whether this is a group that will pull together or fall apart when faced with the reality of the moment (dealing with injuries, etc.)—a very important factor for your own survival prospects.

I said at the beginning that communication and sharing were of great importance in this situation. Now, at the end of our discussion, do you realize the importance of that statement?

Have you assessed your group of travelers yet? Perhaps you do not always travel with the same group. Whatever your situation, I am sure you are able to sense some "vibes" from the group of people you are with.

Public transportation may not be the most desirable place to be during the quake, but, after the quake, a group holding together can be a tremendous plus. It is a very positive thing, especially from a security point of view. At times like this, there certainly can be safety in numbers!

Conclusion? The standard, oft-repeated comments:

—Know your journey.
—Know your own limitations.
—Be aware of your location.
—Work out a plan for each area.
—Be prepared supply-wise.
—Be prepared survival-wise.
—Make your go-or-stay decision early, then do it.
—Never forget the bottom line in this situation: welfare of
  self is job one!

Discussion of public transportation regarding *other* disaster situations is not undertaken here, on the assumption that the early warning systems in effect for these situations will have suspended such travel in the light of impending evacuation procedures.

Now to the sad stuff, The Bureaucracy, Chapter 11.

CHAPTER 11
The Bureaucracy — When?

This book outlines for the average family (in California and certain other portions of the nation as a whole) the *foreseen* circumstances that will be in existence at the time of a major natural disaster. In the case of California, an 8.+ earthquake of severe intensity.

Remember: average citizens have control over only two aspects of their lives when it comes to their own survival needs—in their HOMES and in their CARS.

This means that, apart from family time in the home, and the act of traveling, all citizens, from senior citizen to minors, are completely vulnerable to and unprotected for CATASTROPHE!

As a result of this failure of the bureaucratic system, many thousands (and possibly millions) of citizens will perish unnecessarily. It is important, in this the quiet time, to expand on some of the issues that, after all, are outside the control of the citizens themselves. In the aftermath of this crisis, perhaps justice will be served. In those areas found to warrant such action, criminal proceedings may help to ease the grief so cruelly imposed by this neglect by all involved with *the* bureaucracy!

At the federal level, laws have been enacted and funds are allocated. In order to comply with these laws, lower levels of government have spent these funds in various ways. At the state level, instructions have been issued (again, in order to comply with federal directives regarding "Disaster Preparedness"), usually taking the form of pamphlets of one kind or another, leading to "drills" taking place at the "people" level.

Throughout the state, great sums of money have been spent by all emergency agencies (fire, police, etc.). Together, with newly established agencies of varying titles (ostensibly to "co-ordinate efforts of the agencies concerned"), these efforts usually involve the use of advanced communications networks, which are used to dispatch rescue workers in general.

It has not yet been accepted by these "experts" that dispatching, as we now know it, will not be possible. Dispatching involves the action of a person sitting at a receiving point, who takes given information and, as a result of the information received, dispatches others to designated points. This can involve services from taxi service to pizza delivery. In our discussion, we are referring to the dispatch of rescue workers from a command post *under normal conditions.*

Obviously, normal conditions not prevailing, the whole present system requires a revamping. Fire, police and ambulances will be grounded just like the rest of us! Much publicity is given to all these rescue activities; but, in the light of known facts, which are verified recently in field performance) we must face the fact that:

A. Not only is the citizen *still* at grave risk, but

B. The agencies involved will suffer great trauma, not only because of the complete failure of the established systems, but because they will be forced to witness the tragedy unfolding before their eyes and realize that they are powerless to control the situation. Hindsight will reveal that

C. Politicians and appointees are not qualified to direct emergency planning. Skilled planners with disaster experience, using computer statistics already in hand are required.

My first survival manual, *Survive I Dare You, the Earthquake Awaits,* was conceived in 1980, researched through 1982, and written and published by 1984. Unable to find a publisher (I couldn't even give it away!), the manuscript was finally self-published and, without any distribution activity, 10,000 copies were sold, mainly by word of mouth. In that work, I dealt with this very subject—"The Bureaucracy—When?" At that time I wrote these words:

It is very obvious to the most casual observer, and very frightening to the more careful observer, that the members of the bureaucracy are completely ignorant of the magnitude of a major earthquake and the resultant havoc.

Looking at those words today, ten years after they were first written, we have to sadly conclude that *nothing has changed.* Our officials either are not aware of or refuse to accept the facts of such a catastrophe. Using a conscience-salving approach, they allow over-active planning in the wrong areas (ie: communications and misdirected publicity).

Examples?

Publicity for Universal City Tours Earthquake attraction:

Boy (excitedly, looking up at father): "Come on Dad, let's do it again! That was *fun!*" Poor boy, what a shock he has coming!

Statement by local officials of building industry:

"Stick-built houses generally do well in earthquakes." Where? Certainly not in Big Bear and Landers!

Well-known T.V. anchorman at a Los Angeles station as a minor trembler rocked the studio during a newscast seen by millions: "Don't see any ducking under the desk here, folks. But if it makes you feel more secure, by all means put up some supplies." (Spoken with a fixed, condescending smirk.)

The list is long, but the point I make (and will continue to make as sincerely as I can) is that this is *not a game*. This is serious! As I have so often said, most of these culprits are well-meaning folks. They just have no concept. They are part of the it-can't-happen-here brigade, and the if-it-does-happen-I'll-deal-with-it-when-it-comes group.

Some of the biggest culprits are members of the American Red Cross. Whether by command policy or local member incentive (I am not sure which), I am continually faced, when sharing a platform with these people, with "Just do as we say and we will be there to help you. We always have!" Surely the results of recent disasters, such as Hurricane Andrew, have brought home to these people the facts that they do not have any supplies or plans of any kind that will aid victims in the first vital few hours. Somehow, past events and visibility at disasters has led to the mistaken assumption on the part of the public that the Red Cross (the very presence of the logo itself) is a magic wand that makes it all better.

The statistics of 8.+ earthquakes is staggering:

October 16, 1920:	Kansu	8.6	180,000 dead
September 1, 1923:	Kwanto	8.2	140,000 dead
May 22, 1960:	Chile	8.9	10,000 dead

This is, indeed, *not a game!*

It is very easy to sit and lambast the bureaucracy for its failures. Negative criticism, at best, is non-constructive; at its worst, it is in poor taste. Even though the successful measures for survival are not presently in place, we must in no way accept that such measures are not possible. *They are!!*

They need to be understood before they can hope to be implemented. Let me list, in order of priority, what is required:

1. Action at the citizen level:

In London, during World War II, a civilian defense force (low-paid and mainly volunteer) sustained a whole citizenry during almost three years of continuous bombardment which, like earthquake, had no warning as to location.

In Japan, volumes of data have been accumulated over the years regarding cause and effect.

Teams of highly skilled earthquake scientists have spent years not only studying but also producing guidelines regarding building design and construction. As far back as the late '40s, studies indicated the development of "vertical shift" earth movement (1971 San Fernando recorded nine feet of such movement).

The crucial facts, as yet ignored, which were established in London more than fifty years ago are that:

—Without medical attention in the first hour, severely injured victims will not survive.
—Without medical attention in the first five hours, victims in debris will not survive.

Recent history has shown us that, under existing conditions, search and rescue and medical aid on a major scale is at least *forty hours away*. Since most citizens were evacuated prior to Hurricane Andrew, workers there did not have to face the awesome task of rescuing people caught unawares in buildings—imagine what horror there will be in a disaster situation which allows no time for evacuation!

The present Neighborhood Watch program can be easily converted into "Disaster Watch," having stockpiles of search-and-rescue inventory at the Street Captain's house. All that is required is training by the Sheriff's Department, who, at present, control this activity. Expansion into the outlying areas will be required. A very simple manual could be prepared to effect this activity (see Diagram 26).

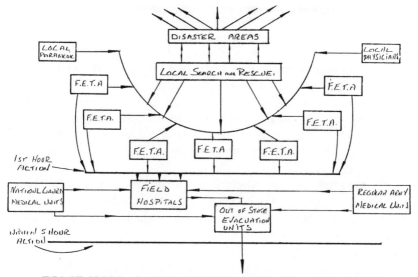

DIAGRAM 26—BASIC CITIZEN-LEVEL DISASTER PLAN

In thousands of outlying areas in the United States lie small communities who are usually several miles from the nearest anything. The hospital is miles away, local fire and paramedics are non-existent, and, at the moment, any help for victims in the first five hours is not a possible reality.

2. Action at local government level (cities, towns, etc.):

Allocation of open areas designated as Field Emergency Triage Areas could be made. These FETA sites must be made known to the general public and the Army/National Guard medical units. These sites should be selected by knowledgeable locals who are very familiar with the area. These sites must be so situated as to be accessible to all the surrounding areas and take into account that access will be either on foot or by helicopter.

All victims will be taken to these sites first. If local hospitals are still standing and operable, the resident staff will be swamped by incoming injured from the local vicinity. All fire and paramedics will proceed on foot to the FETA site.

The civilian search-and-rescue units will be in action from the first minutes after the initial disaster and will have victims there to service within the first hour. The order to paramedics and firemen will be: *be there!*

3. Action on the level of state government:

The state government must co-ordinate with the federal government the development of specialist units of both the National Guard and the Regular Army Medical Units. Both groups would be on twenty-four-hour standby and in constant communication with each other. As soon as disaster strikes, the standby National Guard will, via helicopters, all-terrain vehicles, and foot where necessary, distribute all of the stockpiles of medical supplies required by the Regular Army medical personnel. The *already-prepared* loads of field hospital services will be taken in by helicopters later as a support operation.

Through training, this whole action must aim to have skilled personnel with supplies at the FETA sites in the first hour after the event itself. Injured victims will be there; you can take that one to the bank!

4. Logistical, strategic storing of supplies:

In support of the state government action, these items will be required at the state and local (city/township) level:

—Blood and plasma for a minimum of 50,000 casualties in the first five hours.
—Stretchers and field first aid kits as backup for the citizen DW (Disaster Watch) Corps for the same figures.
—All medical dressings required.
—Supplies of all emergency medications, vaccines, antibiotics, anesthesia, surgery requirements etc.
—Morgue requirements.
—Cots, blankets and pillows.

Computer modems already compiled for Desert Storm could be used for this purpose.

In concert with these four actions:

5. Commencement of debris control:

Predetermined assigned open areas designated for Wrecked and Abandoned Vehicle Elimination (WAVE) activity should be established.

In the first five hours, in order for the rescue work to be effective, these must be pre-planned actions to address the problem of abandoned vehicles. Disasters such as Hurricane Andrew have demonstrated that debris of all kinds builds up and bogs down rescue efforts. Should the disaster strike at A.M. or P.M. peak travel times, up to 1,000,000 vehicles will clog the freeways and surface streets.

Obviously, traffic flow will not resume for weeks, but space must be cleared for helicopter landing sites for evacuation of freeway victims.

6. Mass evacuation plans:
Due to the foreseen mass devastation that will occur in California (especially in the greater Los Angeles area), it will not be possible to house those who cannot support themselves (for lack of survival preparation or other reasons) in the areas in which they find themselves stranded. It is not logistically possible, given the circumstances and lack of unaffected areas.

Following the guidelines in this manual, the Stay population, sitting it out on the freeways, cannot be expected to remain there until the freeways open again (an event which may be up to six months away). The picture of complete destruction of both our major freeway and surface street facilities does not yet seem to be in focus for our officials.

The logical approach will have to be evacuation to outside areas like Nevada, Arizona, etc. If financing becomes available, the production of my Emergency Survival Dwelling Unit (ESDU) will be a decisive factor. In the meantime, alternative plans have to be produced to meet this problem. Another Tent City?

7. Presently established systems:
The only system presently in place is that of communications, which is effective only in a recording and reporting function. It is of no value at the citizen level because dispatching of required services (police, fire, etc.) is not possible under these circumstances. Development of a program of local Disaster Watch, as outlined in Diagram 26, will produce the decisive action needed at the citizen level. These proposals will in no way interfere with the existing plans presently in place in the bureaucracy.

Our concerns are for *now.*

Sadly, after some twenty years of bureaucratic research and planning, conditions still exist that continue to complicate the survival scene at both at citizen and corporate levels. Let's consider some of these situations without attempting to prioritize them.

Communication

It has long been a sore point for me that there is such a lack of communication between elected officials and the general public (*us*).

One tires of failing to hear or see evidence of positive actions of any kind on officials' part, either singly or as a group (and that includes the highest level of officialdom in the state). Or that they are in any way concerned about our safety in the event of an earthquake. Oh, not the little trembler that we all live through, but the major catastrophic disaster that we know they are aware will one day come. We know that through news releases; as early as June 17, 1983, Sheriff Sherman Block said:

> The dead would number 3,000 to 14,000 depending on the time of day of the tremor, and between 14,000 and 55,000 would be injured seriously enough to require hospitalization. Studies have shown that more casualties would result from explosions of toxic substances, ruptured pipelines, and the like, than from earth movement and building damage.

Now, that statement having been made in 1983, what was the follow-up? Here's another quote from the same press release (Remember, this is *1983*!):

> The best thing for private citizens to do is look in the front of their phone book and find out the kinds of things they can do for these critical hours immediately following an earthquake when they're gonna have to be pretty self-sufficient because the emergency sources obviously are going to be overtaxed.

Wouldn't it be more reassuring to see a press release like this:

> At the Governor's press conference today, it was decided that the actions of the Emergency Planning Task Force would, in the future, be made public. No matter how terrible, the public has a right to know, and not only that, understand what is being done.

I wish! Just to say "Read your telephone book" is both an insult and a travesty, for it ignores those who are illiterate, those who are not bilingual, and those who do not have access to a telephone book. Besides, who established the telephone book as an authority? The directive "Turn off the services and get some food and water" was shown to be inadequate during the first minor quake of the '80s. What does reading the phone book do for the elderly, the blind, and the handicapped stuck in their wheel chairs? Communications?

Somebody is communicating with somebody, but not down to us.

Other issues that concern us all have been dealt with in a manner which can be labeled "phony baloney" or "pulling the wool over everybody's eyes" (including, yes, the good old bureaucracy itself). Some "for instances"?

Schools

All school districts are by law mandated to have a disaster plan (whether it is effective or not is neither here nor there). However, each school principal is responsible for *developing* his or her *own* disaster plan. At first glance, this is an excellent idea. Who knows better the site needs than the person at the site? Right? Wrong!

The major problem is that this allows for a vast array of opinions from self-styled experts who have spent their lives in other-than-disaster situations! No two agree on supplies and type of foods to be stored. And as for water? Toilets? Having to sleep 300 students (small campus), 700 students (medium campus), and 1200 students (large campus) outside? The logistics alone require an expert! This is only the tip of the iceberg.

—Most schools could *not* turn off the major gas main. (The tool is lost, the valve is frozen, or other such problems arise.)
—Most schools have *not* taken care of the problem of broken glass.
—Most schools do *not* have adequate supplies of food and water. Five days' supply of water for 500 kids equals a minimum of 2,500 gallons, just for starters.
—Most schools have a thirty-to-one student-to-adult ratio due to budget cuts. Handicapped or elderly teachers increase the risk.
—Most schools have no full-time nurse on campus.

Schools have to rely on overworked, underpaid and, at present, low-morale-level teachers not only to provide search, rescue, and first aid at the onset, but also to provide and organize after-care for what could be a minimum of five days.

All students are required to remain on campus until picked up by a parent or designated alternate. What about the parent who is one of the Stay brigade from Chapter 3? Or perhaps (God forbid) injured or killed? Do we have any plans? School boards do not involve themselves enough, or in some cases at all, in the down-to-earth planning of this, possibly the greatest disaster to befall modern America.

Perhaps the saddest aspect of all is the very safety of the buildings on the average school campus. Old-fashioned designs make rapid evacuation nearly impossible in many situations. Portable buildings are often on unstable foundations. In many areas, schools are in violation of regular building codes (there seems to be a loophole just for schools). Were you, as a parent, aware of that? As long as schools comply with the written manual, practical or not, and hold the required number of drills, the perception is that all is well. The last thing on the list of school considerations, ironically, is the most important. The priority of the lives of both student and faculty, under present conditions, will remain where it is: last.

"Don't rock the boat!" Tragically, most parents assume that their offspring are in a safe environment. Others refuse to get involved. I once heard a parent at a seminar I was giving for a P.T.A. group turn to her small son and say, "Don't worry about any of that stuff; as soon as the shaking stops Mommy will jump in the car and come and get you, fast." The sad thing was that she believed it!

The problem is seriously compounded by our expectation that teachers bear the responsibility for providing services demanding a level of skill they neither possess nor are given training for. A fireman just out of training is termed a rookie. What are teachers with *no* training called as they valiantly undertake search and rescue of their students?

Let's now go on to a broader issue. Substances which pose a health hazard are required, by law, to carry a disclaimer, such as "This product is known to be hazardous to your health. Use at your own risk." What about sub-standard buildings that house chemicals and do not conform to earthquake standards? There are known to be at least 20,000 of them in California. What about those sub-standard buildings used as factories in the downtown so-called distressed areas? Where are the toxic chemicals referred to by Sheriff Block? How many are in the sub-standard buildings? Shouldn't those buildings have a disclaimer on them? Something like "This building was inspected and found to require repairs to bring it to earthquake safety standards," with the date of the inspection recorded on the notice. Doesn't the public have a right to know? Isn't this knowledge open to the public?

What if a person is killed in a building known to be below-code? Can the owner be sued for concealing this information? Why not?

What of places of employment, many of them union firms, that are housed in buildings that allow workers to risk their lives each work day? Where are the politicians who spent all that time trying to work out a budget yet dedicated no time to disaster safety? A right to the "good life" or a right to die unnecessarily?

Is that why so many commercial buildings are vacated and not purchased again, left to sit and rot? Too expensive to bring to code? But as we now know, each one is a great fire waiting to happen! If a building is known to be earthquake-unstable, and the owner has no intention of fixing it, why not pull it down and get it cleared up now, while all is quiet?

Vehicles transporting the general public are subject to strict safety codes. Why are buildings that house workers not subject to the same laws? What is the point of enforcing tough building codes for new construction in an area overflowing with weak structures that are known to be unsafe? Future headlines are so predictable: "The So-and-so Towers, known to be lacking in earthquake safety, as expected collapsed with the first wave. All of the 2000 conventioneers from around the country perished. Their names are not known since the records also perished."

Are there any of you reading this brave enough to ask your boss, "Say, Boss. Has this building ever been checked for disaster safety?" Could this lead to a test case for wrongful dismissal, I wonder? Very tongue-in-cheek? Of course. Very timely? Ditto!

After the 1971 San Fernando earthquake, a report was published by the U.S. Department of Commerce and the U.S. Department of the Interior, mainly to help government and utility workers plan for the future. There was a list of thirteen separate recommendations. I have paraphrased certain sections for reader convenience. I have included only the sections that I feel have the most to say to us survivalists.

Section 1. The hazard of *non-earthquake*-resistive structures was re-emphasized. Old structures, particularly unreinforced masonry bearing-walls with weak mortar, performed poorly.

Section 3. Surprisingly large ground motion was recorded, exceeding in some places the El Centro and Taft records, which have guided earthquake-resistive design for thirty years. The high *vertical* [italics mine] motion recorded and reported by eye-witnesses probably increased the damages.

Section 4. Re-assessment of some designs of bridges and overpasses. Particular attention should be focused on the poor behavior of many one-story industrial and commercial structures, since they comprise the majority of construction other than residences.

Section 6. Greater caution is required relative to building in the zones of larger faults. It goes on to talk about increased mapping of faults, which is now already done.

Section 7. Confidence increased in California public-school design and criteria; however, non-earthquake-resistive school buildings performed poorly.

Section 9. Modern, one-story frame buildings performed reasonably well. However, reconsideration of code provisions and enforcement is indicated, particularly for two-story construction and masonry chimneys.

Section 11. *Greater attention to the hazard of broken glass is needed.* [italics mine]

This information is recorded here as a reinforcement to the call for better current survival procedures. My readers know by now that I start at the worst possible point! I would like to spend some time on this report, if only to emphasize some points to the bureaucracy.

This earthquake was in 1971; it lasted for about sixty seconds and had a magnitude of 6.6 with an intensity of about VI or VII. A fairly mild trembler. Vertical movement was pronounced and caused some surprise. This same type of movement later almost caused the collapse of the San Francisco Bay Bridge in 1989.

The report on schools, houses, and overpasses deserves some attention. Ever notice how many older school buildings in California have those large metal overhangs to keep the sun out of the rooms? I have seen some that have been very thoroughly plastered over. This, of course, increases the weight of the structure already destined to fall and block the entrances.

The report says that houses, especially two-story ones, need attention to code compliance and design. Let me stress chimney weakness in these homes (for more detail, refer back to Chapter 4); measure the height of the chimney and allow room for it to drop. It will!

Also worthy of emphasis (my video addresses this subject at length) are the hazards of the overpass. These hazards are a cause of great concern for us survivalists. When stopping in traffic, we must remember to give them a wide berth. They will be a bear to climb over on the way home, as it is!

When is this information going to be put in to the California Highway Code Book? So far, earthquakes are ignored. I wonder if it will ever be mandatory to carry a survival kit in the car?

Despite Section 11 of the report, I have still not seen one government office of any kind (federal, state, or local) that in any way protects workers from the hazard of broken glass. No matter how many times I point this out at seminars, or even during safety talks in Civil Service offices, and no matter how pale people go as I point out the danger two feet from their faces, when I go back later, the once-shocked employees are still sitting there doing their thing and the glass is still not covered. Modern transparent tape is invisible, so what's the problem? A scarred face is not a pretty sight, especially on a child!

As we stated earlier, pamphlets are issued and, in order to comply with the law, drills are held. Token compliance is alive and well. Unfortunately, that will not suffice after the quake when all the dust has settled.

We often hear, "But there are already laws on the books that cover that." How often has that one been put forward as a political defense, in a wide variety of issues? In some instances, it is true. In the case of earthquake survival, *who is responsible for seeing that laws exist and that those laws are enforced?*

So much for the bureaucracy and what "they" *could* do. How about some *can*-dos? Some city and/or county ordinances, perhaps, over which we citizens exercise a little more control? Some examples:

—All water trucks on construction sites are to be left in the open, fully charged each night.

—No earth-moving equipment is to be locked inside a building except for repairs.

—All school buses must carry first aid adequate for the passenger load. (I've been working on that one for years!)

—All supermarkets must have clear, unobstructed exits. The installation of security barriers as an anti-shoplifting device must be eliminated, as they create a safety hazard.
—Stock (inventory, to use the proper terminology) must be stored in the storage areas, not on the top of shelving in

the shopping aisles where it adds to public endangerment.

—All malls must have a designated person responsible to shut off the services in an emergency.

—All mall exits must be clearly marked as "Emergency Exits."

Perhaps we should have a competition to see who could come up with the longest list of, shall we call it, the I'm-not-going-to-put-up-with-it-anymore list or the When-are-you-going-to-get-around-to-this list. Sadly, there is so much that *can* be done but, without a concerted effort, is not likely to be.

As an answer to those who call me an alarmist, let me speculate about some figures. I'll use a low-middle figure of the 12,000-55,000 injured that Sherman Block predicted and use 25,000 people injured as a backdrop to the following consideration:

If it takes a paramedic only five minutes to service one victim, and it is agreed that victims cannot wait more than five hours for attention (if they are going to live, that is), the equation goes something like this: one paramedic at five minutes per case should be able to treat ten cases in an hour, right? Well, that's only one minute to go from one case to the next? Oh, well. Let's call him Fast Eddie! That equates to fifty cases per paramedic in the allowed five hours. Does he carry that sufficient supplies with him, I wonder? At fifty cases per paramedic, the five-hour time-frame means we will need 500 paramedics; each of the paramedics will be working for five hours straight, without a break for re-stocking or transportation time. And, of course, the five-minutes per case treatment time is highly unrealistic!

Then, of course, where do we take these 25,000 casualties? During the L.A. riots, I seem to remember hospitals complaining of being "swamped" with twenty-five cases.

How about 2000 paramedics as a realistic figure, and fifty hours as not even scratching the surface of the enormity of 25,000 injured victims all at once? The sad fact for me is that, after ten years of my screaming as a survival specialist at the powers that be, the bureaucracy still believes in the dispatch-as-normal theory. No road obstructions, no collapsed overpasses and all systems go.

Fortunately, the officials in other disaster areas have taken positive steps toward increased public awareness and safety through forced evacuations (with some complaining), tight building codes, etc.

I could go on for many more pages and take up many more issues, but this is, after all, a family survival manual, dedicated to positive actions you can take. This whole chapter could well be added to the-devil-you-know section, for it is my firm conviction that only when we fully accept the inadequacies of the powers that be (who hold our fate in their hands), can we fully accept *our* responsibility for *our own* survival.

If we DON'T, who WILL?

Addendum to Chapter 11

After I had put this particular chapter "to bed," over the next few days several things occurred to me as afterthoughts that should be just offered as food for thought. You know what they say about hindsight?

—Prisons. It is all very well to say something like, "We'll let the authorities worry about that one," but, as we know, the authorities either think that it will all take care of itself in a routine manner, or they do not think of it at all. For all you prison workers, and friends of such, if the earthquake happened on your shift, what would you do? Perhaps some dialogue is required?

—Airports. Since airports are the province of the bureaucracy, has anyone thought about the travelers in the air, on the ground, and about to take off? It must be noted that I have, in this text, advised people in crowded spaces to find the open areas. Since airports have all that lovely, safe, open ground called runways, what happens if all the travelers crowding the terminals rush out into the open spaces and a jumbo jet comes in to land? Better have some dialogue here too!

Since they issue the permits, how about the following cases for the bureaucracy?

—Rock Concerts.
—Large conventions.
—County fairs.
—Special events (Olympics, etc.).

—Professional sports.
—Religious gatherings (in stadiums, that is).

How about the zoos? Can you imagine backyard survival with a tiger looking over the pile of rubble that once was the wall?

How about another competition for the longest list of "Who takes care of that?"

Having expressed to the bureaucracy that I am "mad as h—- and I'm not going to take it anymore," I should probably calm down and move into an area that allows for personal action in a positive manner. This would be Chapter 12, The Survivor's Medicine Chest.

CHAPTER 12
The Survivor's Medicine Chest

A short reference was made in Chapter 4, in the discussion on backyard survival, to the subject of the survivor's medicine chest. What's the concept here? Good question. I always like to feel that we are on the same wave length!

Only recently, in the last two years in fact, did my research in the survival field lead me into this whole topic of "being ill." So far, all my thoughts were concentrated on casualties and victims—the people in disaster and the search-and-rescue scene. Somewhere, in this period of time, it dawned on me that "Hey, the shaking has stopped, it's E plus about seven days, the aftershocks have even calmed down a little; now normal feelings and emotions are beginning to return—'Mummy, I got a tummy ache!'"

Let's go back to pre-disaster time. What sort of a family were you health-wise? Most of us fit some well-defined patterns, I believe. We have:

—Good health coverage with a reasonable deductible, or
—Good plan but some deductible, or
—No health plan at all, but Medi-cal or Medicaid, or
—Nothing but over-the-counter medications or county aid.

Consequently, our health-care patterns are established within these boundaries. Admittedly, family traditions come into play in this situation. People tend to follow in the footsteps of their parents. Some, it seems, are always at the doctors; others have to be dragged there. In the case of a disaster, we will all be put into the same boat; habit or not, there is no doctor!

Reasonableness, I believe, is practiced by reasonable people and, in the main, most of us resort to the doctor's office when common sense or instinct directs us there. Now, however, neither common sense nor instinct will secure the services of that worthy practitioner. We will have to cope best way we can. . .*on our own.*

As I delved into this problem, being a true survivor, I at once sought out the "devil" in this piece. I wanted to know the depth of my problem. Considering myself in the backyard, it was reasonable to assume that there might be some accidents or minor aches and pains and, reflecting on a family situation (raising my four sons), it was very obvious that there was a whole range of situations that were more than mere possibilities. Research of available written materials and the purchase of some of them quickly led me to the conclusion that there is not one single good "sick book" out there!

First aid? Yes. Specialized works on herbs, botanicals, and the like, there was aplenty. But ailments? Then I found Dr. Isadore Rosenfeld, M.D., and his book titled, *The Best Treatment.* It was the jacket that really caught my eye. The blurb said, "One of America's most trusted doctors tells you exactly what to do for every ailment and disease."

Upon reading this and putting myself in the backyard situation, even if I only got *some* of the ailments and diseases, I thought that this book would have to be my salvation! To my surprise, I found that this book, for the most part, was like going to my own doctor. Everything recommended by the good doctor/author needed a prescription! Oh, there were a few "home remedies." These were so old-fashioned, though, that any camper learned them long ago. So, I was back to square one! What to do? All the outside opinions that I could solicit fell into one category: "You're in a no-win situation, pal. Either you'll have the A.M.A. on your back for practicing medicine without a license, or the faddists will be annoyed because you didn't mention this, that, or the other. Leave the whole thing alone!"

But I'm still stuck in my backyard without a doctor! What can I do? What of all the people out there that have never heard of home remedies? Even less about Grandma's pet cure-alls? A predicament indeed! The only answer I came up with went something like"These are hard times for us all. Survival is for those who dare, those who care, and those who prepare." In pursuance of this principle, the following guidelines are presented in a sincere effort to:

1. Aid, as best as possible, the "clueless," and
2. Stimulate every other survivor who has any clue at all to dig up, read books, ask around, and, as best you can, put together a "Home Medicine Chest"!

For all concerned, this is mine. This what *I* do, this is what *I* take. If you want to follow along, fine. It's a free world! The following applies to *me*, and in no way is suggested as a remedy or procedure for you to follow. That's called a disclaimer. Anyway, your Grandma was probably smarter than mine!

Now let's get logical here.

First, I had to try to foresee what it was I was likely to run into. Surprisingly, except for accidents, it was not that much. Here's my list:

Allergies	Fever	Sore throat
Bite	Fungus	Splinters
Burns	Gas	Sunburn
Constipation	Indigestion	Upset stomach
Cough	Insomnia	Urinary infections
Diarrhea	Itching	Worms and parasites
Eye problems	Nausea	

This may appear to be a rather compact list, but as we go along, you will see that it can be made to be very all-encompassing. First, then, allergies.

Allergies

Allergic reactions, generally accepted to mean a condition of watery eyes and sneezing, can arise under backyard survival conditions even though there was little or no previous history of such symptoms.

In Chapter 4, under the heading "Personal needs," you remember we were asked to pack any special medications. If you are one of those allergy sufferers of long standing, there is no doubt that you will either have a prescription drug from your doctor or keep an over-the-counter remedy on hand. For the rest of us, the following seems to be the most recommended.

First of all, cleanse the stopped-up nose and throat with a solution of salt or borax water. First, mix one teaspoon salt or borax in a pint of warm water. Let stand for at least an hour. Shake well and use as a gargle. Also, placing a little in the palm of the hand, snuff the solution up the nose repeatedly until the passages are clear.

If the eyes are swollen and irritated, bathe them in a solution of aloe vera juice and water.

Obviously, if you can locate the cause of the irritation, remove it.

One of the by-products of the disaster is the fact that the absence of buildings and other structures allows the wind to be much stronger. Of course, since it blows unobstructed for greater distances, hay fever-like symptoms will result. If wind-blown dust seems to be the root of your problem, wear the paper masks during the time of the strong winds.

I have found that inhaling good, old-fashioned eucalyptus does wonders for my stopped-up nose and bronchial tubes. Place ten drops in a small saucer of hot water, place a towel over the head and gently inhale. This really clears that stuffy feeling. It is also very good for croupy children.

Bites

At first glance you may feel that the subject of bites belongs more to first aid and the first aid kit than here in the medicine section. I do want to place emphasis on bites in the medical section because, when we think about survival and preparing for disaster, we are inclined to overlook bites as they affect a person who is allergic to bee stings and other insect bites. I've found that people are much more likely to remember allergic reactions when packing for a picnic or a day in the country than when packing for survival.

You have been reminded constantly about packing away essential medications in your survival gear. This is another reminder. If you are allergic to bee stings, in particular, be advised that the bees do fly and work in the winter and, although you may not have noticed it, they are out there. In the open conditions following a disaster, you will be vulnerable, so please be on the lookout and make sure you have a protective kit with you.

We also should be concerned about canine attacks. After a disaster, especially when fences and walls are down, animals very often take off in sheer panic. Without restraints, they run great distances before fatigue slows them down. Then, finding themselves in unknown locations, their first requirement is water, followed of course by the need for food. In Coventry, a city ordered destroyed by Hitler, the noise of the twelve hours of bombing had the animals in a totally wild state. Not rabid by any means, but most certainly dangerous. We noticed how quickly they banded together in packs.

Under the conditions of backyard survival, we must be aware that, without the protection of fences or walls, we will be open to attacks from wild packs of dogs, and of course vulnerable to their bites. For city dwellers, rabies should not be a problem, but be aware of an animal's appearance and behavior. Frothing at the mouth or the complete absence of fear are good indicators of a possible rabid condition.

For non-campers and non-outdoorsy types, this is scary stuff! Now, let's get to the positive and what we can do as after-care.

Bee stings, of course, first require the removal of the stinger and cleansing of the bite area. I remember, as a lad, how we took great joy in removing the stinger and followed up with a very ritualistic sucking of the painful area to remove the venom! All of this was carried out with loud sucking sounds and much spitting of the resultant saliva accumulated in the mouth "so as not to swallow the poison." I am not sure if I was taught this practice or if I saw it in a "B" movie, but I know I taught all my sons to do this. It works!

A less dramatic approach is to wash the area with a good antiseptic (peroxide is good), or the good old mouthwash will do. If there is a lot of swelling, cold salt-water soaks will help. A cup of warm sweet tea helps to counteract the shock effect in children.

Animal bites require a more serious approach, depending on the degree and severity. If there is an open wound or tear, we are faced with a potentially serious problem. Follow the first-aid approach:

—Stop bleeding.
—Examine and determine the degree of severity; *be calm.*
—Determine the following—Is the wound deep? Is the muscle torn or are muscle fibers exposed? Are sutures (stitches) required?

If the severity requires it, transport the victim to the nearest first aid center. Otherwise, dress and cover the injury as you would any other:

Cleanse the wound by pouring clean water over the whole area to remove any dirt and debris prior to covering. If possible, soak the area in warm salt water for a few minutes to reduce the shock as well as to clean the area. Now, examine the wound. Is any flesh missing? Did the animal (usually canine) tear the skin while shaking its head? Or was it a bite-and-run situation? The answer to these questions will determine how to dress the injury. Obviously, a large crater left by an animal tearing at the bite site is a serious problem; healing is difficult and infection is a danger. Never pack such a hole with dressing or pads, even if they are sterile. The problem is that the wound will dry out and the dressings will stick inside it, requiring long soaks to remove them. If you are able, use "butterflies," gently close the wound, and dress with a 4"x4" pad first; then apply the zinc oxide tape over the dressing to hold the wound site together. Not too tight now!

In the case of a gaping wound, one too large to close, lay a very large dressing soaked in aloe vera or tea tree oil across the whole wound and dress it so as to leave the injury site safe from invasion by the dressing. A nice cup of tea, one of the sedative kinds (comfrey or horehound) will help to soothe the patient.

Over the next few days, be observant for signs of infection. As soon as possible, apply a covering of antiseptic ointment and expose to the air when possible. Healing for this kind of wound is very slow.

Burns

In the section on backyard survival, I stressed the importance of being careful about the potential for accidents. Usually, the accidents we do have are the minor cuts and bruises associated with using hand tools (eg: opening cans, sawing wood, hammering, etc.). However, care must be taken with our number-one enemy—FIRE. (Observe that I used capitals!) So many leaders and parents can testify that, when out with the Scout troop or the family, burns were the only injuries to be encountered, especially with young and very inexperienced children.

Backyard survival does indeed lend itself to burns of all kinds. We must be prepared for this kind of injury. There are two main kinds of burns:

—From water, known as scalds, and
—From fire, which produces nasty burns of varying degrees.

We could add a third type, from accidentally picking up hot things, such as usually pots or fry pans.

Burns are not pleasant and, with care, can be avoided. As with all conditions, the golden rule is to always stay calm and, as a first step, determine the degree of burn. The rule of thumb is:

—No blister, first-degree burn,
—Blister, second-degree, and
—Burned skin and a nasty-looking crater, third-degree and
  a serious cause for concern.

The first treatment for all burns is to get the part into clean, cold water for as long as it takes for the pain to decrease. Third-degree burns should, as soon as possible, be attended to at a first aid unit.

For a first-degree burn, apply a dressing soaked in aloe vera juice and, as soon as possible, open to the air after applying a little salve to keep the area moist.

For second-degree (blistered) burns, pop the blisters with a sterile needle and leave the deflated skin in place. Apply a dressing soaked in aloe vera cream or honey. Keep the burn moist.

For third-degree burns, if you are unable to get to a first aid station or a physician, you have a problem. My first instinct is to leave well enough alone and stay with the admonition to get to a physician or first aid center. Yet, if I accept the self-appointed task of walking you through a survival situation, I must have the courage not to leave you up a creek without a paddle with a third-degree burn! So, here it goes. A third-degree burn is tough on all concerned. Under backyard survival conditions, we should not encounter the same type of burns as in a house or vehicular fire. But, there are dramatic instances where this type of burn may occur. Setting a tent on fire or catching the clothes on fire are nasty examples. If the burn is confined to a limb or part of a limb, you may, if you simply have no alternative, start treatment yourself. If, however, the body is involved, you *must* transport to a first aid unit or go yourself to a place where you can secure transportation by helicopter. Third-degree body burns can, most certainly, be life-threatening.

As with all burns, the first action is to get the burn into clean water. This puts the "fire" out of the burn, as long as the part is in the water and out of the air. Do not put butter or any ointment on third-degree burns. For the first twenty-four hours, moisture is required. The burned areas dry out very quickly and great scabs and painful dry scales form. The major problem with this type of burn is infection. Boil all water to be used as cold soaks, and sterilize the basin that is used for the soaks. Use rubber gloves and sterile dressings. If possible, keep the area draped for the first few hours, pouring the sterile, cold water or aloe vera juice over the dressing to keep it moist and prevent it from sticking to the wound.

Healing will take place at the bottom of the crater first, and you should see signs of healing in the first forty-eight-hour period. Now, you may begin a regular routine of applying a dressing soaked in one of several different medications. Honey, aloe vera creme, and tea tree oil are all remarkable in their effect. Once you apply any of the types of medications mentioned, change the dressings only every two or three days. If the patient says the burn is not causing discomfort, leave well enough alone.

Increase the fluid intake with all burn conditions. Give as much protein as possible. Use the protein wafers from the car kit, if necessary. Take the victim's temperature frequently during the first forty-eight hours and daily afterwards. Be vigilant for signs of infection or fever. If one occurs, seek help immediately.

Soothing tea and anything that helps to relieve pain and tension is helpful, but we need the patient aware of sensation as much as possible. Otherwise, we will not know what is going on. Despite what you may have seen on the movies, knocking the patient out with alcohol, etc., is not recommended! With care and cleanliness, the wound will heal. But, as soon as possible, get the victim to a doctor.

That should finish the dramatic situations that we may encounter. Now let us move on to the more likely conditions we will most certainly run into.

Constipation

Change of diet and lack of fresh fruits and vegetables are likely to cause constipation. Treat with cascara, garlic tablets, or aloe vera juice. If you suffer from this condition often, you probably have some over-the-counter remedy in your kit. Stay away from sugar and dairy products if you encounter constipation.

Coughs

Due to the changing atmosphere and winter conditions, croup-like symptoms can very often appear in both adults and children. When living outdoors in damp, wet conditions, keep the mouth closed and breathe through the nose. If this is not possible because of congestion, use the paper mask and put a few drops of eucalyptus oil on the mask to help to clear up the stuffy condition.

One of the best remedies I know for coughs and chest congestion is Grandma's Syrup. This is made by placing a one-inch slice of onion in a saucer and covering it with brown sugar. Leave it overnight, and in the morning a black syrup will have started to form. Take one teaspoon of this syrup every four hours.

Eucalyptus oil and camphor oil, inhaled as steam over a bowl or rubbed on the chest for constant inhaling, both help the condition. Gargle with salt water to keep the throat clear.

Diarrhea

We can expect many bouts of this troublesome condition. We must always be aware that diarrhea can be an indication of a more serious problem, one involving dysentery or some other type of infection in the intestines.

First, be sure your hygiene standards are as high as you can keep them. Increase the fluid intake. Diarrhea and dysentery quickly lead to dehydration, especially in children. So, in the fluid-control measures, a mixture of molasses and water will restore nutrition. Barley water and soy bean water (the liquid residue from boiling these beans) can be used with the molasses. Brown rice water is also good. Ginger is wonderful.

Take garlic capsules, reduce intake of all dairy products, fruits and fruit juices, increase salt intake, and get rest.

Fevers

Fever, the elevation of body temperature, is usually the indication of some action by the body in the battle with infection. The old adage "stuff a cold and starve a fever" is generally accepted. So drink plenty of liquids but avoid solid foods. Rest, reduce activity, and drink chamomile tea. I increase my vitamin A, protein, and garlic intake also. Make some chicken and barley soup (use soup powder base). I also take lemon juice and honey. If you are inclined, increase amino acid intake.

Fungus

Backyard conditions—lack of showers, keeping the same socks on too long, other conditions we are not accustomed to—are factors which contribute to fungus-type conditions. Athlete's foot, under-arm rash, this kind of thing.

For the feet, use a pinch of permanganate of potash crystals in a pint of water, soak the feet for half an hour, and dry well. For fungus patches on the skin, a light application of gentian violet, though ugly, is effective. Another old remedy for athlete's foot is to rub garlic between the toes. Increasing my intake of garlic, zinc and B-complex is also an asset.

Gas or Flatulence

I know with every "tenderfoot" that arrived either in the Army or the Scouts, the change of diet, especially the reduction of animal fats in the food intake, always seemed to produce a condition of extreme gassiness. Any of nature's mints will quickly help alleviate this condition. Drinking mint teas or chewing mint leaves (if you have it growing) and drinking lots of liquids (as much as supplies allow) help. You have to wait for the body to adjust.

Indigestion

Upset stomach, queasiness, nausea, and all like stomach maladies are usually caused by "intake" problems (eating tainted food). Rarely does the change of diet have anything to do with indigestion. When I suffer from indigestion, I go on a fast for a few hours, drink some mint tea, and increase my garlic intake to balance my bacterial count and leave it at that. We of course are aware that chronic indigestion is a possible symptom of ulcers, etc., but once the stress of driving to work and job-related stress are eliminated for a while (in the course of our backyard living conditions), this condition should clear up!

Infections

What do I mean by infections? There are many kinds, of course. A sore throat is an infection, and we could say that an upset tummy is an infection. But in the backyard survival scene, our main concern regarding infection is centered around the after-effects of a wound or burn that goes bad on us. . .when infection has clearly set in.

A good rule to go by: SOAK IT! As in the go-soak-your-head type of soak. My own preference is with the very old procedure of a hot soak followed by a cold one. Put the wound into a hot container of liquid, as hot as is comfortable, for about fifteen minutes, then transfer it at once into the cold liquid for five minutes. This action really gets the blood flowing and frees up clogged areas around the wound. In all but burns, use epsom salts or salt to aid in the drawing-out process.

After the soaks, re-dress the wound with a good poultice. This is another old-style treatment. If there is a lot of pus and "weeping," use a poultice of grated soap and sugar, or, if you have it, use slightly moistened bran flakes as a poultice. When the dressing is removed, continue the soaks until the wound is cleaned out. (For the uninitiated, a poultice is a "pudding" of ingredients, "pudding" meaning the consistency required to be effective and, at the same time, comfortable on the painful infection site.)

As soon as the infection is defeated, return to healing medications.

Insomnia

The conditions we are experiencing in our backyard survival situation could possibly have some anxiety attached to them. Young people, camping out for the first time away from family and friends, experience anxiety resulting in insomnia, the inability to rest or to sleep.

To me, sleep as such is an overrated pastime. You should find that going to bed with the daylight will result in waking with the sun, well-rested and ready to go. One finds that the best cure for insomnia is *routine*.

Here we are, suddenly free of a routine that has been in existence for many years. Until a new one takes its place, we are out on a limb, so to speak. Replace that routine with a new one and the problem will clear up.

Of course, your insomnia could be the result of worry, in which case nothing I could say will change the situation. Stop worrying and go to sleep. Worry, per se, is negative. Good survivalists are positive. You may find that a nice cup of soothing tea such as chamomile will help.

Itching

See Fungus.

Laryngitis

See Cough.

Nausea

See Indigestion.

Sunburn

Sunburns, and exposure of all kinds, are included because people who work inside all the time and who are suddenly faced with an outdoor situation often react unfavorably to sunlight for lack of skin pigments.

If you fit this category, remember that prevention is the best cure. Make sure you have a sunscreen (minimum 30 SPF) in your gear. Stay out of direct sunlight for the first few days. Wear a hat that will shade your face, and keep your sleeves rolled down. After a while, you may adjust. If not, stay protected. Use a good moisturizing cream; aloe vera is excellent and natural.

If you are truly sunburned, treat it as if you would a burn. Keep the skin moist and, of course, stay out of the sun. A good home remedy is to place several plain tea bags in hot water and, when cool, apply to the burnt areas with a cotton ball or cloth well-soaked with the cold tea. This will put out the fire.

Within the framework of these basic conditions, you should have a good foundation to take care of the backyard "doctoring" needs of most minor and sometimes-serious conditions we may run into. Usually though, your backyard is a pretty safe place to be.

Kids falling out of trees? Well, that's another condition altogether. If you go back and look at the chapter on backyard survival, you will remember the safeguards we talked about. Reflection on the complete lack of medical services should make the whole family more safety-conscious.

Take time to talk to your pharmacist about these very items we have just discussed. You will find he is a fountain of knowledge. Go to your local health-food store. They, too, have many home remedies that are natural and inexpensive. Additionally, you may pick up some ideas and habits that will become part of your daily routine long before the disaster happens.

Here is a list of the items I have in *my* medicine chest. You may find them useful, but remember—I am not in any way making any recommendations!

2-oz. bottles of each of these oils:
Oil of camphor
Oil of clove
Oil of eucalyptus
Oil of methyl salicylate mineral oil
Oil of peppermint
You can make a fine liniment using equal parts of the first
four oils (½ oz. each) in 6 oz. mineral oil. Shake well.

Good for sore muscles.
Boric acid powder
Large quantity of mineral oil
Calamine lotion
Coconut oil
Hydrogen peroxide
Castor oil
Sodium bicarbonate
Sweet oil
Rubbing alcohol
Glycerin
Epsom salts
Witch hazel
Mercurochrome
Good antibiotic ointment
Suture kit
Rubber gloves
Paper face masks
Q-tips
Aloe vera, plain and gel
A good burn kit and Silvadene
Tea tree oil
Kyolic

Add any personal remedies you like.
The snake-bite and bee-sting kits are in the first aid kit, right?

This is my personal anti-oxidant kit for pollutants:
Vitamins E, C, and B12
Pantothenic acid
Beta carotene
Selenium
Zinc
Folic acid
Glutathione
Tanalbit
Chlorella

Read and ask all you can about the danger of pollutants. You remember that in Chapter 4 we talked about this danger possibly causing evacuation. Nobody, it seems, wants to talk about the dangers of airborne pollution from the chemicals in our areas. I stress again that this is information that you will have to dig up for yourself.

I have not yet found a non-technical book on the subject of anti-oxidants that we as lay people can understand. Yet I know from my own sources and from the media coverage of Desert Storm that our military personnel carry capsules with them to be taken when exposure to chemicals is imminent. Why this information is not readily available. . .? Again, remember that we are on our own!

As far as the text for survival is concerned, this, my dear reader, is it! It is my hope and dream that my idea for the formation an organization of interested Survivalists will become a reality. In the meantime, do take care and, above all, take *Action!!!*

Epilogue

During the months that passed while this update of my first survival manual was in progress, life, as it revolves around my small part of the world, went on as usual. Many earthquakes happened and my phone did not ring off the hook, even though my services are free. (But, on reflection, I realize that my bookings did pick up a little!)

Whether it was the fact that I was even more deeply involved in my survival obsession or that, since I had written the words, they were jumping off the page and stirring my brain to greater realization—whatever the reasons—I found myself addressing audiences with an even greater intensity and urgency than before. In the process, I began driving myself even harder, with my letter-writing campaign taking on new dimensions in volume and stringency (that is, as far as the budget for postage would allow!).

What, I asked myself, accounts for the difference in my own feelings? After all, none of this is new to me! The more I pondered, the more elusive the answer became. Then, as though a wind suddenly blew the fog away, realization hit home. . .hard! I thought of phrases like:

—The rich get rich and the poor get poorer. . .
—United we stand, divided we fall. . .
—Don't call me; I'll call you. . .

These and many similar phrases all have a common theme. . .polarization! Our society is becoming more and more polarized.

Reflection about recent audience reactions, the depth of questions from participants, and personal contacts after the meetings (when the informal stuff happens) served to reinforce my first conclusion. The general public is getting polarized into action and non-action groups. This was further brought home to me when a friend stopped me in the store the other day with, "Since my wife went to your family survival seminar, my life has not been the same." Further conversation revealed that his home was being "survivalized," and the process, it seemed, was involving the whole family! A note of praise for his fired-up wife; obviously. . .she cared.

It seems to me that, now more than ever, society has taken a clear stand regarding survival. One group is fired-up and hungry for information, while the other group (yes, you guessed it), no matter what is said or written, still maintain a What-me-worry? attitude. Yes, it seems that Kilroy still lives!

In spite of this conclusion, I am sticking to my personal slogan of "I'll go anywhere, anytime to talk about survival." I must admit, however, that I respond more to the "turned on" group and am less obsessed with swaying the others than I used to be. (Hey, I can only *plant the seed* of survival action. I can't do it for you!)

To those of you who are turned-on to survivalization, I would like to announce the formation of Survivors Unlimited, a nation-wide group that shall be formed to promote personal and family survivalization whenever possible, at all levels of their daily lives.

To the boss, the union, work mates, schools, and, especially, the Bureaucracy, we will speak out. "It is my right as a citizen to know what you are doing about my family's and my survival" shall be our slogan!

A bi-monthly publication called *Survivors Unlimited* with regular features plus reader feedback will be available soon. Price will be $30 per year. Watch for information on the Prodigy Service or write for update and application form. *Do not send money!*

Surely the heightened awareness will result in an increase in the percentage of "survivalized" families and individuals, as well as the potential for the development of specialized products modernizing backyard survival (portable wind/solar generators, water filters, portable shelters—the list of "needs" is long. All it takes is input and effort). If you agree, now that you have read this far, act now. Say "Yes, I want to become involved." For more information, write to:

Survivors Unlimited
1036 E. Ave J, Ste. 155
Lancaster, CA 93535

Epilogue, as defined by Webster, is the "final note or speech." So, for me, comes the final note of this, my attempt to share my personal wisdom regarding disaster survival. It is knowledge gained with a high cost in personal mental anguish and pain. I share this knowledge with you, hoping you use it in a positive manner.

In the days since I first started this journey, my own sadness is constantly being compounded by the indifference shown by the majority of folks with whom I come into contact. Constantly I am reminded of that young lady on T.V. from San Francisco. . ."But nobody told me how bad it was going to be. . ."

I want to go out into the streets and yell as loudly as I can,

"But I DID. . .It was you who didn't listen. . ."

I cannot close without a grateful word of thanks and praise for my wife Kacey, who, hour after loving hour, sat and changed my British colloquialisms so that my American readers do not need a British/American dictionary to decipher this text. Thanks Love. . .and thank you all for at least reading this far. . .

Please. . .act *now*. Thank you, and always remember, "Think Survival!" It pays, you know!

Your letters are always welcome. You can write to me at the following address: Ted Wright, 1036 E Ave. J, Ste. 155, Lancaster, CA 93535.

Suggested Further Reading

Back to Eden by Jethro Kloss. Back to Eden Books Publishing Co., Loma Linda, CA 92354.

The Healing Foods by Housman & Hurley. Rodale Press, Emmaus, PA.

Rodale's Basic Natural Foods Cookbook. Simon & Schuster, Inc., New York, NY.

Prescriptions for Nutritional Healing by James & Phyllis Balch, M.D., C.N.C. Avery Publishing Group, Garden City Park, NY.

Adventures in Sourdough Cooking and Baking by Charles D. Wilford. Cal-Gar Corporation, 33 Beach Rd.,Burlingame, CA 94010.

Sprouting for all Seasons by Bertha B. Larimore. Horizon Publishers, P.O.Box 490, Salt Lake City, UT 84010.

Cooking and Camping on the Desert by Choral Pepper. The Naylor Company, Book Publishers of the Southwest, San Antonio, TX.

The Soybean Cookbook by Dorothy Van Gundy Jones. Gramercy Publishing Co, New York, NY.

Oven Drying by Irene Crowe. Sheed & Ward, Kansas City, MO.

Fighting Radiation and Chemical Pollutants by Steven R. Schecter, N.D.

Vitality Ink, P.O. Box 294, Encinitas, CA 92024.

Australian Tea Tree Oil First Aid Handbook, Cynthia B. Olsen. Kali Press, Fountain Hills, AZ.

In order to claim personal loss due to disaster, you will need the following forms, which you can get from any office of the I.R.S.:

Publication #547 (an instruction book)

Form 4684 and the accompanying instruction sheet

I urge you to obtain these forms now and store them with your personal papers; *after* a disaster, such forms may be difficult to obtain, adding to your hardship.

Products

As this text goes to print, I am excited to share with you the products I currently have on hand or have in the development phase. All are available through my company, Earthquake Survival Services, at very reasonable fees. Please contact me at the following address:

Ted Wright
Earthquake Survival Services
1036 E. Ave J, Ste. 155
Lancaster, CA 93535

Video Tapes: *The Getting Ready For Survival Series*   ($19.95 each)

1. *The Auto*
How to prepare your vehicle with both Go gear and Stay gear to meet your travel survival needs.

2. *The Home*
How to complete your own home and backyard inspection and how to take the steps needed to prepare you and your family for complete backyard survival while maintaining a good quality of life.

3. *Water and Food*
How to prepare water for safe use and the "how tos" of backyard cooking, including recipes, food storage, and step-by-step instructions for putting together your own food torpedo.

4. *First Aid and the Home Medicine Chest*
How to put together a home medicine chest to meet your family's ongoing first aid and medical concerns.

Audio Tape Set $9.95 per Set

Home and Auto
Two one-hour cassettes describe the perils to your home and
auto and precautions necessary to protect your survival
needs in your everyday routine.

Plans Available $14.95 per Set

The Backyard Survival Shed
As described in this text.

Products in Development

The Emergency Survival Dwelling Unit (ESDU)
As described in this text, this unit supports a family of four.
Inquiries are welcome.

About the Author

Ted Wright was born in London, England, during a period of violent changes. As a teenager, he survived the bombing of his city in a backyard shelter for almost a year. He joined the Eighth Army "Desert Rats" and traveled from Tobruk to Rome with the "Green Howards" Special Forces unit, until an encounter with a tank ended his career as a "grunt."

He earned his degree in Physical Therapy from City of London University and worked with the R.A.F. Rehabilitation Center as well as in private practice. Having studied sports medicine, he also became the "Honorable Team Attendant" to Great Britain's 1948 Olympic Team.

Ted came to the United States in 1960 and moved to California, where a radio newscast about earthquakes in 1980 changed his life. Believing he had valuable, practical input because of his vast life experiences surviving all kinds of disaster, he became an active voice in the disaster survival field through lectures, seminars, books, pamphlets, videos, and audio cassettes.

In 1984, Ted formed Earthquake Survival Services as a means to "get the survival message to the people" through development of educational products and services. He works with the Los Angeles County Sheriff's Department as a volunteer presenting lectures and conducting seminars on disaster survival. His homespun, no-non-sense style and British accent makes him a popular speaker.

Ted Wright lives in Lancaster, California, with his wife Kacey.

Hampton Roads publishes a variety of books on metaphysical, spiritual, health-related, and general interest subjects. Would you like to be notified as we publish new books in your area of interest? If you would like a copy of our latest catalog, just call toll-free, (800) 766-8009, or send your name and address to:

Hampton Roads Publishing Company, Inc.
891 Norfolk Square
Norfolk, VA 23502